SPRING 64

A JOURNAL OF

ARCHETYPE

AND

CULTURE

Fall and Winter, 1998

SPRING JOURNAL

WOODSTOCK, CONNECTICUT 06281

ACKNOWLEDGMENTS

To Princeton University Press for quotations from the *Collected Works (CW)* of C. G. Jung (Bollingen Series XX), translated by R. F. C. Hull, edited by Herbert Read, Michael Fordham, G. Adler, and William McGuire, and published in Great Britain by Routledge and Kegan Paul, London. Other quotations have been acknowledged throughout in appropriate notes and references.

Spring is printed in North America, text on acid-free paper.

Spring is the oldest Jungian journal in the world. It was founded in 1941 by the Analytical Psychology Club of New York. In 1970, James Hillman transferred its editing and publication to Zürich, Switzerland. From 1978 to 1988, it was edited in Dallas, Texas. Since 1988 it has been edited in Connecticut.

Contents

Spring 64: *Histories*

Imagine how different your education might have been if, when you were in school, the History Department was called the Histories Department. Your Histories teacher would have had to give you a pretty good account of what happened—no bluffing and no more pretending there was this one great big unified consciousness that you had to accept. Your own sense of learning might have changed from one of simply receiving the cultural information of the past to one of actively engaging in its interpretation, perhaps even "dreaming it on" a little yourself. After all with so many histories of an event to choose from, you would have to choose the one that suited your imagination—a radical idea if ever there was one. Well, forget it. The History Cops of Consciousness (liberal or conservative) would never have permitted it. Some of you might even have chosen to live in a noncommittal kind of world where, since everything was open to interpretation and nothing was fixed, you would leave all Histories alone and not settle on any, making you a perfect little ironist, if a bit of a nerd; and, of course, no more French madeleines for you!

In preparing this issue of *Spring*, which deals with the ways people remember and interpret psychological events and their history, we realize that *Histories* is definitely a plural. Over the years, interpretations of the life and work of C. G. Jung—many dealing with the same events or themes—have ranged from the politely deferential to the crudely contemptuous, from portraits of him as a genial professional to portraits of him as a sensational sham. The same has been done to Freud and virtually everyone else who has been at all significant in the field of psychology in this century, from James to Skinner, from Kohut to Bettelheim, from Laing to Erikson. The histories keep appearing, the interpretation of events, and sometimes even the events themselves, keep changing.

The reader who is dismayed by all this, like the student who cannot choose, can of course just say, "I don't want to know any more. I have my version of the story and that's it." Worse, the reader can begin to insist on one version of the story because it is the one most comfortable. Yet, it is part of psychology itself, inherent in the practice, that its own history will be plural, and plurally interpreted, that its exponents will be overly loved or overly hated, that the "facts" will be conveniently denied as often as they are bravely embraced.

If all this begins to sound like you are about to read an issue of *Spring* that is more like Mel Brooks' *The History of the World, Part Two* than a serious engagement with soul, hold on. Our *Histories* issue gathers several of the most respected analysts and scholars in the world today—Italy's foremost analytical psychologist, Bianca Garufi, London's great Jung historian, Sonu Shamdasani (winner of last year's Gradiva award from the National Association for the Advancement of Psychoanalysis for his book, *Cult Fictions*), and Glasgow's distinguished scholar of German culture, Peter Bishop. And this issue begins with what we think is the most profoundly argued paper on the depth of soul that we have ever published in this journal—Wolfgang Giegerich's brilliant objection to what Jung ultimately did with psychology.

Far from your being left out of these histories, then, we think you will find yourself even deeper into them than you have ever been before. After all, what are histories (the most image-laden of all the arts) but depths?

—The Editors

Letter to the Editors

Dear *Spring*,

I recently received *Spring 62*, along with the unexpected extras you sent (*Healing Fiction* and *Poetic Imagination and Reverie*). Thank you so much for going out of your way to make a subscriber feel appreciated. You'll be receiving my renewal soon.

On a more critical note, and very belatedly, I want to express my extreme disappointment at your 1994 decision not to publish Wolfgang Geigerich's article responding to James Hillman's "Once More into the Fray." I have given a lot of thought to the questions raised by that debate, and your editorial statement that *Spring* isn't the place for "long-standing dialogues that can be accommodated in other ways." *But there are no other ways!* Indeed *Spring* is the place, the *one* place, where such a dialogue can and should occur. I say these things now because I finally wrote Dr. Giegerich and requested a copy of "Once More the Reality/ Irreality Issue: A Reply to Hillman's Reply," and having just finished reading it, I am reminded of how challenging and worthwhile the ideas are. I certainly don't expect you to respond to my complaint so long after the fact, but I felt obliged to lodge it anyway, if only to satisfy myself. Despite my criticisms, a new *Spring* is always exciting, and I look forward to it with anticipation.

Yours truly,

Michael Caplan
Toronto, Ontario

Is the Soul "Deep?"

Entering and Following the Logical Movement of Heraclitus' "Fragment 45"

WOLFGANG GIEGERICH

Is the soul "deep?" This question does not seem to make sense within depth psychology as the soul's depth is one of the presuppositions given with the very definition of the field. The well-known "Fragment 45" (Diels)[1] of Heraclitus'—"You would not find out the boundaries of soul, even by travelling along every path: so deep a measure does it have"[2]—has often been taken as the earliest formulation of the insight into the depth of the soul, and for this reason Heraclitus has been considered one of the ancestors of depth psychology.

But does this dictum really advance the thesis of depth? And, if it should turn out that his statement is about the depth of the soul, what then is the precise meaning of "depth" or "deep" in this case? These are questions that can reasonably be posed.

Focusing on an ancient text with such questions in mind does not make the following discussion a philological or historical study. Its interest is in the soul, but since the soul cannot be approached directly, this style of psychological investigation has to take the form of commentary on given "documents of the soul." The psychological question

[1] *Editors' note: The Fragments of Heraclitus* were first edited by H. Diels and were published in his book, *Fragmente der Vorsokratiker* (Berlin, 1922).

[2] G. S. Kirk and J. E. Raven, *The Pre-Socratic Philosophers* (Cambridge: Cambridge UP, 1977), 205.

Wolfgang Giegerich is a Jungian psychoanalyst in Steinbach, Germany. His most recent book is *The Soul's Logical Life* published by Peter Lang.

is not, cannot be, what and how the soul is, but how the soul is reflected in its manifestations. We are not as naive as to want to take on the soul directly. We have understood that psychology is the study of the reflection in some mirror and not the study of what the mirror image is the reflection of. This turn to the already reflected is not a trick to get at the otherwise invisible soul after all, and not a second-best substitute for "the real thing." On the contrary, we know that the already reflected is psychology's "real thing."

Apart from the question of the range of meanings of the Greek word used here for "deep" (*bathýs*), three features of our quotation demand attention.

> 1. If one approaches our fragment with the expectation that it is the *locus classicus* about the soul's depth, one is surprised to find upon closer look that Heraclitus does not say that the soul is deep. He uses the word "deep" with respect to the soul's *lógos* (which in the above English version has been rendered as "measure"). The *lógos* is deep. Whether this also makes the soul deep is an open question.
>
> 2. We tend to connect "depth" primarily with verticality. Thus James Hillman, after quoting our fragment, stated, "Ever since Heraclitus brought soul and depth together in one formulation, the dimension of soul is depth (not breadth or height) and the dimension of our soul travel is downward."[3] And in a footnote to the quotation, he adds, "Soul is not in the surface of things, the superficialities, but reaches down into hidden depths, a region which also refers to Hades and death."[4] Now, is it not strange that the fantasy which Heraclitus presents to us in the longer part of this fragment is one of horizontality, a movement on the surface of the earth? When Thomas Mann opens his novel, *Joseph and His Brothers,* with the sentence, "Deep is the fountain of the past," we know immediately that the perspective is downwards. However, here there is no image of a fountain, no suggestion of "abyss," "ground," "underworld," "bottom," or "bottomlessness." There can be no doubt that Heraclitus is

[3] James Hillman, *Re-Visioning Psychology* (New York: Harper & Row, 1975), xi.
[4] *Ibid.*, 231, note 6.

primarily thinking in terms of breadth. He speaks of "every road (or path)," of traveling, of borders, limits. Roads always follow the surface of the earth. They may go up a hill and down into a valley, but they never leave the surface, and they serve the purpose of taking you horizontally from here to there (the journey to the Underworld does not proceed on roads). Furthermore, the word translated as "to travel," *epiporeúesthai*, with its prefix *epi-* explicitly suggests horizontal movement. It is typically used for the marching of an army and for any traversing of an area, an aspect which is reinforced in our quote by the idea of the boundary or border, which you encounter after having completely traversed a region or country. There is also an additional word in the text, *ion* (present participle of *iénai*, to go, to walk), which in modern translations is frequently left untranslated because its meaning is felt to be contained in that of "traveling," but which is apt to strengthen the fantasy of horizontal movement. And conversely, there is nothing in the text to suggest a climbing or descending. Of course one might think that Heraclitus' argument could have been: the horizontal movement is inadequate to the soul, therefore we have to come to the conclusion that the proper dimension of soul is the altogether different one of depth and downwardness and *not* horizontal extension, *not* breadth. But as the word *hoúto [bathýn]* (so [deep]) shows, there is no contrast established between the first and the second parts of the fragment, the horizontal fantasy precisely leading up to and supporting the final statement.

3. How strange that Heraclitus would, when thinking about the dimension of the soul (*psyché*), come up with the image of traveling along roads at all. Nobody today whose purpose it is to search for the limits of soul would start out from the idea or image of a search in the outside world, because it is understood that the soul's limits are not to be found there in the first place. Is not the soul something invisible, immaterial, nonspatial, and above all, something in us to begin with, so that any movement along roads in external reality (regardless of whether it is meant literally or metaphorically) is on principle simply missing the point? Unless, of course, Heraclitus' *psyché* is not defined to be

> "inner" (inside humans) versus "outer" but extends out into the world. Then this would logically be where it is primarily to be sought. Whatever the Greek or the Heraclitean notion of soul might be, the choice of image makes it clear that *psyché* must be such that to search for its boundaries out there by traveling along every road has some plausibility, even if perhaps only a preliminary one. It cannot be part of the psyche's *a priori* definition to have its locus in ourselves and to consist of what is going on in us, our emotions, thoughts, images, desires, etc.

The last part of our text about the depth of the soul's *lógos* is not the important part of our fragment. It presents only the result or conclusion of a thought process, a result that is hardly more than a brief, abstract *name* for the insight to be transmitted. The insight itself, what it amounts to and the way it is acquired, can be learned only from the first sentence about the search for the psyche's boundaries. It will not do to jump on two single words ("deep" and "soul") in the text, and regardless of the context and thought process in which they occur, attribute to them whatever meaning we ordinarily associate with them in order to exploit them for our purposes. Also, we must not stand in awe in front of the alleged mystique that "the soul is deep" and mindlessly repeat this slogan as a static article of faith. "Fragment 45" expressly speaks of traveling. But even if it did not, we would still have to honor Heraclitus as a thinker and our fragment as an instance of living thought, in other words as movement. It would be an insult to Heraclitus to intimate that all he wanted to do with this fragment was to lay down a kind of "golden word of wisdom" about the soul's depth; not wisdom, not a gnome, not a static and finished truth but a thought. We have to enter into the precise and intricate thought process that Heraclitus condensed into this fragment and think it, reconstruct it, that is to say, follow its internal movement; we have to unfold what he presents in the nutshell of one sentence. In order to do this, we must leave behind all the baggage that we bring along, all our preconceived ideas about the nature of the soul, even about its "depth," and in fact submit to the very journey upon which our text sends us, in order to find out where this movement leads and what its results are.

Heraclitus sends us out to search for the soul's boundaries. In order to do this, we are supposed to go forward and travel along not one road, but along every (possible) road, in all possible directions, and we are to travel each of these roads, as it were, all the way (as the sense of "traversing" contained in *epiporeúesthai* implies). The philosopher subjects us to a mental experiment; it is obvious that empirically we could not travel every road to its end (especially during an age when traveling a road meant to walk by foot or to ride on horseback). Life is too short, our physical strength too slight. No, we do not have to physically leave home. We have to set out on an expedition in the mind. Suppose, Heraclitus tells us, there were no limitations at all as to time and strength, no human shortcomings, no finite nature of human existence, and we had the capability to actually travel every single road all the way (one could even extend his idea by including our modern technical means of transportation—motor-ships, aircraft, spacecraft—and transform Heraclitus' statement into the following: suppose we were capable of searching every spot in the universe)—we would discover that we cannot find the boundaries of the soul.

The idea is by no means the human impossibility of ever getting to the limits of the soul. The problem is not a practical one. Heraclitus is not trying to tell us that this task is too immense or difficult for us. Rather than about us and our insufficiencies, the fragment is speaking about the nature of the soul, as the last sentence concerning "the depth of its logos" makes clear. The point is that on principle the soul's boundaries cannot be found; they could not even be found by a superhuman. That is to say there is no boundary, the soul is limitless, infinite. This is a difficult thought. What does it mean?

One might think it means that one's travel could go on and on, endlessly. But such a sense of infinity is not supported by our fragment. This would be what philosophically is called the "infinite progress" and what has been shown by Hegel to be the "bad infinity" of "bad metaphysics." The insight that Heraclitus has gained and pronounced would not have been taken to heart, or we would not abide by it, because we would still be hoping for some boundaries, even though it has been understood that we will never arrive. Heraclitus' insight is definitive, that is, it puts an end to any search for the boundaries of the soul. His insight *a priori* renders any attempt to find out the limits of the soul absurd. This entire project is frustrated, negated; it is shown to be not only futile but also unreasonable from the outset. We do not end up with the indeterminateness of a "depth" in the sense of an endless extension into the distance (regardless of whether it be horizontal or vertical). No, the whole orientation towards a bottomless depth, the infinitely self-perpetuating expectation of an end to one's search in some unreachable future has been ruthlessly cut off; no, "not yet," in a forever deferred future, but the conclusive "no" that here and now terminates any flirting with the idea of a limit of the soul out there.

The result that we end up with is paradoxical. The insight is that the soul has "no limits," but this insight turns out to be in itself a terminating thought and as such a new limit. The final outcome of Heraclitus' reflection is not a total limitlessness at all. The closure that cannot be found in fact or *in re* (as the soul's closure) turns up anew in the mind, inside our thinking as its closure, as a limiting thought that terminates our endless expectations and our search for a boundary. Heraclitus' reflection, rather than altogether depriving us of a sense of boundary, brings about a transportation of "boundary" from the sphere of the real into that of the mental or notional, from the "object" (the soul, psychological reality) into the "subject," from the ontological to the logical.

Another paradox is that we have to actually undergo the search for the boundaries by traveling every road in order to find out that this search is unreasonable.

The soul has no limits. This is a contradictory idea. "Border" means two things: a) limitation, end, constriction, enclosure and b) a bordering on some other, something new, foreign, and in this sense an opening to new regions or countries. If the soul has no boundaries, this results in a reversal with respect to the two aspects of "border." Where "border" means limitation, the soul is unlimited, infinite; where "border" means opening to an outside, we have to realize that the soul has nothing that it borders on and that "soul" thus implies absolute confinement.[5] Conversely, this reversal of the natural order of things shows that with his "no limit" insight, Heraclitus is not merely using the word "soul" but is touching the reality we mean by "soul," for the soul is an "inverted [or upside down, inside out] world" (Hegel), it is *contra naturam.*

[5] This is not physical or imaginal but logical confinement. There is no narrow prison cell outside of which freedom would begin. In this prison you are free to go as far and wherever you want. It is imprisonment in the infinity of the soul.

We are hopelessly enclosed by the soul. There is nothing outside the psyche, no other, nothing new. The notion or logic of the soul precludes a beyond, an "abroad." We cannot get out. There is never a point where there would be a demarcation line separating what is inside the soul from what is out there. We are hopelessly stuck in the soul, that is to say, in its absolute interiority; no exit,[6] no escape. I want to elucidate this notion of absolute interiority in the sense of an inescapable enclosure by turning to another text from another civilization in which—*mutatis mutandis*—"the same" idea is presented in much more detail and plasticity, although with respect to the presence of God rather than to the psyche It is a text from the *Old Testament*, *Psalm 139*, lines 1 through 16.

> O Lord, thou hast searched me, and known me. Thou knowest my downsitting and mine uprising, thou understandest my thought afar off. Thou compassest my path and my lying down, and art acquainted with all my ways. For there is not a word in my tongue, but, lo, O Lord, thou knowest it altogether. Thou hast beset me behind and before, and laid thine hand upon me. Such knowledge is too wonderful for me; it is high, I cannot attain unto it. Whither shall I go from thy spirit? or whither shall I flee from thy presence? If I ascend up into heaven, thou art there: if I make my bed in hell, behold, thou art there. If I take the wings of the morning, and dwell in the uttermost parts of the sea; Even there shall thy hand lead me, and thy right hand shall hold me. If I say, Surely the darkness shall cover me; even the night shall be light about me. Yea, the darkness hideth not from thee; but the night shineth as the day: the darkness and the light are both alike to thee... My substance was not hid from thee, when I was made in secret, and curiously wrought in the lowest parts of the earth. Thine eyes did see my substance, yet being unperfect; and in thy book all my members were written, which in continuance were fashioned, when as yet there was none of them.

What Heraclitus presented summarily in one sentence and in the one thought of traveling "every" road, the psalmist spells out. In his

[6] Heidegger translates *peírata* (boundaries) on the basis of his understanding of the Greek sense of *psyché* as *Ausgänge* (*der Seele*) ("exits, openings or outlets of the soul"). See his *Heraklit*, Gesamtausgabe, vol. 55 (Frankfurt am Main: Klostermann, 1979), 282, 297, 303f.

mental experiment the psalmist really travels every possible road in all directions. Whether he were to go to the end of the world in the east where the sun rises or in the west where it sets in the ocean, whether he were to go up to Heaven or down into the Underworld, he is forced to realize that he would nevertheless be enclosed in God's presence. Whether he be in motion or at rest, he cannot escape. Even the seeming privacy of his thoughts and the darkness of night (or the darkness, we might add, of the "unconscious"), indeed, even the prenatal past is not an area that would provide at least some theoretical outside. What the psalmist expresses is the insight into his being inescapably surrounded on all sides, in time, empirical and cosmic space as well as in the inner realm of one's thoughts and feelings. Everything, his whole existence, is absolutely contained in an absolute ("autonomous," "objective" and *a priori*) knowledge, a *being known* that is experienced as an imprisonment.

If there is no escape and no outside, then there is only interiority: absolute interiority. It is absolute, because this interiority is not the counterpart of an exteriority. This interiority is unchallenged: infinite. Our habitual notion of interiority or the "inner" is abstract or external, because according to it the inner has its other, the external, outside of itself, on the other side of the border between them, and it, the inner, is just as external to the outer world. Our psalm drives home the realization that every conceivable "outside" is already (*a priori*) "inside" this all-encompassing knowledge. We are thus forced to advance to a sense of an "inner" interiority that has interiorized even the notion of an "outer" into itself. On the level of consciousness reached by the psalmist and by Heraclitus, a "real" outside has become inconceivable. We are absolutely locked, be it into the interiority of a being known by God (*Psalm 139*) or into the interiority of the psyche (Heraclitus, "Fragment 45").

Driven by the wish to get out, the psalmist tested every imaginable kind of "outside" in his mental experiment and experienced how the hypothesis that there could be a way out was falsified. In this way he painfully acquired for himself a new status of consciousness determined by the notion of an inescapable interiority. Even though Heraclitus gives us only the briefest condensation of his mental experiment, we can assume from what he said that his thought process was "the same," and we see that it led to the same result. The first aspect of this result is the imprisonment character of our containment in the soul. But there is also the other aspect of the "no boundary" insight: that of the infinity of the soul. It is unlimited. We already know that this infinity cannot mean an unending extension into the distance, neither spatially nor in time (past or future). The knowledge that there *is* no boundary works as a new, unsurmountable boundary at which, as if by a brick wall, our striving to get to a limit in the endless distance is repulsed. It is thrown back upon and reflected into itself. The new boundary is the absolute prison wall that is absolute because it does not separate freedom outside from imprisonment in here. Inasmuch as the soul's infinity is itself absolutely enclosed in its absolute interiority, it cannot escape further and further into extendedness. It is turned back inside, forced within, interiorized into itself.

But when the relentless orientation towards spatial extension into an endless distance is forced back and has to return within, where can it go? It inevitably has to explode the literal, natural, namely spatial notion of the "inner" and thus to open up an entirely new dimension, that of "intension." But no, "explosion" is already wrong; it is still tied to the extensional orientation. We have to speak of an implosion. But again, this is not the adequate expression, implying too violent a process. The infinite interiority or interiorized infinity comes about through the alchemical, logically negative process of an internal putrefaction, corruption, fermentation, sublimation ever deeper into itself of "whatever is there."

However this conquest of the dimension of an intensional or "inner" infinity amounts to nothing less than a breakthrough into spatial thinking altogether. And this in turn is the breakthrough into the mode of imagination and into that of reflection, of thought proper. Heraclitus is driven beyond the imagination. Similarly, the psalmist is driven beyond the imaginal, beyond myth. Not only all empirical places on the surface of the earth and the whole world of nature, but also the strictly imaginal or archetypal *topoi* Heaven and Underworld are once and for all sublated in favor of the new dimension of an all-encompassing, all-pervasive knowing. The importance of the mental sphere is emphasized by the inclusion of one's hidden thoughts (plans) and as-yet unspoken utterances in this aforecoming being known. There is a radical, revolutionary shift as to the locus of human existence. Now human existence has its primary place within an inescapable "being known" and no longer, as in the times of polytheistic myth, in naive, simple being, in the cosmos, in nature. What we witness in this psalm is the origin of a first awareness of "consciousness," in other words, of a real consciousness, of consciousness, and thus the beginning of a sense of the psychological. The (innocent, natural[7]) being-in-the-world (and thus ontology) is superseded by a being in the notional sphere of reflection, consciousness, logos as "broken" (reflected) or sublated being—from *mythos* to *logos*.

Because this psalm is a text from the *Bible* and on the surface speaks about and to God, we tend to read it theologically, in terms of piety. But a theological reading cannot do it justice. It would belittle its importance and neutralize its revolutionizing impact by enveloping it regressively in a conventional faith. Our text is above all an essential document in the history of the soul, bearing testimony to the rise of a new status of consciousness. We must not be blinded by the word God and our "natural" reaction to it. This text is not about God, as if God were first of all a given positivity whose nature would here be described. Many mythical gods had the attribute of being all-knowing. But in the world of myth, the god was the "substance," and his knowing was one of his "attributes" or qualities. Here it is the other way around. The text is about an inescapable knowledge. The psalmist does not want to flee from Him, who happens to be all-knowing but from (His) knowing, (His) spirit, (His) presence. The psalmist rose to the insight of an inescapable containment in a nonspatial realm of reflection or of an "objective" (not subjective, not his personal) self-knowledge ("*con-scientia*"), and as was to be expected, he gave this absolute containment the name "God."

But whether "God" or "psyche," the actual experience in the psalm and in the Heraclitus fragment is analogous, the only difference being that in each case different moments of the same experience are being stressed. The Biblical text, by personifying this sphere of reflection, emphasizes its wholly-otherness, its objectivity and autonomy *vis-à-vis* the I, whereas the aspect that the newly discovered "being known" is a self-knowledge is kept in a subliminal condition. The psalmist feels the need to distinguish and distance himself from this self-knowledge. This

[7] I use "natural" in a psychological, alchemical sense, not in an abstract, naturalistic or positivistic sense (as in biology or physics). The natural in terms of human existence is an animated, spiritual natural to begin with: the imaginal perception of the world. Myth and ritual are what is natural to the soul.

is why the motif of escaping is in the foreground. It is terrifying to find oneself expelled from the innocence of one's native embeddedness in myth and to awaken to an awareness of the reflectedness of existence. The psalmist's fleeing is driven by his wish to return into the innocent, unreflected state of being-in-the-world (that state of being characterized by myth and ritual)—a forerunner of the romantic longing *Retour à la nature*. But the first emergence of this longing to be relieved of the burden of consciousness (in the sense of *Selbstbewußtsein*, a consciousness of consciousness) and the attempts to escape the broken, reflected state of being already come with the insight into their futility; no indulging in a nostalgic illusion. In fact, it is probably only through the feeling of the loss of oneness, the loss of an embeddedness in myth and ritual, and through the insight into the impossibility of a return to the innocence of being that the new sense of "in-ness" in a self-knowledge is acquired. The attempt to get out of his containment in God's knowledge is, dialectically, the mode in which the psalmist really acquires the idea of this containment for himself and settles in it, definitively removing human existence from its surroundedness by myth and instead grounding it in reflectedness; precisely by trying to escape he brings the insight of his inescapable containment in God's knowledge home to himself.

Heraclitus, by contrast, is not especially interested in getting out. He would want to positively reach the boundaries by traversing the whole space of his containment in psyche from here to there. From the outset his view stays much more within. And his notion of *psyché* is accordingly one that stresses the connection of this "objective" reflection to the human being, to ourselves, as our psychological existence. From his version of the insight, it is not too difficult to get to our modern notion of the *psyché* as self-relation, self-reflection. But of course in the idea of self-relation the otherness that was highlighted in the Biblical text is not totally lost either; it is inherent in it as a sublated moment, inasmuch as the self that does the reflecting and the self that is being reflected are both identical and different.

The different realms and things in the imaginal have boundaries. For example Heaven, earth, and the Underworld are clearly demarcated spheres. Sea and land, valley and mountain border on each other. If the soul has no boundaries, it cannot be of an imaginal nature. The insight gained by Heraclitus that the soul has no boundaries puts an end to any thinking about it within the realm of the imagination and all the more so within the space of sensory intuition. When in the logical status of consciousness reached by Heraclitus it comes to the soul, thinking in spatial terms as such is reduced to absurdity. The soul is not *res extensa*, it cannot be conceived in terms of extension, regardless of whether literal or imaginal extension. The soul is *res cogitans* and the appropriate approach to it is thus in and by thought. If we accept the message of Heraclitus' fragment, we have to realize that the realm of psychology begins where the imagination has been superseded.

There are two obstacles to this understanding. 1) With the terms *res extensa* and *res cogitans* we enter the territory of Descartes. In many quarters and in archetypal psychology, Descartes meets with contempt. He is treated like a (psychological or intellectual) criminal responsible for the fundamental split expressed by the opposition of the aforementioned terms. This is not only unfair but also unpsychological. Descartes did not *do* anything; he is not responsible for, not guilty of, a splitting. He merely expressed the split that was constitutive for the modern soul condition and thus a modern truth. If anyone is "guilty" here, it is the soul. Descartes conscientiously did her bidding, no more. In a way we can see this distinction or opposition of his already prefigured in Heraclitus' dictum. Blaming Descartes is a defense (in the psychoanalytic sense of the word) against having to acknowledge the fundamental psychological revolution that has long taken place and brought about an irrevocable rupture, experienced as the loss of myth and the estrangement from "nature." Expressed in positive terms, it was the acquisition of a broken, reflected, and reflecting consciousness. We do not have to fight or undo Descartes. We have to take him further, "think him onwards" (to play on Jung's formulation, "to dream the myth onwards"). This is why when I say that the soul is *res extensa*, the latter expression is not exactly identical with the meaning and function it has in his thought.

2) There is the idea that by resorting to the imagination, this split could be healed again. The imaginal is imagined (not thought!) to be neither a Cartesian *res extensa* nor a *res cogitans*. It is supposed to be exempt from this distinction. It is said to be an intermediary third. But things are not as simple as that. To be sure, the way Descartes' oppositional pair is set up, the imaginal does not fit in, just like that. But this does not mean that it would not be covered by his scheme. On the contrary, it is nothing

but the compromise formation between his opposites. If it does not belong on either side and is not a totally different third either, what else can it be? It exists as the whole opposition collapsed into one, but in such a way that within this One the opposites are internally immunized against one another, and their dangerous conflict is thus defused and suspended, stalemated. As such the imaginal in modern psychology is the disguised internalization of the very Cartesian split as a whole that it openly scorns and for which it is said to be the solution. Why?

Image is shape and shape is spatial. On this count, the imaginal is undoubtedly *res extensa.* But it is extended matter only as far as the content of the image is concerned. Its logical form (as image in the imagination or as idea in the mind) is, of course, not extended. Through its form it partakes of the nature of Descartes' *res cogitans.* By holding content and logical form of the image strictly apart, each to one side, the idea of the imaginal is the trick that allows having it both ways. It is the trick of trying to do justice to *res extensa* and *res cogitans* at once while preventing the self-contradictory nature of this undertaking from becoming apparent and effective, which would lead to its self-destruction. The trick is to camouflage the simultaneous obedience to both and to systematically distribute the opposites neatly each on one side. The sanity of the mind is thus rescued. The fall into the contradiction and the ensuing dialectic is avoided. Imaginal psychology can indignantly reject the diagnosis of its being firmly rooted in Cartesian ground: when the character of the extendedness of the content of its images is pointed out, it quickly insists on its non-extended ideational form; and when conversely the ideational character of the form or status as images is stressed, it disowns having any part in the *res cogitans* and produces as counter-proof its connection, by way of metaphor, with the sensory, physical world.

The standpoint of the imaginal is the (hypostatized, reified) act of skillfully switching between the Cartesian opposites, so that it never has to show its true colors. As the movie projector's speedy sequence of separate images creates the impression of one continuous moving image, so here the speed and the subliminal nature of the switching back and forth makes its act character and the inherent contradiction between the two sides disappear in the impression of a static, in-itself, reconciled image. The idea of the imaginal is not really a third, not really something new and other beyond the Cartesian opposites. It is the artfully produced illusion of something other, a splendid show.

Here it may be time to return to the final sentence of Heraclitus' fragment: *hoúto bathýn lógon échei*—"so deep a measure does it have," "so deep is its meaning," "such is the depth of its meaning," to cite only three of a multitude of translations. It has already become obvious that Heraclitus' fragment is not concerned with depth in the sense of verticality and a downwards movement but also not with extension in a wider sense. This is why the translation, "so deep a measure," is ruled out for us, also for linguistic reasons; for Guthrie's argument against Kirk's thinking in terms of "vast extent" is conclusive: "but *bathýn lógon échei* would seem a rather recherché phrase to express simply 'so extensive is it.'"[8] The Greek word *bathýs* like Latin *altus* means both deep and high (cf. "altitude"), in other words vertical extension, but it can also have quite different meanings. It (and the noun *báthos*, "depth") can be used in a decidedly horizontal sense to indicate width (such as that of a shore, the wide extension of a courtyard or the depth of a battle-line). Indeed, Plato uses the plural of the noun to refer to all three dimensions of a solid (length, height, and depth). It can also have nonspatial meanings and designate the density of a forest or of a fog, the thickness and length of hair, the intensity of a color, the strength of a storm, the high degree of wealth or of a debt, the craftiness of a person, the profundity of an argument.

So we might think that we are better off with the other translations given above that speak of the depth of meaning. For now depth is used no longer literally but metaphorically, imaginally. Apart from the fact that this would be a rather banal, trite wisdom for the discovery and formulation of which one would hardly need a philosopher of the rank of Heraclitus, does the metaphorical depth get us any further? By no means. In fact the move to the metaphorical merely obscures that nothing has changed as to one's dominant orientation. If the soul has "so deep a meaning," I am still and remain, standing at the place where I have always been and from there look into an assumed distance. Whether I am doing this literally in external space (in the area of physical vision)

[8] W. K. C. Guthrie, *The Earlier Presocratics and the Pythagoreans*, vol. I, *A History of Greek Philosophy*, (Cambridge: Cambridge UP, 1962), 477, note 1.

or metaphorically in the realm of the imagination, or in "the depth of feeling" (e.g., through the puer's nostalgic longing, *póthos*, for far away and fundamentally unreachable places) makes no difference. Whether depth of measure or depth of meaning, in both cases it is the same refusal to get going to the boundaries and to get Heraclitus' message about the pointlessness of any orientation into the distance (a message which I cannot really get unless I have relentlessly tried to get there and actually experienced a failure).

Heraclitus does not, as we with our talk about the depth of the soul's meaning, end up with the vagueness of an undecided question, and the boundary does not fade away in an endless distance, that is to say, in the fuzziness of a mysterious and mystifying idea of depth. Heraclitus has come to a definitive conclusion. He did travel all the way to the boundary, for how else could he have found out the truth about it? The question about the boundaries is decided. And it has consequences. There is a closure. We have to see through the intellectual idea of the depth of the soul's meaning and the analogous feeling attitude of *póthos* and recognize it as the (however glorified) neglect or hesitation to actually try to get to the end. By holding on to the idea of "depth," one pretends that there might still be some boundary and a beyond after all, only so far away that our arrival there is forever postponed, deferred. One simply ignores that the "no boundary" insight has long been acquired, and that thereby any longing into the distance and any imagining in terms of vast extent has once and for all been cut off.

This small example concerning the idea of the depth of the soul brings to light the structural deficiency of the imagination if it is supposed to be the predominant function for approaching the soul and for understanding its nature, in other words, its deficiency for doing psychology. "The soul's depth" is the formula describing in a nutshell the nature of the imaginal approach: with this stance one is just day-dreaming of something that is by definition not supposed to ever be actually attained. One is just "tele-visioning"—envisioning, peeping, viewing, romantically expecting (*ex-spectare*, "to look out") from a distance into the endless distance. The imaginally understood image is nothing but the visualized or reified "depth" (endless distance) itself. It can be adored from afar but cannot be known. The imaginal stance allows one to stall, to hold back, to reserve oneself, inasmuch as belief in the soul's depth arrests midway, or prevents altogether, the internal movement that the Heraclitean statement speaks about. The imaginal stance speaks with a split tongue. It says, "no boundary," but it continues to be on the lookout for one. The insight of the "no boundary" does not come home. The recoil is avoided. The old orientation out and away into (literal or metaphorical) space is rescued and the reflection into itself, this essential result of Heraclitus' motion, does not happen. In this way the *real* depth aimed at by Heraclitus is avoided—that depth which is of the soul's *logos*, logical "depth," the "depth" of thought, in contrast to sensory, imagined, or felt depth. If you follow Heraclitus' movement, you start out from thought and end up with thought.

I said that Heraclitus did travel all the way. But his traveling was neither literal movement nor imagined movement. He did not picture his journey and where he would arrive. Nor did he stay at home. What he did was travel without leaving home and stay home by way of the most extensive traveling, that is to say, he traveled in thought: he thought through the idea of traveling every road to the boundaries all the way, with all its consequences, just as the author of *Psalm 139* did. Their traveling was negated, sublated, alchemically decomposed traveling from the outset (which already comes out linguistically in what is in translation the subjunctive—"would not find," "if I were to ascend to heaven"). It is only in thought that you really arrive at the soul's boundary, which however is that sublated boundary consisting in the very insight that there is no boundary. It is only in thought that you arrive in soul country. For the imagination there cannot be the insight that there is no boundary, because it resorts to the idea of depth, which is the noun for the act of deferring the boundary forever and thus for avoiding closure. It keeps the boundary question in the dark. Heraclitus' thinking-through to the end of the idea of a (literal or imaginal) search for the boundaries of the soul, and in fact his arriving at the inescapable insight that there is no boundary out there in the realm of extension, amount to a closure of the mode of imagining (which is always space-bound). He conquers the non-space of thought for the soul, thereby removing the soul from its exile in myth or mythically imagined nature and returns it into its native country. He fetches the boundary that was not to be found out there back home as the "determinate nought" (Hegel) of "outside boundary," as sublated border, and as the inalienable property of the mind: as truly inner or internal boundary.

The imagination inevitably has to imagine the border out there, in the distance, at the margins. But Heraclitus (logically, not physically) draws the border or margins inside, into the center, thereby establishing interiority (a revolution that the perceiving and imagining mind cannot survive; it is at once sublated and becomes thinking consciousness). For the real "inner" is not something located inside of something else. It is not a location at all; as a location it would still be an abstract or external notion of interiority. No, the real "inner" is what has nothing outside of, or external to, itself, no boundaries that would be out there, at its margins. The true inner is defined as that whose interiority has, in a revolutionary reversal, surrounded the very notion of "outside," "margin," or "border" and internalized it into itself. The inner is thus what has the outer truly within and not outside of itself. Only this self-contradictory, "crazy" relation is what constitutes interiority. But something that has the outside (its own outside) truly inside itself can, of course, not be imagined any more. It can only be thought. And because the "land" of soul is constituted by interiority, it is accessible only to thought. It is in itself an Inverted World, and as such, unimaginable.

What becomes of the boundary when it has truly been interiorized? It now can be seen to be the contradictory nature or dialectic of the soul's logical life. As such, it is the liquefied, vaporized, sublimated border, border no longer as a static line but as a living *complexio oppositorum.*

Now we are in a better position to understand what the last sentence of our fragment—"so deep a *lógos* does it have"—means. Far from suggesting a mysterious depth of the soul, an endless extension of its measure or its meaning, it tells us how *bathýs* (unfathomable, complex, intricate, subtle, counternatural, "twisted," "crazy") its *lógos* is. Why *lógos*? Why not, for example, "how *bathýs* the nature of the psyche is?" The answer is that the status of consciousness reached here does not allow Heraclitus any longer to naively speak of a "nature" of the soul. He says the soul's *lógos* is "deep" because soul is not an existing entity, not ontic. It is sublated nature, sublated myth, or it is logical. It is nothing else but the relation of a dialectical reversal, an inversion. It is absolutely misleading to say that the soul is deep. When we say this, we inevitably imagine it as a "something" that extends out into an imaginal distance. But the soul is not a "something," it is "reflection into itself." It is a logical relation, a relation that exists only in and for the mind. It is the status of absolute interiority, which, as we have seen, is that unimaginable, because self-contradictory, relation of outer and inner where the outer is inside the inner and the inner thus encloses all, even its own outside. The external is now only a sublated moment within the internal.

This is why Heraclitus', "so deep a logos does it have" is somehow analogous to the psalmist's, "Such knowledge is too wonderful for me; it is [too] high, I cannot attain unto it." In both cases it is a question of logic, of conceptual comprehension (which is experienced as "deep" or as "too wonderful"). In "Fragment 45" as well as in *Psalm 139* we witness the first emergence of the conscious awareness of this unheard of new dimension of absolute interiority or internal infinity. The psalmist calls it "such knowledge" (the all-encircling knowledge of God). Heraclitus calls it the psyche whose boundaries cannot be found out there (because the psyche as internal infinity is itself the all-encompassing boundary).

The idea of an all-encircling and inescapable knowledge is too wonderful, too high—in short, incomprehensible for the psalmist, because his is only the first dawning of the insight of the inescapability of consciousness. He is, as it were, getting a glimpse of something that explodes the stance of mythologizing or imagining consciousness, but he is getting this glimpse from "beneath," while he is still viewing from within this old stance of consciousness. Therefore he necessarily experiences it as an incomprehensible wonder, because within it he naturally does not have the logical means to comprehend it. But this of course does not mean that what he caught sight of would be incomprehensible and absolutely irrational. On the contrary, it is that new form of consciousness that in all essential regards orients itself in life by means of the abstractness of rigorous thought and conceptual comprehension, because it has sublated the modes of sensory intuition and imagination. It cannot be imagined any more. So the problem with it is not at all that it is truly incomprehensible (as the psalmist suggests), but that it is unimaginable. Having within the horizon of a perceiving and imagining consciousness caught sight of what is utterly beyond this horizon and implies the destruction of the imagining mode as consciousness' dominant mode amounts to a summoning to be initiated into the new logical level of consciousness through a logical revolution. You cannot have an inkling of the inescapability of reflection without having fallen under an obligation: to allow the new "content" to alchemically decompose your old frame of mind and the old logical constitution of your world. What at first appears as a content of consciousness is in truth the seed of what wants to become a new form of consciousness at large.

This is where the idea of the soul's depth comes in. It, too, expresses the dawning awareness of something that explodes the horizon of the imagination, but it also defuses this "content," which threatens to decompose the whole status of consciousness, by re-integrating it into the old status of consciousness. It holds what wants to be the promise of a new form of consciousness down in the status of a mere content of the old, imagining consciousness, freezing its internal dynamic, its corrupting, fermenting power. How can it do this? By depriving it of its logical, notional, intellectual claims and challenge and instead translating it into the harmlessness and fuzziness of a mere romantic feeling. Emotions, feelings, are an excellent packaging for safely storing the logical or "metaphysical" dynamite of contents away. If you construe a conflict as an emotion or feeling, you have successfully removed it from the battlefield of truth and reduced it to the banal level of personal, subjective, or interpersonal problems. Emotions, if taken *per se*, are in the life of the soul what the *ad hominem* argument is in a discussion. The intellectual substance of "depth" in "the soul's depth" is near zero. It is a vague feeling. And it is a black hole that swallows within it all precise thinking. It is the name for the "unthoughtness" of Heraclitus' message to us, and for the refusal to allow it to work on our consciousness.

I expressed the view that what Heraclitus and the psalmist discovered explodes the whole sphere of mythological imagination. But we now have to realize that the idea of absolute interiority, of an internal infinity, of an all-surrounding logical life and an unreachable boundary is not new. In fact, it is a constitutive idea of mythology itself. There is the Greek myth of Okeanos, the "origin of the Gods," "the generation of all," the corresponding Egyptian myth of the primal Ocean Nun, the "World Encircler" and "Father of the Gods," and the Germanic uroboric Midgard Serpent, to mention only three examples from different cultural spheres. I will concentrate on the Greek myth. Okeanos[9]

[9] See my paper, "Deliverance from the Stream of Events: Okeanos and the Circulation of the Blood," in: *Sulfur 21* (Winter 1988), 118-140.

(the name is said to be of Semitic origin and to mean "circling") is the mythic image of the soul's logical life as stream (continuous streaming, fluidity), as unending circulation (returning into itself), as unreachable outermost border of the world separating Being from Non-Being, and thus as all-encircling as well as all-permeating circumference of Being. If the world-encompassing Okeanos separates Being from Non-Being, what is outside of its limits is nothing. In other words, the world has no outside, no beyond. Okeanos is not a border between two realms, like borders in ordinary reality, from which proceed, as it were, two vectors, one out and one in. Being the outermost end of the world, he exclusively points inwards. All rivers, springs, wells, the entire sea, they all continuously originate from him and flow into the world. He is the generation and circumference of all that exists. You could not reach this boundary, because however far you might go and whatever distant and unheard-of place you would reach would *ipso facto* be encircled by all-encircling Okeanos. Okeanos is in this sense much like what we call the horizon, which one cannot reach either, because it moves along with one wherever one goes.

In the image of Okeanos the mythological imagination imagined its own engendering origin—the constituting principle of mythologizing itself. Okeanos is the image of the world's absolute containment, the world's inescapably being locked in, thrown back upon itself. He is the image of the internal boundary of everything in the world. Thanks to this boundary everything is "inner." There is, for mythic experience, no "outside world," nothing "external," no natural world in the modern sense of a *res extensa*. The world is not positive fact, not "whatever is the case," not mindless matter, not mere *Vorhandensein*. As long as there is an Okeanos, it is *a priori* a world in itself reflected, which is what makes it imaginal. Okeanos guarantees the absolute interiority and inner infinity of the whole world, and thus also of everything that exists in this world. By locking everything within, Okeanos is what enables and forces (potentially) everything to be experienced as "inner," as animated, spirited from within by an ultimately divine image as its soul. This is why Okeanos is the Father of all the Gods—the father, we might say, of all images. He prevents things or events from being seen in terms of extension and exteriority by forcing all thinking and all vision into that interiority of each thing or event that is the divine image, word, or meaning it contains.

But if mythology already contains the idea of absolute interiority and is even conscious of the fact that this is what it is constituted by, what is new with Heraclitus' and the psalmist's insight? It is not the content or substance. The content is ancient mythological stock. New is only the logical form in which this substance is now conceived. Already myth *is* logos, *is* reflection, *is* thought, *is* absolute interiority. But it is logos cloaked in natural imagery, it presents absolute interiority projected into its other, the "extended matter" of the imagination, in other words in a mode opposite to what it is about. This is why myths are paradoxical: Okeanos, who represents the idea of absolute interiority, is imagined as a river out there at the margins of Being. Thus this is image necessarily turns our orientation towards the outermost distance and holds it in a spatial fantasy, while at the same time telling us that all rivers flow from out there inwards; in other words, that the essential movement goes in the opposite direction. By contrast the psalmist does not imagine a world-encircling river any more. He thinks of an inescapable knowledge. He and Heraclitus reduce the idea of the literal or imaginal move into the distance to absurdity and thus overcome the imaginal mode once and for all, thereby sublating the ancient idea of an absolute containment, by both overcoming the mythical idea of an Okeanos and regaining it in the mode of reflection and on the level of conceptual thought.

It is with this revolutionary change of the mode or form of consciousness that psychology becomes possible as well as necessary. As long as the form of consciousness was truly imaginal (mythic), there was no place for psychology, because then the soul, as it were, spilled out into and all over nature. It "extended" itself. However psychology is the soul returned to its home ground, reflected into itself, not into its other, nature. As long as consciousness was informed by myth, humans could still feel that they lived in the world, in nature, in the cosmos. This is impossible for us. We know that we live in soul, in consciousness, in God's knowledge, and that the world is irrevocably outside.

In order to understand Heraclitus' fragment and to put it into perspective, we have looked at *Psalm 139* as well as at the myth of Okeanos. It now remains for us to clarify how the Heraclitean conception relates to Jung's psychology and vice versa. Jung writes (*CW 8*, § 380), "We are in truth so wrapped about by psychic images that we cannot penetrate at all to the essence of things external to ourselves."

Does this not sound like an (unintended) rewording of Heraclitus', "You would not find out the boundaries of soul, even by traveling along every path?" This is no exit out of psychic reality. We are totally surrounded by soul. Clearly, this is the idea of the psyche's absolute interiority in itself.

But then we also have to note that in the same sentence Jung posits an essence of things external to the psyche, which is incompatible with the "no exit" idea. Jung simultaneously holds two mutually exclusive views. It is not that with the second view the soul's absolute interiority is relativized. Rather, as absolute interiority it is suspended in the opposite conception, in a linear orientation of extension and exteriority. Even if it is practically inaccessible, theoretically there nevertheless does exist for this stance an exit out of the psyche; the soul does have an "outside" of itself. Jung operates with the idea of a beyond on the other side of "a barrier across the mental world" (*CW 18*, § 1734), in other words with the idea of an outer boundary that Heraclitus as well as the psalmist had reduced to absurdity. This second stance is diametrically opposed to the insight Heraclitus had gained. Jung leaves the boundary "out there," and unreachable, while Heraclitus had interiorized it into the soul.

Thus Jung is speaking with a split tongue; he has two separate truths that he holds apart by means of a systematic distribution. When "doing" psychology (when speaking within the field of psychology), he totally subscribes to the "inescapable interiority" idea, sometimes even giving psychology the rank of a super-science, a "science" of the sciences (inasmuch as all sciences are expressions of the psyche, too). But when he reflects about psychology and presents his overall theory of knowing, he ultimately invalidates psychology by embedding it in an overriding stance for which precisely the essence of things is located beyond that unsurmountable boundary, in the "things external to ourselves." What from within psychology is personally felt and explicitly declared to be of utmost importance, to be the essential (our processes of transformation and individuation with all the precious images of ultimately divine matters they involve us in) has only ("nothing but") the logical status of a kind of personal entertainment in a bubble that has both the real essence and the essence of real life outside of itself. Psychology is fenced in, encapsulated in a reserve or asylum, one could also say in a playhouse. Within this playhouse it is free, infinite, or, putting it the other way around as Jung did, it does not have "the advantage of a 'delimited field of work'" (*CW 9/i*, § 112), but psychology as a whole is defined as a "de-limited field." You have to play dumb and suppress your knowledge about the real state of affairs (namely, that the essence is out there) in order to be able to take psychology seriously. In other words you have to act as if you were taking it seriously.

That the essence of things outside of ourselves is said to be totally out of reach, and the barrier to be unsurmountable even for "the boldest leap of speculation"[10] has the result that for all practical ends and purposes the exit out of the psyche can be neglected. Within psychology it does not take effect. But this does not alter the fact that the (practically ineffective) idea of something external to the psyche psychologically is powerful. It is what determines the theoretical validity and logical status of things psychological. Psychology is under the spell of the orientation towards an "outside."

The ruling power of this orientation is not even destroyed for Jung by the fact that his view involves him and us in a (faulty, undialectical) contradiction. For if it is true that we are so wrapped about by psychic images that we cannot penetrate at all to the essence of things external to ourselves, we cannot know in the first place that there are things external to ourselves, because this idea would necessarily also be no more than a psychic image. It would be a fantasy on the part of the soul, a soul content that the soul within itself projects outside of itself. Within psychology Jung insisted that projections have to be withdrawn. But when it comes to the soul's projected imagination of its own other, he instantly dropped the psychological approach insisting on taking this (soul-internal) projection of something external as bare fact. Whereas within psychology the soul was all-surrounding, psychology itself was set up as bordering on, and totally encircled by, an external other—"real" reality.

Why would Jung resort to such a split-in-itself, dissociated conception? This question strikes at the heart of his psychology and touches on its basic fault. An answer would involve a thorough analysis of his psychology including a fundamental critique of his notions of "the unconscious," "the inner," "psychological reality," "personality," and "Self," as well as of his psycho-biography. This is beyond the scope of the

---

[10] Jung, *CW 18*, § 1734, translation modified.

present paper. Some aspects of an answer I tried to provide in my article, "Jung's Betrayal of His Truth: The Adoption of a Kant-Based Empiricism and the rejection of Hegel's Speculative Thought."[11] Here I want to point out merely one benefit of this dissociation.

By fundamentally "doing psychology in," (i.e., defining it as having to do with an "inner" in an abstract, external sense, so that he would have two mutually exclusive ultimate commitments, and by correspondingly inventing himself as two alternating subjectivities in the form of personality No. 1 and personality No. 2), Jung could continue operating on the level of the contents of consciousness without having to become conscious of and take responsibility for the problem of the logical form of consciousness. I have stressed that Heraclitus, by fetching the notion of boundary from out there onto the home territory of the soul as the self-contradictory, inverted notion of its inner or internal boundary, had decomposed or corrupted once and for all that form of consciousness that orients itself primarily by means of sensory intuition and imagination. Instead he advanced to a thinking, reflecting form of consciousness as the only adequate mode in which to think about the soul. Two and a half thousand years after Heraclitus, Jung hoped to get away, in his conception of the new field of the psychology of the unconscious, with staying at the old level of consciousness and feeling exempt from having to think of the prime matters of soul. The split to which he resorted enabled him to provide, on the one hand, a playground for all the mythical images and ideas of the soul, a playground unhindered by any metaphysical claims that they would inevitably involve a modern consciousness in, and on the other hand, to pay tribute to the reality that the times of myth (of a oneness of soul and nature, of an imaginal form of consciousness) were irrevocably bygone and that we had long arrived on the level of a broken, reflecting consciousness. He satisfied two opposite needs, not, however, by logically reconciling them but by switching back and forth. In other words, he acted the rupture out instead of remembering, interiorizing it.

I used the image of the playhouse for psychology and said that psychology is free and unlimited within this playhouse, whereas the playhouse itself is defined as a "delimited field." Of course it is the

[11] *Harvest 44*, No. 1, 1998, 46–64.

personality that is the reality reflected in this image. The structural setup of psychology with the duplicity of a total surroundedness by psychic images and of an unreachable reality external to ourselves is perfectly mirrored in the idea of the unconscious *in* the personality (the abstract "inner") and the real world all around it (the abstract "outer"), which in turn is mirrored in the distinction between the subject- and the object-levels of dream interpretation. Here, too, we see how Jung acted out. He internalized the psyche into the person instead of reflecting it into itself. This is the result of his clinging to the mode of sensory intuition and imagination which forced him to absolutely hold on to something positive and empirical-factual, the human personality. It prevented him from "remembering" the soul's need for an internalization, which, if "remembered," would have been an absolute-negative interiorization.

His acting out on the theoretical level is what most distinguishes his conception from both that of Heraclitus and that of the Okeanos myth. The latter two did not act out nor were they split. They were both "whole." The unshakeable foundation of Jung's setup was the abstract, external, unpsychological border (his "barrier through the mental world") that separated "inner" and "outer" as mutually exclusive opposites standing, as it were, back to back, much as the two half-circles in Jakob Böhme's "broken" mandala.[12] This dissociation was the tribute he had to pay to modernity, and it was what drove his "striving toward wholeness." Because Jung externalized the abstract boundary (i.e., left it "out there"), he did not penetrate to a psychological (interiorized) notion of the inner. As his internalizing the inner into something external, namely into the "positive fact" called human being shows, his psychology remained subject to positivity and external thinking, as much as he tried to acquire a sense of soul.

The Okeanos myth is totally different. It started out from a non-abstract idea of boundary, from absolute interiority, but it externalized this only secondarily by imagining it. This secondarily externalized true interiority resulted in humanity's real being in the world, being in nature, which in turn meant that humanity was able to experience nature from within: as animated, divine, full of meaning. With Heraclitus the situation is again different. Like Jung he started out with the external, abstract

[12] See Jung, *CW 9/i*, Fig. 1, § 297.

idea of boundary. This shows that from the outset he was in "reflection" and no longer in "myth." Embeddedness in nature was once and for all bygone. But then he drew the external boundary within, thereby opening up the dimension of absolute interiority on the level of reflecting consciousness and paving the way for a true psychology.

Another small example may illustrate the fact that Jung tried to achieve on the level of contents (observable, empirical, i.e, external "facts") what he had theoretically excluded and vehemently prohibited on the level of logical form (his own thought, the theoretical setup of psychology). I am talking of his theory of synchronicity. In his well-considered thought, the "inner" was, on the one hand, separated from the "outer" (the object external to ourselves) by an unsurmountable barrier, as we have seen. But, on the other hand, Jung showed them to be united in certain empirical (so-called synchronistic) events, a union which seemed to promise no less than an ultimate overcoming of the gulf between physics and psychology. Through the observation of "facts," he tried to get in through the backdoor what he had thrown out through the official, dedicated entrance. How can a psychologist put the burden of proof or authority on the empirical, on the observation of external facts? How can he want to get himself out of the firing-line, posing as an innocent, neutral observer? The implications of the theory of synchronicity absolutely threaten, indeed shatter, our accustomed world-view. But Jung did not take responsibility for his theory. *He* was not to blame. He had nothing to do with it. He had not on his own come up with a "metaphysical" claim of an ultimate oneness. He had only *discovered* certain "empirical facts" about the deepest, psychoid nature of the collective unconscious. Shameful.

The subject, you yourself, your own thinking, have to take responsibility for whatever is stated in psychology, because the only entrance to psychology is through my (each person's) own subjectivity, which in turn is only accessible speculatively by reflecting myself in some other (in a given manifestation or document of the soul) and through absolute-negative interiorization. It is not accessible empirically through introspection, which is merely a literal, positive return home, inasmuch as it looks at the subject only as its new object of study, never reaching psychological interiority.

We see Jung was still trying, as it were, to "travel every road out there" in search of the boundaries of soul. Declaring himself to be an empiricist means he believed that he had to find the truth about the soul "on the street." But two thousand five hundred years after Heraclitus and more than one hundred years after Hegel, he could have and should have known that psychology begins with the return home—not a literal return in space, but a logical one through the logical reversal of the ordinary relation of inner and outer. By cementing his empiricism, Jung in contrast to Heraclitus protected this empiricism from its having to suffer its own natural fate: its sublation through the inevitable experience of not finding out the boundaries out there. Jung arrested the search midway by resorting to ideologizing. He claimed that the road is the goal. This claim is ideological because it cloaks a subjective refusal (the refusal to expose his empiricism to its fate) in an allegedly objective truth. But what this claim says is not simply the truth. What it amounts to is the freezing of the search, not in the physical or imaginal sense of immobilizing it (halting it in its movement), but on the contrary, in the logical sense of freezing its movement as movement, so that it can go on and on and on. It can never arrive anywhere. The search cannot find its natural end. It is endless in the sense of "bad infinity." In other words, his claim is the ideological equivalent to the sentiment expressed in the idea of the soul's depth. Despite his revolutionary moves in many areas of psychology, Jung was, in the very heart of psychology (namely where it is a question of its logical constitution), a reactionary. By staying on Heraclitus' "roads," he protracted the modes of sensory intuition and imagination and defended against the necessity of entering thought, which would have transported him to the outermost boundary of the "no" instantaneously. Thus he successfully prevented the experience of the recoil of his outwards movement (his empiricism), of its being thrown back upon itself and the ensuing reversal of his logic. The road is not the goal. The goal is the actual, committed arrival at, and ever deeper penetration into or submission to, the "no" of the "no boundary" insight, in other words, the absolute-negative interiorization. The "road as the goal" is the positive negation of the goal. Yet psychology requires the negative negation.

It is not enough to teach the *unus mundus* and the *complexio oppositorum* and not enough to have and experience dream or visionary images thereof. That is not psychology at all, because it is still projected into positive "fact" or natural "event." What good are images from the unconscious of the self and wholeness and of an *unus mundus*, if the systems of the unconscious and consciousness and of humans and world are divided against each other by an unsurmountable barrier? Has wholeness become real if I dream an image of wholeness? Is a divorce or an estrangement between husband and wife healed by seeing a movie about a perfect marriage? What good is the experience of synchronistic events if the union of physis and psyche occurs only in the "object" out there—the event—but excludes its own inner from this union; namely me, my subjectivity, my conscious mind? That it does exclude my mind is obvious from the fact that I have to experience synchronistic occurrences as miraculous (as "too wonderful, too high, I cannot attain unto them"). Jung's answers to the problem of the great split in the Western soul and of the psychic opposites are mock solutions because they sidestep the actual problem. They must sidestep the actual problem because they are systematically set up to occur on one side only—that of the images or experiences—when the actual problem is the division between the two sides—the images there and our subjectivity or thought here. This is why any approach concentrating on facts, feeling experiences, images, the imaginal, jumps too short. It stays on one side of the split that it wants to overcome.

There is one answer to the problem of the split and the opposites. It is that I have to slowly and painfully learn to become able to think, to conceptually comprehend, the union of opposites—where true thinking does not mean that I push ideas around in my head, but that I exist as this living comprehension, as the existing Concept (Hegel). This comprehension has to have become the explicit and real logic of my conscious awareness of my being-in-the-world.

The neurotic split in the Western psyche is not actually pathological. What makes it pathological is that it is not understood—not understood as a "symptom" of the fact that in the history of the soul consciousness has advanced to an awareness of itself as a determining factor and as one half of a whole, an awareness that simply requires thought and dialectical logic. It requires the alchemical corruption of the empirical stance into a speculative one. The painfully experienced split is no more than an invitation to consciousness to allow itself to be initiated into thought and to become thinking consciousness *sensu strictiori*. It is only because this invitation is refused, consciousness stubbornly cocooning itself in the innocence of its outdated imagining mode, that the split becomes neurotic, pathological. The neurotic split is an artifact. It is our letting the "barrier through the mental world" remain out there as a positive barrier. In other words, it is our neglect to (like Heraclitus) interiorize it, to reflect it into itself (not into ourselves, our "inner"). Jung tried to locate and cure the split out there, in the psyche of the person. But this is not where it is. The soul is not split, it is not in need of wholeness, because it is always whole. The split is in Jung's (and our) frame of mind. It is produced by his obstinate empiricism, image-fixation, and speculation phobia, that turns the soul's inner boundary (its internal contradiction or the dialectic of its logical life) inside out, translating it from the negativity of the soul into the positivity of imagined realities, so that the inner boundary all of a sudden appears as a hard "barrier" or positive rupture between two separate, unambiguously distinct, ontologized realms—the positivized inner (or psychic, "the unconscious") and the likewise positivized outer (or the "objective" world); exactly like the two back-to-back half-circles of Böhme's split mandala. But, of course, you need the split out there if you want to be the innocent neutral observer and psychology to be a natural science.

Why do we have neuroses? Apart from the external (not yet psychological) aspect of the contingent conditions lying in one's personal biography, there are two psychological reasons. The first is that the soul's internal boundary (its dialectical life) is turned inside out, resulting in (1) a factually existing split or rupture and (2) a positivizing frame of mind. The second reason is that, due to this compulsion to positivize, the personality is identified, (i.e., becomes identical) with the now abstract, external boundary and thus has to personally exist as the embodied barrier that holds two sides apart and dissociates them.

Returning from the individual neuroses to the cultural neurosis, we can say that the personality has become the existing boundary by having been interposed, like a wedge, right into the whole of experience so as to be the partition wall dividing this integral whole into two opposite classes of experiences, those that "seem to us" to be "derived from a 'material' environment to which our bodies belong" (the outer), versus "others, which are in no way less real" but "seem to come from a 'spiritual' source" (cf. *CW 8*, § 681), such as our dreams, fantasies, thoughts. We call this intercepting, interposed personality, the "ego personality." Existing as the embodied border that splits the world into two, "the physical world" here and "the spiritual world" (*ibid.*) there, it is fundamentally Janus-faced. It has two separate truths, two antipodal "source(s) of psychic contents that crowd into my field of consciousness" (*ibid.*), two opposite orientations. It switches between looking out (extraversion) and turning in (introspection, introversion); it *is* the neurosis. That the ego personality *is* the neurosis does of course not mean that in all cases it would also have to have a personal neurosis in the clinical sense. On the contrary, the more it *is* the neurosis, the more it is likely to be free from neurotic disorders. The more it is plagued by an individual neurosis, the more it probably refuses to exist as the neurotic split. And Jung's typological doctrine is the celebration and justification of the neurotic split by raising it to the rank of a general theory.

The insight into the "ego personality" as the head of Janus supports our view that "inner" and "outer" are both equally external. They are like looking left and turning around to look right, or like looking north and turning around to look south. Dream images as such are not "inner" in a psychological sense. They are "inner" only for the mindless understanding of everyday consciousness that takes the mere name "inner" for the real thing, clinging to an external sense of the inner-outer opposition. Dream images are just as much outer (empirical) facts as the stones, trees, animals, people I experience in the physical world, and they have their real inner, namely me ("my field of consciousness"), likewise outside of themselves. That we arbitrarily call a class of objects *vis-à-vis* ourselves (thoughts, feelings, dream, and fantasy images) inner is only a sign of the ruling abstract sense of boundary and of the internalization of this external boundary into or its identification with the positivized human personality. And it is the sign of a defense against the soul and its absolute-negative interiorization, its reflection-into-itself. It is the sign of a wish to do psychology but nevertheless to keep the "I" out so that it can be the self-identical empirical scientist. And it is a sign of the avoidance of thought, logic. If a certain class of phenomena are supposed to be the "inner" as opposed to others as "outer," and if there is a hypostatized object called "the Self," I myself as subjectivity am exempted. I do not have to become aware of myself. It is all out there.

However psychology begins where any phenomenon (whether physical or mental, "real" or fantasy image) is interiorized absolute-negatively into itself, and I find myself in its internal infinity. This is what it takes; psychology cannot be had for less.

Interestingly I can "get out" and feel exempted only by getting in the center of experience as such, so as to be the dividing barrier. This contradiction results from the dialectical nature of existence. The ordinary ego personality and the consciousness of the scientist are the barrier in that they hold the archetypal, religious, metaphysical aspects of experience behind their back as so-called superstitions or are at least "merely subjective" in order to have only positivized facts in front of themselves.

Jung, the psychologist of the collective unconscious, invented a second way of getting out by getting in even deeper. How did he preserve his neutrality? He did not simply turn around so that he would look at the psychic images while having the positive facts of reality behind him. Rather, he widened our ordinary vision or our ordinary sense of the real so that it would include the ordinarily ignored archetypal aspects. We already know that extraversion and introspection are equally external. How then did he exist as the barrier and what did he keep behind his back? Jung kept the religious, metaphysical dynamite contained in the soul's archetypal fantasies and ideas behind his back. He could look at the mysteries of Gnosticism, Christian dogma, metaphysical conceptions, even at the weirdest delusional ideas and superstitions without a threat to his common sense, because he had interposed himself right in the middle of these ideas or images, dividing their archetypal content as legitimate psychological interest ("psychological reality") from their inherent claim to truth, which had to be excluded by penalty of one's sanity of mind.

In other words, Jung repeated the same division with which positivistic science rid itself of any religious or metaphysical implications, only now on a deeper, more refined level. He applied it precisely to what the other sciences had systematically excluded. The cleaver with which he was able to interpose the scientific ego personality into what science had hitherto had to keep behind its back was his invention of a second, special kind of reality or truth, the aforementioned psychological reality. This ingenious invention permitted him to subject even the archetypal ideas or the imaginal to the same positivizing that formerly had cleared "nature" from any archetypal "projections." "When psychology speaks, for instance, of the motif of the virgin birth, it is only concerned with the fact that there is such an idea, but it is not concerned with the question whether such an idea is true or false in any other sense. The idea is psychologically true inasmuch as it exists" (*CW 11*, § 4). Here we see not Occam's but Jung's razor at work. The archetypal substance is cut apart, castrated, deprived of its claim to truth, reduced to the factual "occurrence" (*ibid.*) or existence of its abstract content. This is—*horribile dictu*—archetypal positivism, positivism applied to the imaginal itself. Psychological truth is here defined precisely as what excludes real truth; real truth which has to be kept behind the psychologist's back. So Jung rescued the imaginal contents for the scientific approach by paying for it with their soul—their claim to truth. Nevertheless he sold the resulting leftover as the definition of psychology. He did all this in order to avoid falling into dialectical logic and speculation.

But now we have to realize, too, that the personality as the head of Janus already is the dialectic, the existing Concept, only turned inside out and thus in its frozen, hardened shape as literal border or dissociation. This is also why it needs and has the sentimental idea that "the soul is deep" to console it for and disguise its own logical petrification. In the romantic sentiment it has the split-off other side inherent in the dialectic (other than its contradictory nature), namely the dialectic's interiority and fluidity as the soul of all reality and as logical life (an interiority that is now, in the guise of this romantic sentiment, also abstract, externalized, reified). If Heraclitus can be considered the father of psychology, psychology has to learn from his fragment: (1) that the notion of soul hinges on actually getting to its boundaries and thus on a sense of opposition or contradiction (inner–outer), (2) that getting there is only possible through and in thought, and that it is negative arrival, or arrival at a "no;" being permeated by this "no," (3) that such an arrival leads to an absolute-negative interiorization of "boundary," resulting in an interiority through which (4) the boundary is decomposed as the positive barrier that it used to be for the imagining mind and is vaporized into the fluidity of living dialectics. Such is the depth of the soul's *logos*.

“Yes, In You the Tempest Rages”

The Archetypal Significance of America for Jung, 1909-1913

THOMAS J. MARTINEZ

AND

EUGENE TAYLOR

While interpreters of the Western analytic tradition continue to focus on Jung’s life and work from a Eurocentric point of view (Charet, 1993; Noll, 1995, McLynn, 1996), little attention has been paid to the archetypal significance that America held for Jung in his own process of individuation or to the manner in which Jung’s ideas have been assimilated into American thought and therefore have become Americanized.[1] We believe a case can be made for the idea that without the American response there would have been no Freud and no Jung as we know their ideas today. Freud came only once and promised he would never come again; Jung traveled to America on seven occasions during his lifetime. Nevertheless, a large part of the success of their respective theories rests with their American visits and the American response to

[1] The Americanization of Jung and Freud is considered in Taylor (1999). See also Martinez (1998) “Anthropos and Existence” for Jung’s influence on the development of archetypal themes in the work of American existential psychoanalyst Rollo May.

Thomas Martinez is an adjunct professor of psychology at the Sage Colleges in Albany, New York, a psychotherapist practicing in Saratoga Springs, and a Ph.D. candidate at Saybrook Graduate School and Research Institute in San Francisco. Eugene Taylor is a lecturer on psychiatry at Harvard Medical School, senior psychologist at Massachusetts General Hospital in Boston, and a faculty member at Saybrook. His most recent book is *Shadow Culture: Psychology and Spirituality in America* (1999).

their ideas. Freud's one visit continues to be analyzed over and over, mainly from the same Freudo-centric perspective, while several, but not all, of Jung's visits continue to be recounted as part of psychology's history (Hornstein, 1992; Rosenzweig, 1992). As a topic unto themselves, the frequency and nature of Jung's excursions to the United States have yet to be fully analyzed (McGuire, 1983; 1995). This essay, which focuses on Jung's psychoanalytic years and friendship with Freud, is an attempt to fill that void at least up to 1913. The evidence suggests that not only did a process of Americanization immediately begin to take place for Jung, but also it appears that America became an archetypal symbol for him. And it seems that America played a central role in his personal journey toward self-knowledge.[2]

The 1909 Visit

As is already well-known, Jung traveled to America for the first time in August, 1909, together with Freud and colleague Sandor Ferenczi at the invitation of G. Stanley Hall, an American psychologist

[2] Sonu Shamdasani takes issue with two key parts of this hypothesis: first, that there is no such thing as an "archetype of America," a conception that stretches the definition of the archetypes beyond what Jung had intended; and two, Shamdasani prefers "to avoid depicting Jung in his own psychological terms, due to the resulting circularity." We differ significantly on these points. With regard to the archetype of place, Jung's various remarks on "the archetype of transformation" (38; 135-147), leaves no doubt that he certainly did recognize the archetypal significance of place in the individuation process. His retelling of the story of Moses and Khidir, and his use of the "journeying" motif central to the story, as a metaphor and symbol for "going into the darkness that lies behind consciousness" (135), is particularly informative for demonstrating the transformation experience. Jung writes: "The character of the self as a personality comes out plainly in the Khidir legend (142)…it gives an almost perfect picture of a psychic transformation or rebirth which today, with our greater psychological insight, we would recognize as an individuation process… The legend expresses the archetype of transformation admirably" (147). If we look at Jung's life in this way, as storied, myth-like, well-traveled, or journeyed, and above all as a "symbol for going into the darkness that lies behind consciousness" (135)—as being shaped by the archetype of transformation, then America emerges as the most compelling place for insight into the meanings concealed in that darkness. We believe that America was not only essential for Jung's maturation as a psychiatrist, but that it also served as a spiritual homeland during his encounter with Freud and place of transformation and rebirth for many years after their break in the fall of 1913. To support this assertion, we show how the image of America and significant archetypal figures and themes associated with American culture appear as symbols of destiny and self-realization in *(continued)*

and president of Clark University (McGuire, 1974; Rosenzweig, 1992). The nature of this initial visit was to celebrate the twentieth anniversary of the founding of Clark University.

At Clark, Hall had been involved competitively with Harvard University and William James, his old mentor in psychology, on a number of fronts, one of which was pioneering developments in abnormal psychology. James and the so-called Boston School of Abnormal Psychology had attracted the attention of both psychologists and medical doctors by premiering the work of Pierre Janet and the French school of dissociation. Hall would no doubt be able to steal some of the spotlight by inviting Freud, Janet's Viennese counterpart, whose controversial sexual theories were just then becoming well-known. In addition Hall had been founder of the Child Study movement and he believed Freud's ideas, especially on child development, could be used to attract attention to this struggling movement.

Jung's dreams at crucial points in his life.Thus echoing the conclusions of Hillman, Casey, Corbin, and others on the relation of image, archetype, and place (Samuels, 1985), we see America as both a symbolic or imaginal place and a geographic locality essential for Jung's individuation. America as an indispensable place for Jung's transformation experience is rooted first in the dream image of an American journey recounted in the text (see *Excursus: Jung's Dream of an American Journey and the Archetype of Transformation*) and in his mature understanding of the archetype as a psychosomatic concept with certain psychoid properties and a propensity for transgressivity. Jung (1969) writes: "The psychoid factors I call archetypes. These are indefinite, that is to say, they can be known and determined only approximately. Although associated with causal processes, or carried by them, they continually go beyond their frame of reference, an infringement to which I would give the name "transgressivity," because the archetypes are not found exclusively in the psychic sphere, but can occur just as much in circumstances that are not psychic (equivalence of an outward physical process with a psychic one)" (515).

Here Casey is also helpful when he observes: "It is not a matter of reducing archetypes…but of recognizing the strictly coeval status of psyche and cosmos. Both are essential: Neither can be eliminated from an adequate archetypal analysis. Archetypes, then, have a foundation equally in psyche—which is to say in imagination, for "image is psyche"—and in the material world: and this is the case whatever their ultimate configuration may be" (1991, 11). With regard to using Jung's terms to refer to his own process of individuation, we subscribe to the idea that Jung's iconographic picture of the unconscious was his own unique map, and is, in fact, applicable only to him (Taylor, 1997). This is why he urged others to go out and create their own mythology, not take over his wholesale. So if his system is applicable anywhere, it is most appropriate to apply to himself.

We know from recent scholarship that Hall had invited Wilhelm Wundt and a number of others, including Freud, to speak, but all had turned him down. Freud had cause to reconsider a second invitation when Hall increased the honorarium. In the interim between refusal and acceptance from Freud, and following close upon the news that Ernst Meumann could not come, Hall had invited Jung almost as an afterthought. This suggests that Hall's motive for approaching Jung remained ancillary to his primary interest in Freud.

For their part Jung and Freud discussed the matter briefly but intensely. Jung had a secret yearning for America because he believed that his talents would be recognized and that he might acquire wealthy patients there (Rosenzweig, 1992, 39). Prior to his discussion with Freud about the pending trip in 1909, Jung had been retained as a consultant to Harold McCormick, a psychotic patient who moved in and out of asylums and whose wealthy family was descended from Cyrus McCormick, inventor of the reaper. Various members of this family were also intermarried with the Rockefellers. Eventually Jung would take a number of them as patients, and they in turn would provide significant support for launching the Analytical Psychology movement in the United States and in Europe (McGuire, 1993).

A few years before their discussion of the pending Clark conference, Jung had already made his feelings known to Freud about the New World. In *The Psychology of Dementia Praecox*, which he sent to Freud when it was first published in 1906, Jung included an analysis of a dream recounted by a young husband who reflected Jung's own predilections toward America. According to Jung:

> A friend once told me the following dream: I saw horses being hoisted by thick cables to a great height. One of them, a powerful brown horse which was tied up with straps and was hoisted aloft like a package, struck me particularly. Suddenly, the cable broke and the horse crashed to the street. I thought it must be dead. But it immediately leapt up again and galloped away. I noticed that the horse was dragging a heavy log along with it, and I wondered how it could advance so quickly. It was obviously frightened and might easily have caused an accident. Then a rider came up on a little horse and rode along slowly in front of the frightened horse, which moderated its pace somewhat. I still feared that the

> horse might run over the rider, when a cab came along and drove in front of the rider at the same pace, thus bringing the frightened horse to a still slower gait. I then thought, now all is well; the danger is over (1910, 57-58).

In his analysis of the dream, Jung later reports a number of associations which show that the dreamer had:

> ...a great desire to make a high ascent and also to travel [but]...had been obliged to give up the idea of a journey to America... According to Freud, the dreamer must be represented [and] is usually the chief actor. This is undoubtedly "the powerful brown horse." The powerful brown horse resembles him firstly, because it can work hard, secondly, because the brown colour was described as a healthy tan such as mountain-climbers have. So the brown horse may well be the dreamer (1960, 58-59).

Excursus: Jung's Dream of an American Journey and the Archetype of Transformation

Freud suspected that Jung himself was the dreamer. Jung responded in the affirmative and clearly indicated that the "yearning for an American journey was a distinct part of his contemporary personality" (Rosenzweig, 1992, 39). While we concur with Rosenzweig on this, we go further still and maintain that Jung's dream[3] locates the image of America as an already existing symbol in his psyche—prior to the initial exchange of letters with Freud in October of 1906, and long before he voyaged to America with Ferenczi and Freud in August of 1909. Given Jung's subsequent returns to America and his rapid maturation in the years immediately following the 1909 trip—including the years of friendship and disenchantment with Freud—we view the initial dream and image of America as an expression of the archetype of transformation for Jung. Here Jung himself provides the lead, when late in life he returns to the significance of the skyscraper motif and the meaning of America for his self realization. Jung writes:

[3] See Michael Vannoy Adams (1991) for a different interpretation of the dream. Adams' excellent paper refers to the dream as "Jung's dream of the brown horse and heavy log" and focuses extensively on the horse symbolism.

> Through my acquaintance with many Americans, and my trips to and in America, I have obtained an enormous amount of insight into the European character: it has always seemed to me that there can be nothing more useful for a European than sometime or another to look out at Europe from the top of a skyscraper... In America...I became aware [that] I was still caught and imprisoned in the cultural consciousness of the white man" (1973b, 247).

These reflections of Jung's late in his life indicate that America played a vital role in his awareness of cultural consciousness and was an important aspect of his self realization and individuation. Hence Jung's "dream of an American journey" is not only foreshadowed by the 1909 voyage to America but also hints at elements of destiny, personal transformation, and freedom to the intrigue surrounding his numerous returns. This is to say that Jung's path to individuation, as a matter of destiny or fate, necessarily involved the real geographical locality known as America and was preceded by an anticipatory dream and archetypal fantasy of a journey to the New World.

How we understand the word "archetypal" within the context of Jung's visits to America and encounters with Americans can be defined by establishing a connection between the dream image of America, its geographic counterpart, and the elements of destiny, personal transformation, and a desired freedom from the presumptions and often tyrannical restrictions of psychoanalysis. Here Jung's remarks are helpful.

> In the course of this process [individuation] the archetypes appear as active personalities in dreams and fantasies. But the process itself involves another class of archetypes which one could call the archetypes of transformation. They are not personalities, but are situations, places, ways and means that symbolize the kind of transformation in question. Like the personalities, these archetypes are true and genuine symbols that cannot be exhaustively interpreted, either as signs or as allegories. They are genuine symbols precisely because they are ambiguous, full of half glimpsed meanings, and in the last resort inexhaustible. The ground principles, the *archai*, of the unconscious are indescribable because of their wealth of reference, although in themselves recognizable (1980, 38).

With this in mind we might then envision the actualization of the archetype as the concrete manifestation of the unconscious and begin to understand what Jung means when he states: "Everything in the unconscious seeks outward manifestation, and the personality too desires to evolve out of its unconscious conditions" (1973b, 3). James Hillman is also instructive with his recognition that "fantasy locations...place the ideas in a geographical image" (1985, 30). America can be understood as an imaginal place and as a geographical location: a place of immense growth and transformation for Jung.

Jung was also aware of the symbolic importance of color in the process of psychological transformation. His 1906 paper, "Association, Dream, and Hysterical Symptom," dating from the same time period as his dream of an American journey, shows this clearly. Jung's analysis of a twenty-four year-old woman suffering from hysteria at the Burghölzli reveals "that the disturbances in the Association Experiment formed around the same contents, as the contents of dreams... Thus the dream is a channel for the complexes to be acted out [and] complexes are personified in dreams" (C. A. Meier, 1987, 35). The central figure in the drama of this woman's dream series was "a black man [who] she often imagined and who stretched out his black hand towards her" (Jung, 1981, 354), especially just before sleep. This "black man of dreams and visions" (389) was seen in Jung's psychoanalytically influenced interpretation as a symbol for the woman's forbidden sexual desire for the doctor and ultimately as "escape into illness...the desire to remain ill" (390). Beyond the transference and projections though, the "black man of dreams and visions" awakened something sleeping in Jung. What was to be transformed in America had something to do with the dark element within Jung. We will see how this motif, which first surfaced in America as "the imprisoned cultural consciousness of a white man," returned again years later in Africa with a clearly American connection. Finally Jung's essay, "Concerning Rebirth," makes this unequivocal. The archetype of transformation presupposes the presence of the larger personality [Self] and a dynamic encounter with the unconscious. Thus when we speak of Jung's dream of an American journey, we are speaking of a dynamic encounter with the unconscious and Jung's subsequent transformation in the geographical location known as America.

Psychoanalysis and the New World

When Freud informed Jung that he had turned down Hall's first offer, Jung replied that it would have been good "to speak in America if only because of the echo it would arouse in Europe." Freud was well aware of this possibility but dared not think directly about it. When he later decided to go, he convinced himself that he really did not like America but would go for the sake of his own curiosity as a naturalist, as he had always wanted to see a porcupine (Gifford, 1972).

The trio sailed from Bremen, Germany on 21 August and arrived eight days later. Once in New York the group, whose ultimate destination was Worcester, Massachusetts, was joined by Austrian-born New York psychoanalyst Abraham Arden Brill, and a few days later, by Toronto-based physician Ernest Jones. Freud later said he would never return to America, partly because he had become sick from eating the food. At one point Freud, Jung, and Ferenczi all came down with indigestion at the same time. They took the opportunity to visit the museums and the opera and even saw their first motion picture, and Freud met with the Bernays family, relatives who were living in the city.

A significant event in this progression occurred when Jung and Freud took a walk in Central Park and discussed one of Jung's dreams concerning "Jews and Aryans" (Rosenzweig, 62-63). According to letters that both Freud and Jung wrote to their families, the walk was pleasant and several topics were discussed. Freud wrote home noting only the ethnic diversity in the park, especially the number of Jewish children playing, while Jung wrote home describing an exchange about "a sociological problem with psychoanalysis" involving "Aryans and Jews." However Rosenzweig gives the impression that Freud remained neutral and was probably shocked to hear Jung's blatant anti-Semititic comments. Rosenzweig refers to Jung's comment as a "racist dichotomy" and further says, "It is remarkable, not hitherto noticed, that the difference between Aryans and Jews was important to Jung as early as 1909" (63).

We disagree with Rosenzweig's analysis of the episode. First, Rosenzweig is factually incorrect on several points. For instance it is generally agreed among scholars of Freud and Jung that one of the reasons Freud embraced Jung was that he was both a gentile and a Swiss as well as an outsider of Freud's immediate Vienna circle, which was made up wholly of Jewish followers. Jung would not only bring international recognition to psychoanalysis but also rescue it from being labeled merely an ethnic cult.[4] Secondly it is almost certain that Freud and Jung talked about these racial matters as "the sociological problem of psychoanalysis,"[5] and the topic was not endemic to Jung's personal views. It is known that Jung had over-identified with German *volkist* culture since he was a boy and that the histories of the *volkist* movement before 1900 all stress the strong anti-Semitic cast within that folk subculture.

However the larger question of Jung's anti-Semitism is an important one and should not be glossed over (Maidenbaum & Martin, 1991; Samuels, 1993). And it is important to ask, "What was the origin of his racial statements about Jews and to what extent was it societal or individual?"[6] The evidence suggests that his views were significantly influenced by the German *volkist* culture with which he had over-identified in his youth. Moreover, we would expect that if he held such prejudices, Jung would feel the same antithetical feelings against all minority groups. We will see this is not the case with his perception of blacks. Indeed, the color black and its contrast with whiteness was to figure in a number of dreams Jung would have that would refer to the archetypal significance of America in his individuation process.

---

[4] One need only compare the original German edition of Freud's works to the Standard English edition by James Strachey to see that Strachey significantly anglicized Freud's text by substituting English folk and fairy tales for ethnic Jewish jokes and punchlines that Freud had actually employed in his writings. (Gilman, 1993).

[5] Jung wrote to his wife, for instance, saying "We spoke a good deal about Jews and Aryans, and one of my dreams clearly pointed up the difference" (62).

[6] This is the central distinction made by scientists involved in the experimental study of prejudice. Gordon Willard Allport, for instance, a pioneer in this field, found perfectly healthy decent middle class personalities in South Africa, whose prejudiced attitudes toward blacks was the worst he had ever seen. His investigations suggested that in a racially prejudiced society, the more well-adjusted a healthy person is to their surroundings the more they will reflect the larger normative prejudices of the mainstream group. See Allport (1954) *The Nature of Prejudice.* Jean Paul Sartre's (1948) *Anti-Semite and Jew* lays the problem bare from the standpoint of existential psychoanalysis, while Adorno's classic *The Authoritarian Personality* examines the problem of prejudice from the perspective of attitudes and abuses related to power. Compare also with Freud's own attitude, according to Jones "an amusing incident...was when in one of his fanciful moods he predicted the extinction of the white race in two thousand years and its probable replacement by the black one. Then, he jocularly added: "America is already threatened by the black race and it serves her right." (Jones, 1955, 60)

Another significant event took place a few days later when Freud was plagued by an attack of prostatitis. This was an important episode because Jung had to assist Freud out of an embarrassing moment when Freud had urinated in his trousers during a visit to the Psychiatric Clinic at Columbia University.[7] Freud was particularly afraid that this would recur during his lectures at Clark, and Jung offered to psychoanalyze Freud for the unconscious elements involved. When Feud produced a dream but would provide no further associations, because he said, "it would undermine my authority," an irreparable schism opened for the first time between them that would eventually lead to a complete break in their relationship.

After spending a week in New York socializing and sight-seeing, Freud, Jung, and Ferenczi departed on Saturday evening, September 4, for Worcester (Jung, 1973b). They arrived at Fall River, Massachusetts, early the next day and traveled by train to the on-going activities at Clark (McGuire, 1974; Rosenzweig, 1992). Once in Worcester the group stayed at the Standish Hotel, with Jung and Freud moving to the residence of G. Stanley Hall the next day (Jones, 1955). On Tuesday, September 7, Freud delivered the first of five lectures on psychoanalysis, while Jung gave three lectures on his experiments in word association beginning on Thursday of that week. The highlight of the trip for Jung was undoubtedly Friday evening when he was able to meet William James. The two of them spent several hours together discussing their mutual interest in psychical research (Taylor, 1980, 1985). It was probably at this time that James received his copy of Jung's medical dissertation, *On the Psychology and Pathology of So-Called Occult Phenomena.* This may not have been the only time they met.[8]

The closing ceremony on Saturday, September 11, culminated with the conferring of honorary degrees on both Freud and Jung. But again, to show Jung's ancillary status, Freud received the honorary doctorate of philosophy in laws, while Jung was awarded the honorary doctorate of philosophy in education (Rosenzweig, 1992). On Monday, September 13,

---

[7] Rosenzweig reveals these details for the first time (64-65).

[8] Jung referred to meeting James on two occasions. The second time could have been on a brief trip Jung took through Boston just after the Clark Conference, when he traveled up to Gloucester to see Mrs. Peterson, or it could have been during Jung's return visit to America, March, 1910.

Jung, Freud, and Ferenczi traveled west to Niagara Falls and then spent four days at the Adirondack Mountain retreat of J. J. Putnam, a retired Harvard professor of neurology and chief of the Neurological Department at Massachusetts General Hospital. The psychoanalytic contingent, minus Jones and Brill (who returned to Toronto and New York respectively following the activities at Clark) spent several more days in New York City before sailing for Europe on Tuesday morning, September 21 (Jones, 1955; Jung, 1973b; McGuire, 1974).

Jung's Preeminence Over Freud

While historians continue to maintain that Freud's lectures at the Clark Conference were a landmark event, there is abundant evidence to show that Freud was not the focus of the conference nor were his lectures the most well attended. Even the newspaper interviews Freud had given were contrived by Hall rather than being any kind of spontaneous recognition of Freud's importance. Jung was more well known in Boston psychotherapeutic circles than Freud, having established a name for himself as early as 1905 with his word association studies (Taylor, 1998). He was first introduced to professionals in psychology and psychiatry by Adolf Meyer and identified through his Swiss connections to August Forel and Eugen Bleuler. Even after Jung became identified as a spokesman for Freud's ideas, physicians and psychologists consistently approached Freud in Vienna by first going through Jung in Zürich.

Brill's recollection in 1955 of his introduction to psychoanalysis shows the centrality and almost singular importance of Jung for the early dissemination of Freud's ideas and the rise of the psychoanalytic movement. After completing his medical training at New York University and the College of Physicians and Surgeons at Columbia University in June of 1907, Brill traveled to Paris to study hypnotism. Discouraged to find that interest in hypnotism and the effects of suggestion "were already outmoded there"(9), Brill wrote one of his teachers at Columbia, Frederick Peterson, who recommended that he travel to Zürich to study with Jung and Bleuler. In August of 1907, Brill visited the Burghölzli, and "a month later joined the group of men...[including] Jung, Abraham, Meier, Riklin, Binswanger and others, working with Bleuler" (10). Brill adds, "I did like it in Zürich [and] remained there for about a year... From that time dates the beginning of psychoanalysis in the United States"(9).

While at the Burghölzli, Brill tells us that he "felt inspired" by the care and attention Bleuler and Jung extended to the residents of the hospital. Brill recalls that Bleuler and Jung not only examined each of their patient's "hallucinations, one by one [so as] to determine what each meant" but also inquired into "just why the patient had these particular delusions." Brill explains, "In other words, instead of registering phenomena, they went into the dynamic elements which produce those phenomena. To me, that was altogether new and revealing"(1955, 10).

While in Zürich, Brill learned from Jung the technique of dream interpretation, the word association method, and the theory of complexes. Brill reciprocated by collaborating with Peterson to translate from German into English Jung's *The Psychology of Dementia Praecox,* "the first contribution that I [Brill] made in the field of psychoanalysis, and...the first English book on psychoanalysis to be published here [in America]" (1955, 16).[9] By most accounts (Freud, 1959; Jones, 1955), Jung became during the years leading up to the Clark University Conference "a very ardent and pugnacious Freudian" (Brill, 1955, 11) whose efforts were tireless in the advancement of the psychoanalytic movement.

Jung later wrote about his impressions of Americans from this first trip, which by then had fused with the many subsequent experiences he had with American patients. All countries can be typed, Jung said, such as the fixation on the ideal by the Germans and the wish to be seen as the gentleman in England. Jung felt that Americans are looser, walk in a more gangly fashion, talk a tremendous amount, and are less stiff than their European counterparts. But especially, Jung noted, Americans know how to laugh. Jung studied the deep, free, and unrestrained laugh of the American and recounted the following story:

> I was once a guest of a pretty stiff and solemn New England family of a rather terrifying respectability. It felt almost like home (There are very conservative and highly respectable folk in Switzerland, too. We might even better the American record in this respect.) There were Negro

---

[9] There is also an alternative interpretation that this was primarily a Kraepelinean text which, however, did give Freud proper credit for elaborating on the method of symbolism in working with hysterics (Taylor, 1998).

> servants waiting at table. I felt at first as if I were eating lunch in a circus and I found myself diffidently scrutinizing the dishes, looking for the imprint of those black fingers. A solemnity brooded over the meal for which I could see no reason, but I supposed it was the solemnity or serenity of great virtue or something like that which vibrated through the room. At all events nobody laughed. Everyone was just too nice and too polite. Eventually, I could stand it no longer, and I began to crack jokes for better or worse. These were greeted with condescending smiles. But I could not arouse that hearty and generous American laugh which I love and admire. "Well," I thought, "Indian blood, wooden faces, camouflaged Mongols, why not try some Chinese on them?" So I came to my last story, really a good one—and no sooner had I finished than right behind my chair an enormous avalanche of laughter broke loose. It was the Negro servant, and it was the real American laughter, that grand, unrestrained, unsophisticated laughter revealing rows of teeth, tongue, palate, everything, just a trifle exaggerated perhaps and certainly less than sixteen years old. How I loved that African brother (1930, 403-405).

The point was an interesting one from the standpoint of Jung's own identification with the American psyche. He marveled at how people who migrate from one country tend to look like the country they lived in. In a family with six children, three born in Germany, three born in America, it is always easy to tell who was from abroad and who was born in the United States. Moreover, he suggested, white Americans tend to also reflect features of Native Americans and Negroes in an age-old cycle, where the conquerors are only later subtly assimilated to the permanent and most enduring elements of the culture they replaced. Thus, Jung said, there is something of the Negro bound up in every white and something of the white bound up in every Negro, whether each likes it or not. As we will see, Jung, by identifying with the archetype of America, began to have visions of his black counterpart, the *oppositorum* buried in the unconscious, waiting to see the light of day.

The March 1910 Visit

An exchange of letters beginning on 11 February 1910 between Jung and Freud indicates that differences in their visions for psychoanalysis were becoming more obvious (McGuire, 1974). The exchange can be considered as part of the general intrigue that surrounded Jung's next trip to America in early March, 1910. That trip set the stage for Jung's Fordham Lectures in 1912, where Jung used the lecture platform in America to define his own version of psychoanalysis. The break with Freud followed immediately afterward.

Presaging these events Jung wrote to Freud in February, 1910:

> The ethical problem of sexual freedom really is noble and is worth the sweat of all noble souls. But 2000 years of Christianity can only be replaced by something equivalent...An ethical fraternity, with its mythical Nothing, not infused by an archaic infantile driving force, is a pure vacuum and can never evoke in man the slightest trace of that age old animal power which drives the migrating bird across the sea and without which no irresistible mass movement can come into being. I imagine a far finer and more comprehensive task for psychoanalysis than alliance with an ethical fraternity. I think we must give it time to infiltrate into people from many centres to revivify among intellectuals a feeling for symbol and myth, ever so gently to transform Christ back into the soothsaying god of the vine, which he was, and in this way absorb those ecstatic instinctual forces of Christianity for the one purpose of making the cult and the sacred myth what they once were—a drunken feast of joy where man regained the ethos and holiness of an animal. That was the beauty and purpose of classical religion, which from God knows what biological needs has turned into a Misery Institute. Yet what infinite rapture and wantonness lie dormant in our religion, waiting to be led back to their true destination! A genuine and ethical development cannot abandon Christianity but must grow up within, must bring to fruition its hymn of love, the agony and ecstasy over the dying and resurgent god, the mystic power of the wine, the awesome anthropophagy of the last supper—only this ethical development can sever the vital forces of religion. (McGuire, 1974, 294)

Freud's reply of 13 February 1910 goes in part as follows:

> Yes, in you the tempest rages; it comes to me as distant thunder. And though I ought to treat you diplomatically and humor your obvious distaste for writing with an artificial delay in answering, I am unable to restrain my precipitate

> reactions… I am not thinking of a substitute for religion; this need must be sublimated. (McGuire, 1974, 295).

Several letters later Jung writes, "I was very perturbed by your letter—all sorts of misunderstandings seems to be in the air. How could you be so mistaken in me[?]" (298). Freud's letter of 6 March 1910 is conciliatory. Its opening lines read:

> Believe me, there are no further misunderstandings between us… I am neither so forgetful nor so touchy, and I know how closely we are united by personal sympathy and by pulling on the same cart. I am merely irritated now and then—I may say that much I trust—that you have not yet disposed of the resistances arising from your Father complex and consequently limit our correspondence so much more than you would otherwise. (300)

These exchanges can be taken several ways. In one sense Jung is following the path of his own transformation, while Freud, who had no interest in such a process, is trying to establish psychoanalysis as a science. So Freud says, "you are the one trying to establish a religion, not me. I am trying to establish a new scientific discipline." Another way that this passage could be interpreted involves the simple analogy of the young hot-head learning to subsume himself under the wiser guidance of the older master. Hence Freud says, "what I meant was that you have yet to give up your resistances to me because you are still stuck in a father complex—that is, still projecting your father complex into me."

There is yet another interpretation. Ironically, Freud's invocation and image of "the tempest" seems to have prophetically cast Jung, like Prospero in Shakespeare's *The Tempest*, into the role of an exile. Despite the criticisms and misunderstandings of Jung's work over the years (Glover, 1950; Stern, 1976), Jung, like Prospero, survived the experience by way of an otherworldly-like initiation into the reality of the collective unconscious and by transforming himself over time from banished heir apparent and exile, to seer. We might say, too, that just as Prospero found an island in the midst of his exile and fateful "otherworldly" initiation, Jung found America in the midst of his monumental encounter with Freud and the collective unconscious.

Freud's allusion to the image of a "tempest," a storm that enveloped Jung in the months following their return from America, finds not only a fitting allegory and powerful metaphor in Shakespeare's play of betrayal, exile, and transformation, but also an enduring and instructive literary form that insinuates a necessary archetypal trace. There are ironic and uncanny similarities between Prospero and Jung (Cobb, 1984). The archetypal image of America implies that Jung was destined from the beginning of his friendship with Freud to be cast out of and exiled from Freud's psychoanalytic kingdom. Here too, the "tempest" image and motif can be sustained by Giorgione's sixteenth century dreamlike and enigmatic painting of the same name (Settis, 1990). There a lightening bolt pierces the Venetian sky, signaling "distant thunder" and an approaching storm. A scantily clad gypsy woman is seated on the ground below suckling a newborn child. A soldier with spear in hand stands nearby, not far from the time-ravaged ruins of a classical pillar and wall. The painting's figures and elements combine to imply both trace and potion, as well as a vaguely suggestive destiny: "The worlds of alchemy and psychoanalysis, it would seem, are only a step away" (52).

The Report on America

The effects of Freud's demands on Jung seemed to create in the younger man the need for distance. However, this conveys only part of the story, for Jung was also involved with important theoretical innovations, and he knew these would be problematic. On 8 March 1910, Emma Jung (McGuire, 1974) wrote Freud to inform him that, "my husband suddenly left for Chicago today, where his former patient, McCormick is seriously ill" (301). A letter dated 9 March 1910 written by Jung from Paris anticipates Freud's concern and thus announces:

> Now, don't be cross with me for my pranks! You will already have heard from my wife that I am on my way to America. I have arranged everything so as to be back in time for Nuremberg… I shall be back in Cherbourg the afternoon of March 28th, having spent 6 to 7 days in America, enough for the trip to Chicago and a few other things besides. It will also be good for my mental health. (302).

Among these "other things" was a plan to reconnect with William James.

We have one piece of evidence from the 1910 trip: on 31 March 1910, Jung delivered, before The Second International Psychoanalytic

Congress at Nuremberg, Germany, his "Report on America" (McGuire, 1974). Only a brief abstract of Jung's paper survives, gleaned from the notes of Otto Rank:

> Lecturer described a number of impressions he had gained on two journeys in North America. The psychological peculiarities of the American exhibit features that would be accessible in psychoanalysis, since they point to intense sexual repression. The reasons for repression are to be sought in the specifically American complex, namely, living together with the lower races, more particularly the Negroes. Living together with barbarous races has a suggestive effect on the laboriously subjugated instincts of the white race and drags it down. Hence strongly developed defensive measures are necessary, which manifest themselves in the particular aspects of American Culture. (Jung, 1980, 551)

Insofar as we can rely on the accuracy of Rank's summary of Jung's remarks, they appear at first both racist and preoccupied with sex. However, a deeper analysis suggests that Jung's psychic identification with America exposed him to "the American complex," namely, the struggle by the ruling white class to prevent itself from being drawn too much into the indigenous cultural patterns of blacks, hence the white's over identification with sexual repression as a countermeasure. Jung would later explain this phenomenon among white people in Africa as "going black," meaning a return to the unconscious, numinous domain of the primitive psyche.

At the same time, Rank's account is heavily psychoanalyzed. That is, at that time Jung and the others around Freud were more than willing participants in the psychoanalytic interpretation of their experiences, which necessarily gave an emphasis on the status of sexual repressions in normative social adjustment. Here, we have Rank's account and Jung's acknowledgment of the psychoanalytic ideology that they was trying, together with Freud, to advance.

The goals of psychoanalysis with respect to America, as Jung understood them at the time of the Nuremberg Congress in 1910, were simply to expose "the psychological peculiarities of the American's intense sexual repression" (McGuire, 1974, 550). Once exposed, America (and "white America" in particular) would then yield "features that would be accessible in psychoanalysis" (550). Yet even though Jung conveys in the above remarks an impression of cooperation with Freud and of a unified psychoanalytic movement, he continued privately to struggle with the narrowness of Freud's views on sexuality and the limited nature of his vision for psychoanalysis. Jung's memoirs, for instance, indicate that he had already hypothesized, as early as the first voyage to America in late August, 1909, the existence of a deeper level of the unconscious and also sought to advance a broader application and understanding of the psychoanalytic libido.

The 1912 Visit

In September, 1912, Jung traveled to New York for a third time at the request of Smith Ely Jellife of Fordham University to deliver a series of lectures on psychoanalysis. A letter dated 10 September from Emma Jung to Sigmund Freud indicates that Jung, after completing a military obligation, left on Saturday, 7 September. She begins the letter, "The offprints of Part II of *Transformations and Symbols* have just come out and you must be the first to receive one" (McGuire, 1974, 514), and goes on to lament the fact that, "Carl was away nearly all summer....spending only one day here between military service and departure." Jung's late reflections on the publication suggests that this book would, "cost me my friendship with Freud" (1973b, 161).

An exchange of letters between Jung and Freud beginning on November 11, 1912 reveals that the Fordham lectures would indeed prove problematic for their deteriorating relationship, although Jung continued to see himself in the service of Freud and psychoanalysis (McGuire, 1974). Jung writes:

> The psychoanalytic movement over there has enjoyed a tremendous upswing since we were last in America. Everywhere I met with great interest and was well received. Thus I had rich soil to work on and was able to do a very great deal for the spread of the movement. I gave 9 lectures at the Jesuit(!) University of Fordham, New York—a critical account of the development of the theory of psychoanalysis. (515)

The letter then takes on a more serious tone with Jung asserting:

> I have done more to promote the psychoanalytic movement

> than Rank, Stekel, Adler, etc. put together. I can only assure you that there is no resistance on my side, unless it be my refusal to be treated like a fool riddled with complexes... [In the service of psychoanalysis] I lectured in Chicago, Baltimore, and at the New York Academy of Medicine with apparent success. I also gave two clinical lectures on dementia praecox in Bellevue Hospital, New York and another on Wards Island, and in Washington I analyzed 15 Negroes with demonstrations. (516)

The interest that Jung displayed in American culture and race relations, while partially apparent in the aforementioned letter to Freud, was expressed more directly in an interview with an anonymous correspondent of *The New York Times.* The article, based on the interview, appeared under the headline, "America Facing Its Most Tragic Moment," in the paper's magazine section on September 29, 1912. The article expands on ideas Jung alluded to in his 1910, "Report on America," with the exception that there is substantial elaboration on the race problem.

The 1913 Visit

In March of 1913 Jung returned again to America to travel and lecture on psychoanalysis at the Liberal Club in New York (McGuire, 1974). Little is known about this trip with the exception that his friendship with Freud at this point was damaged beyond repair. However, a dream that Jung reported while on an expedition in Africa in 1925 suggests that he traveled as far south as Chattanooga, Tennessee, during the 1913 visit. The supporting text that introduces and clarifies Jung's interpretation of this dream is important for our purposes and appears as follows:

> During the entire trip my dreams stubbornly followed the tactic of ignoring Africa. They drew exclusively upon scenes from home, and thus seemed to say that they considered—if it is permissible to personify the unconscious processes to this extent—the African journey not as something real, but rather as a symptomatic or symbolic act. Even the most impressive events of the trip were rigorously excluded from my dreams. Only once during the entire expedition did I dream of a Negro. His face appeared curiously familiar to me, but I had to reflect a long time before I could determine

> where I had met him before. Finally it came to me: he had been my barber in Chattanooga, Tennessee! An American Negro. In the dream he was holding a tremendous, red-hot curling iron to my head, intending to make my hair kinky—that is, to give me Negro hair. I could already feel the painful heat, and awoke with a sense of terror.
>
> I took this dream as a warning from the unconscious; it was saying that the primitive was a danger to me. At that time I was obviously all too close to "going black." I was suffering an attack of sandfly fever which probably reduced my psychic resistance. In order to represent a Negro threatening me, my unconscious had invoked a twelve-year-old memory of my Negro barber in America, just in order to avoid any reminder of the present.
>
> This curious behavior of my dreams corresponds, incidentally, to a phenomenon which was noted during the First World War. Soldiers in the field dreamt far less of the war than of their homes. Military psychiatrists considered it a basic principle that a man should be pulled out of the front lines when he started dreaming too much of war scenes, for that meant he no longer possessed any psychic defenses against the impressions from outside. (1973b, 272-273)

The African expedition went from November 7, 1925, through March, 1926 (Jung, 1973a). Roger Brooke has already shown that as Jung "traveled into the interior of East Africa, he felt as though he was returning home. But this was paradoxical, for he was both returning to his origins and yet fulfilling his destiny, the purpose of his life" (1992, 53). Concerning the dream recounted above, Brooke concludes that the "existential liberation revealed to Jung [through his experience in Africa] is now seen through the defensive eyes of the [European] psychiatrist." Brooke adds, "In Africa Jung...realized the self as a nonsubstantial openness within which the world could come into being" (60).

We in turn have shown how motifs of journeying and destiny, as well as the capacity for self-realization, appear symbolized by the image of America in Jung's dream of an American journey, long before his monumental encounter with Freud. The dream fortells Jung's subsequent trips to America and anticipates his personal maturation, especially through his travels there between 1909 and 1913. Ultimately Jung speaks to the forthcoming darkness; namely his estrangement from Freud and the psychoanalytic movement. In this sense, the allegories to Shakespeare's

The Tempest and Giorgione's painting of the same name accentuate the potential for dark promise and futurity. They become metaphors not only for Jung's struggle with Freud, but also for the trace elements which are gradually transformed and engender an alchemical world view out of the *prima materia* of the psychoanalytic unconscious. The play of dark and light elements in Jung's early dream analyses combine sexuality and color so as to indicate a hidden and unconscious vestige of primitivity in the dreamer. For example, in Jung's first dream of an American journey, "the powerful brown horse" (1960, 57) represents not only the passion, ambition, and desires of the tanned and healthy mountain-climbing dreamer but the dark depths of the unconscious. America is then imagined as the land of opportunity and skyscrapers where through hard work "one gets to the top" (59) and also prophetically as a symbol of restraint and sexual repression.

The point is that Jung's dream images, even at this relatively early date in his career, convey a profound sense of self-knowledge, futurity, destiny, and knowledge of the world. The image of a Negro barber in Chattanooga, Tennessee, emerges from the unconscious while Jung is in Africa, not only as a defensive measure but as a symbol of transformation and of things to come.[10] In the dream the black barber is ominous, menacing, and dangerously close; not unlike the black man of dreams and visions from the unconscious of Jung's hysterical patient at Burghölzli in November of 1905 or the dark and shadowy figure in Welti's etching, *A Moonlight Night.* However, the image of the barber is also suggestive in its connection with primitivity, ritual, sacrifice, mutilation, and transformation of the alchemical barber in his yet to be written (at that time) "The Visions of Zosimos." In this essay on Zosimos, the barber is gray "because he represents the lead" (Jung, 1967, 60) in the alchemical opus; but gray is also the curious blending of black and white elements.[11]

We know that after 1912, Jung resigned his teaching position and withdrew into a period of intense personal conflict over the course and

---

[10] See Michael Vannoy Adams, 1996, *The Multicultural Imagination* for an interesting rendering of this image and its alchemical transformations.

[11] Hillman's emphasis on states rather than stages in the alchemical work is applicable here, for this would acknowledge the barber as a guiding figure, "an achievement" (1997, 7) in the individuation process because of the figure's connection with darkness and the *nigredo.*

direction of his life. He emerged from this enforced, psychic retreat only after several years, and when he did, he was a changed man. Phenomenologically, it is our contention that the archetype of America continued to function long after the oppressive relationship with Freud was over as a kind of spiritual homeland and symbol of the self for Jung, which he took as an extraordinary symbolic representation of the interplay of opposing tendencies in the psyche and the possibility of integration and wholeness.

The dreams and visions of December 1913 that first overwhelmed and eventually liberated Jung refer to this integrative process in terms of encounter with the shadow, with sacrifice, death, rebirth, and renewal. A central figure in this inner drama was, according to Jung "a small brown skinned savage who accompanied me" (1973b, 181). Here Jung becomes absorbed in the issue of how Americans have reconciled themselves to living with the liberated black race. He takes on this creative tension in his own symbol system, in which the vision of the black American is the factor that saves him from being engulfed by the primitive forces of his unconscious. He declares from his first impressions of America, "Oh how I loved that African brother."

It is our conclusion that the pre-existing image of America as an important value in Jung's psyche adds the element of destiny to the puzzle of his numerous returns to the New World and provides the necessary connection between his unconscious sense of being, as self, and his individuation in the existing world. Jung conveys this sense of destiny when he writes: "My life is the story of the self-realization of the unconscious. Everything in the unconscious seeks outward manifestation and the personality too desires to evolve out of its unconscious conditions and experience itself as a whole" (1973b, 3).

Jung himself then corroborates our view when later, referring to the period of his first American visits and the transformation that followed, he says:

> The years when I was pursuing my inner images were the most important in my life—in them everything essential was decided. It all began then; the later details are only supplements and clarifications of the material that burst forth from the unconscious, and at first swamped me. It was the *prima materia* for a lifetime's work. (199)

Works Cited

Adams, Michael Vannoy. "Dreams as complexes: Jung's Dream of the Brown Horse and Heavy Log." *Quadrant, 24* (1), 1991.

____________________. *The Multicultural Imagination*. London: Routledge, 1996.

Adorno, T. *The Authoritarian Personality*. New York: W. W. Norton, 1982.

Allport, G. *The Nature of Prejudice*. Cambridge, Mass.: Addison-Wesley, 1954.

Brill, A. *Lectures on Psychoanalytic Psychiatry*. New York: Vintage Books, 1955.

Brooke, R. *Jung and Phenomenology*. London: Routledge, 1992.

Casey, Edward S. *Spirit and Soul*. Dallas: Spring, 1991.

Charet, F. X. *Spiritualism and the Foundation of C. G. Jung's Psychology*. Albany: State University of New York Press, 1993.

Cobb, Noel. *Prospero's Island: The Secret Alchemy at the Heart of "The Tempest."* London: Coventure, 1984.

Ellenberger, Henri. *The Discovery of the Unconscious: The History and Evolution of Dynamic Psychiatry*. New York: Basic Books, 1970.

Freud, Sigmund. "On the History of the Psychoanalytic Movement." *Collected Papers of Sigmund Freud* (Vol. 1, 287-359). Ed. Ernest Jones. Trans. J. Riviere. New York: Basic Books, 1959.

Gifford, G. E. "Freud and the Porcupine," *Harvard Medical Alumni Bulletin*, March-April, 28-31, 1972.

Gilman, S. *Freud, Race, and Gender*. Princeton: Princeton UP, 1993.

Glover, E. *Freud or Jung?* London: George Allen and Unwin, 1950.

Hillman, James. *Archetypal Psychology: A Brief Account*. Dallas: Spring , 1985.

____________. "The Seduction of Black." *Spring, 61*, 1997.

Hornstein, E. "The Return of the Repressed: Psychology's Problematic Relations with Psychoanalysis, 1909-1960." *American Psychologist, 47,* 1992.

Jones, Ernest. *The Life and Work of Sigmund Freud: Years of Maturity,* Vol. 2. New York: Basic Books, 1955.

Jung, C. G. (1930). "The Complications of American Psychology." Originally published as "Your Negroid and Indian Behavior." *Forum* (New York) lxxxiii, 1930. Reprinted in *Collected Works: Civilization in Transition*. New York: Pantheon, 502-514.

Jung, C. G. *The Psychogenesis of Mental Disease*. Trans. R. F. C. Hull. Princeton: Princeton UP, 1960.

__________. *Alchemical Studies*. Trans. R. F. C. Hull. Princeton: Princeton UP, 1967.

__________. *The Structure and Dynamics of the Psyche*. Trans. R. F. C. Hull. Princeton: Princeton UP, 1969.

_________. *Letters: 1906-1950, Vol. 1*. Eds. G. Adler and A. Jaffe. Trans. R. F. C. Hull. New York: Pantheon Books, 1973a.

__________. *Memories, Dreams, and Reflections.* Ed. A. Jaffe. Trans. R. Winston and C. Winston. New York: Pantheon Books, 1973b.

__________. *C. G. Jung Speaking: Interviews and Encounters.* Eds. W. McGuire and R. F. C. Hull. Princeton: Princeton UP, 1977.

__________. *The Symbolic Life: Miscellaneous Writings.* Trans. R. F. C. Hull. Princeton: Princeton UP, 1980.

__________. *Experimental Researches: Including the Studies on Word Association.* Trans. L. Stein and D. Riviere. Princeton: Princeton UP, 1981.

Maidenbaum, A., and Martin, S. A. (Eds.). *Lingering Shadows: Jungians, Freudians, and Anti-semitism.* Boston: Shambhala, 1991.

Martinez, T. J. "Anthropos and Existence: Gnostic Parallels in the Early Writings of Rollo May." *Journal of Humanistic Psychology, 38*(4), 1998.

McGuire, William. "Firm Affinities: Jung's Relations with Britain and the United States." *Journal of Analytical Psychology*, 40, 1981.

________________. "Jungian New York," *Quadrant*, 16:1, 1983.

________________ (Ed). *The Freud/Jung Letters.* Princeton: Princeton UP, 1974.

McLynn, F. *Carl Gustav Jung.* New York: St. Martin's Press, 1996.

Meier, C. A. *The Meaning and Significance of Dreams.* Trans. D. N. Roscoe. Boston: Sigo Press, 1987.

Noll, Richard. *The Jung Cult.* Princeton: Princeton UP, 1995.

Rosenzweig, S. *Freud, Jung and Hall the King-Maker: The Historic Expedition to America (1909) with G. Stanley Hall as Host and William James as Guest.* St Louis: Rana House, 1992.

Samuels, Andrew. *Jung and the Post-Jungians.* London: Routledge, 1985.

________________. *The Political Psyche.* New York: Routledge, 1993.

Sartre, Jean Paul. *Anti-Semite and Jew.* New York: Schocken Books, 1948.

Settis, S. *Giorgione's Tempest: Interpreting the Hidden Subject.* Trans. E. Bianchini. Chicago: University of Chicago Press, 1990.

Stern, P. J. *C. G. Jung: The Haunted Prophet.* New York: Braziller, 1976.

Taylor, Eugene I. "William James and C. G. Jung," *Spring*, 1980.

_______________. "C. G. Jung and the Boston Psychopathologists, 1902-1912." *Voices: The Art and Science of Psychotherapy, 21*(3-4), 1985.

_______________. "Jung in his Intellectual Context: The Swedenborgian Connection," *Studia Swedenborgiana, 7*(2), 1991.

_______________. "Jung before Freud, not Freud before Jung: Jung's Reception in American Psychotherapeutic Circles before 1909." *Journal of Analytical Psychology, 43*(1), 1996.

______________. *Shadow Culture: Psychology and Spirituality in America.* Washington: Counterpoint, 1999.

Let It Be
An Interview with C. Toni Frey-Wehrlin

JANIS and ROBERT HENDERSON

In 1964 in Switzerland, along with C. A. Meier, Carl Briner, and Heinrich Fierz, C. Toni Frey-Wehrlin established the Zürichberg Clinic, the first and only inpatient Jungian psychiatric clinic in the world. We met Toni recently on a beautiful summer day on the banks of the Hudson River near Rheinbeck, New York, at the Valeur Mansion where Toni was leading a week-long workshop for mental health professionals. At the age of seventy, his body is somewhat frail, but his mind is quick, and his heart is warm and open.

After receiving his doctorate in philosophy from the University of Zürich, Toni enrolled at the Jung Institute in Zürich. C. A. Meier was his analyst. Later Toni trained under Michael Fordham in London. He has been friends with Adolf Guggenbühl-Craig since they were in boarding school together at the age of fourteen.

Born in St. Gallen, Switzerland, Toni has been married for over forty years to his wife, Rita, and the two enjoy their family of three daughters and four grandchildren. Toni still maintains the private practice in Zürich he opened in 1958. He has been teaching at the Jung Institute since 1960 and has been an analyst and training supervisor for students from five continents attending the Institute.

Toni's written works include: "The Treatment of Chronic Psychoses," "Oedipus in Gethsemane-Archetypal Aspects of Homosexuality,"

Janis Henderson is a psychotherapist and Robert Henderson is a pastoral psychotherapist. They live in Glastonbury, Connecticut. The Hendersons have published interviews with Adolf Guggenbühl-Craig, Jane and Jo Wheelwright, and John Weir Perry.

"C. G. Jung: Light and Shadow," "Reflections on C. G. Jung's Concept of Synchronicity," "Defiance and Compliance: What is a Jungian?," and "Problems of Dream Interpretation." Since he places a high value on spontaneous reactions, he supported in recent years Susan Bach's work with spontaneous pictures by severely ill children (see: Susan Bach, *Life Paints its Own Span* [Einsiedeln: Daimon, 1990]).

Encountering Jung

RH: You have described yourself as part of the almost extinct species of those who actually met Jung in person. What impact has meeting Jung had on you?

TF: It was quite impressive to me that he was such a huge man. He was a tower, an athlete, and a giant physically. That was quite impressive, not only the weight of his personality but his whole physical appearance. That is something I will never forget. If that made a difference to my views on Jungian psychology or not is another question. But the man…he was colossal. You could imagine him as a dairyman in the Alps carrying huge cheeses around on his back. There are pictures of him taking off his jacket, screaming and yelling. Jumping around. He was an enormously vital personality. Full of vitality and energy.

RH: Was his physical appearance overwhelming to others?

TF: I remember a passage from Jones' biography of Freud in which Freud and Jung were talking about alcoholism and Freud fainted. Jung just picked him up and carried him to the sofa.

RH: So he was a strong man.

TF: He was. I remember the passage in *Memories, Dreams and Reflections* where Jung, after his break with Freud, said that getting through his night sea journey was a matter of "sheer force." When Jung was in Africa, some black people started a ritual and became more and more excited, and they started waving their spears and dancing around the fire, and when they became really aggressive and dangerous, Jung felt threatened and suddenly he just started shouting at them in Swiss German as if to say, "How dare you," and soon the whole thing calmed down. And if you have met Jung you would believe it.

RH: How old were you when you met Jung?

TF: Thirty years old. He was eighty.

RH: You didn't have any contact with him?

TF: He was quite withdrawn at that time. He seldom came to the Institute. I don't know if he ever lectured at the Institute. He once gave a student an exam in the fundamentals of Analytical Psychology. He asked him in the exam: "If I were a street cleaner, and you had to explain Analytical Psychology to me, how would you proceed?" And after half an hour the man was flunked.

RH: Where did you hear that story?

TF: That is a story at the Institute. There are lots of stories about Jung, but they are mostly legends. Only Jung and the other person were present.

JH: Do you think he was aware of how strong his personality was?

TF: I am quite sure. And he used it very well. Jung invited projections more than the average person. He also offered a big hook for these projections. Jung often reacted bizarrely to things, if judged from a scientific viewpoint.

RH: You described Jung as a mythical figure. What does that mean?

TF: It means that the projections he constellated were of the archetypal kind. He really was the wise old man, the giant behind the mountains or in the cave. That's how one experienced him. This is something people need. A leading figure in the good sense and in the bad sense, like the Führer in Germany. People need this kind of figure in times of change, when values collapse or change. They need a guiding figure who tells them what is good and what is evil. Jung constellated in a very deep way. He invited the projection.

RH: When you say "invited," are you saying there was something intentional?

TF: No. But real. You know the famous hook for the projection. It just happened to him.

JH: Does that mean that his life was also taken off by the myth?

TF: Absolutely. The big question for him after the separation from Freud was "which myth am I living?" He was convinced everyone was living a myth. He was trying to determine which myth he was living. Then came the famous dream in which he shot Siegfried down from the wagon.

RH: Then that told him which myth he was living?

TF: Yes. That told him that he had been living the myth of the hero up to that point. And after the separation from Freud that was the end of the hero myth. That is why he withdrew from all his official functions at the psychoanalytic society. He withdrew from Zürich University and from the Burghölzli Psychiatric Hospital. He dropped his career. His career could have gone God knows where, but he withdrew into his own inner world. He had his practice, he traveled around the world and wrote his books.

RH: He started to live out of another myth then?

TF: Of course.

RH: He left the hero myth and started to get into the myth of the wise old man?

TF: Yeah, I think he got into a number of myths then. The wise old man, and you mentioned yesterday his book, *Answer to Job*. I think he also identified with Job.

RH: That is a very interesting book. I don't hear too many people talking about that book.

TF: I can imagine. When it came out, I think it was 1952, I was in the midst of my analysis with Meier, and Meier said it was a mistake to publish the book then as it was fifty years too early.

RH: Is that right? It was really interesting yesterday for me when I told you what I thought Jung was saying in that book, to have you say that you thought the same thing. Because I never have thought I understood it even though I have read it many times.

TF: It is very difficult to understand, and I am far from pretending that I understand the book. It is one of the books by Jung that I read every three or four years, and when I find something important, I make a mark in the margin, and I hope that if I ever reach one hundred, the whole book will be marked. [Laughter.] Because you don't see what is in the book unless you have really experienced it. The other book of this kind is *The Psychology of Transference*.

RH: You feel the same way about that book?

TF: I have marked about half of it so far.

RH: Like we were saying yesterday, one thing Jung is saying in *Answer to Job* is that God has a dark side—we call that Satan—and that God is partly unconscious, and because he is unconscious, there are things that happen in the world that happen because of God's unconsciousness.

TF: Yes.

RH: So why do bad things happen to good people? Some of that is because God is unconscious.

TF: Yes. God is like an emotional person. If you are in the grip of an emotion you can say afterwards, "I didn't know myself anymore. I did this and that, but how could I have done or said that? I don't know myself like that, something else has taken over." The complex.

RH: So God gets taken over by a complex?

TF: Yes. I think that is a very difficult thing for you to understand with your theological training. Jung sees God as a person, as a human being.

RH: It makes sense to me if we are born in God's image. I have also had the experience of sharing these ideas in churches, and I can remember in one church, the minister of the church had given a sermon that morning about God being love and good, and I came through with some of these ideas in an evening group. The minister got so angry with me that I thought he was going to punch me. It was very embarrassing for me but that is the kind of reaction that these ideas get, at least in the church.

TF: Where does evil come from then if God is almighty and all loving, why does evil happen? This is where the question comes up of whether Jung was a Gnostic or not.

RH: What do most people misunderstand about Jung?

TF: He is often seen as a mystic. I think this is because he describes things that cannot be described in the language of positive science. I do not think Jung is a mystic. He understood himself to be an empiricist and a scientist.

RH: And yet a lot of medical people who are scientists would discount Jung.

TF: In a paper she wrote shortly before she died, Susan Bach wrote about a case where a man who was from the United States called her for an appointment. She said she didn't have any time but that he could call back later and maybe she could find some time that evening. She hung up and then a client called in order to cancel his appointment—therefore making it possible for her to see the man who had called earlier. She related this synchronistic—that is, meaningful—coincidence in order to demonstrate the "charged" atmosphere of the case. As we were about to publish this paper, a doctor advised us to omit this section because he considered it "unscientific." It would appear that it is "unscientific" to describe phenomena that don't fit a positivist world view.

RH: But would Jung have seen this as a fact?

TF: Of course—and he published such facts. And because he published such facts, he is called a mystic. He was a scientist who made known what he had observed.

RH: As far as the biographies of Jung go, you do not like the idealizing ones.

TF: No, not at all. I like [Paul J.] Stern's book, [*The Haunted Prophet*]. I haven't read it for some time, but I remember some passages that were the same, word-for-word, as things Meier had told me. It is reliable. Stern is skeptical and critical of Jung and why not? I do not think he is hostile. He spent quite a bit of time and energy writing the book.

RH: Do you think the biographies by Von Franz, Van der Post, and Hannah have done a disservice to Jung?

TF: I don't know. In the long run probably not. These things correct themselves. I had to smile at certain passages. For instance, when Hannah writes about Jung's relationship with Toni Wolff, she describes the shifting of Jung's affections away from his daughters as a "sacrifice." So he sacrificed himself and projected his anima on Toni Wolff, and the proof that this was the right thing to do was that all four daughters got married. [Laughter.] For my taste that goes too far.

RH: Do you think enough has been said about the Jung-Wolff relationship?

TF: I believe we know what there is to know about this relationship. I can hardly imagine that yet more correspondence will come to light. The old alchemists sometimes exchanged correspondence about their work with their *soror mystica*. Jung's work is available to us. We know almost more about Jung's relationship to Sabina Spielrein, and from their correspondence one can discern the birth, so to speak, of the anima. In my opinion we know much too little about Emma Jung.

RH: You felt a biography of Emma Jung would be helpful. Why?

TF: I can't imagine Jung's life work being what it was without Emma. Let's not forget that despite being a genius—which is beyond doubt—he was also the poor son of a parson. By going on to marry this immensely rich woman, he was able to build his houses in Kusnacht and Bollingen. It was with the help of her money that he was able to work for six months a year and spend the rest of the time writing his books and traveling to Africa or India. Here's another little anecdote: after she died a friend visited him and Jung said that he had just got a bill for coal and that he didn't know what to do because he'd never paid a bill for coal before. She paid all the bills and for the education of the children. She looked after the children and generally sheltered Jung from day-to-day problems. When she died the money was to a large extent gone. She never said a word. She paid the bills.

RH: So Jung was not able to provide for the family.

TF: No. I found a bill he had written for an American patient for two consultations in the 50s. The total sum was fifty Swiss francs. That would have been considered very cheap and much less than he could have asked for had he wanted to.

JH: Jung didn't have time to get involved.

TF: He didn't have the time, the interest, or the energy for that kind of thing.

JH: He needed someone to sort of run his life in a way to make sure he had clothing and food.

TF: He had to be taken care of.

RH: Everyone we have talked to about Jung has said that Emma was a very wonderful and generous person. She raised the kids and ran the home.

TF: And that is never mentioned in his autobiography. She is mentioned twice in half a sentence. He took her for granted. That was the old system in Switzerland and perhaps everywhere in the world a hundred years ago. The wife was the shadow of the man. I remember a book that came out in the forties or fifties by the wife of a famous man with the title, "I Helped My Husband." [Laughter.]

RH: Is that particularly Swiss?

TF: I would say we stuck to that system much longer. Women didn't get the vote in Switzerland until 1971. Before then they couldn't vote—in the oldest democracy in the world.

RH: So the women's movement has not arrived in Switzerland as it has in the United States?

TF: I think it has now. There was an accelerated development. I can see that in my kids. My wife and I still have the traditional system: I earn and she manages the house. But our children haven't adopted this approach. They wouldn't take it any more.

RH: We hear lots of wild stories about what happened in the sessions with Jung. You have called them legends. Does that mean they may not have happened?

TF: They contribute to our impression of Jung's personality. Perhaps these legends didn't actually happen but they could have happened. They have their value. But remember: who witnessed these events? People came out of a session with Jung and said, "Oh God." [Laughter.] A woman worked with him for three weeks before realizing that he didn't have a beard. [Laughter.] In the fourth week she looked at him and said, "Professor Jung, did you cut off your beard?" [Laughter.] She had seen the Wise Old Man for three weeks.

RH: You talked to a woman who said that? Or is that one of the legends?

TF: That's one of the legends.

RH: That's one thing I liked about you when I was in your seminar in Zürich. You know all the legends, don't you?

TF: I have heard the gossip about Jung, and I like gossip. But I see this in my own practice. Clients have come back after a week or a year to say that they were very impressed by something I had said, and they quote me. And I think, "That is not me. It's impossible that I said that." Now my first reaction might be that the client heard something I did not say because he or she needed to hear it. Or that syntonic countertransference made me say such a thing. I am not like a computer during the session. I am a living system that reacts to the patient. So it's possible for a reaction to come out of a corner of myself that I haven't yet seen.

RH: You have used that word before, "syntonic." What does it mean?

TF: That's from Michael Fordham. In his *Notes on the Transference*, he speaks of countertransference. It is an emotional reaction by the analyst. It can be based on an unconscious complex of the analyst. There is something in the analyst that has not been analyzed yet, and it comes up in the session. It's usually disastrous for the analysis when the analyst's own unconscious stuff comes into the treatment. But it is also possible that a complex wants to come up that is the client's business. But the client can't accept it and fights it, pushing it down. It then tries to come up again not in the client but in the analyst, and then the analyst has an emotional reaction which actually belongs not to him or her, but to the client.

RH: So when you say something to the client it might have originated in the client's complexes?

TF: The anger the client feels towards his or her mother or father might be something he or she fights against. So he or she tells me a story about his or her father or mother, and as he or she is telling it, I find myself getting more and more angry. So I can say to myself that this may be his or her own anger which is coming up in me because I am less resistant to it. I can tell my client that I don't know what this is, but when I hear what he or she says, I find myself feeling more and more angry. I can ask, "Don't you feel this anger?" or suggest that the client may have felt anger but not allowed him or herself to express it

RH: And the more they deny the anger the more you may feel it?

TF: Right. And that is a syntonic reaction. That is one of the few new things discovered and formulated after Jung but in the Jung school by Michael Fordham.

The Jungian Clinic

RH: The Jung Clinic, or as it is called in your country, *Klinik am Zürichberg*, did you begin it?

TF: I was the initiator and cofounder along with C. A. Meier, Carl Briner, and H. K. Fierz. Briner was the husband of one of the first graduates of the Jung Institute in Zürich, Mary Briner. He was also the president of a large Swiss insurance company.

RH: How did the idea for the Clinic come to you?

TF: I came back from England in 1958 following my Jungian clinical training. I had a friend who ran a small psychiatric clinic near Zürich. He asked me to come and do psychotherapy. I needed to start my practice. I saw patients at the clinic, and when they were dismissed, they would come to me as private patients—within two months my case load was full. I got highly interested in clinical work with schizophrenics and would go to the clinic three times a week. On one occasion I returned to the clinic to see my patients after a day or two and found that a patient of mine had been sedated by a doctor. The patient had apparently stopped speaking for a day or two and had become a disturbing element. This episode provoked a very infantile reaction of defiance in me. Like alchemy, you start out with shit, and you make gold out of it. [Laughter.] I thought: if things are going to be like this, I want my own clinic. The economy in Switzerland was excellent in the 60s and we were able to start the venture with ten thousand Swiss francs. That was then about two thousand dollars. I also worked at the Binswanger Clinic by Lake Constance, together with Fierz and a whole team of psychotherapists, all of whom were keen to join the new venture.

RH: Meier helped you?

TF: He was in agreement and was the figurehead and was interested in the research.

RH: He had also been your analyst. So you had a relationship with him.

TF: I had a transference. [Laughter.]

RH: You were the initiator, does that mean Meier contributed just his name.

TF: Yes, yes, but I must admit he also went around and did some fund-raising, which was not very successful. But he did find a man—an ex-patient of his—who was quite wealthy and gave us three hundred thousand Swiss francs interest-free, and with that we were able to purchase the house and pay the expenses for the first few months. We had two patients when we began.

RH: You went out and purchased a house in Zürich?

TF: It was an old villa on the Zürichberg near the big Waldhaus Dolder Hotel. It had ten or twelve rooms and would have been suitable for a family with two children. Later it came out that it had belonged to the von Franz family up until 1946. I remember finding some maps from the Austrian general staff in a cupboard. The late Baron von Franz was a colonel in the old Austrian army. I see this coincidence as a synchronism, and I'm sorry that Frau von Franz never chose to visit the building in its new function, which must have been significant also for her.

There were other flats on the grounds which we were able to expand into as the Clinic grew. And then we bought a third house nearby, also on the Zürichberg. When I was kicked out of the Clinic for bad management, the original ten thousand Swiss francs had been transformed into ten million due to soaring property prices. [Laughter.]

JH: Can you go back and talk about what was going on as you began work in the Clinic. How did you start formalizing what you wanted to do with patients? How were you bringing your training into the Clinic?

TF: I had had my Jungian training and at that time was convinced that Jungian psychology could cure almost anything, that it should be applied. And after all, Jungian psychology came out of the psychiatric clinic. There would be no concepts of the collective unconscious or the archetype without Jung's experience with psychotic people. Jung saw the parallels between what he saw in these people and what he had read in old manuscripts; the archaic fantasies in schizophrenic people which Freud hadn't seen. Freud had a practice for neurotic people.

RH: So you really thought you were reclaiming the territory where Jungian psychology had begun.

TF: That was one side of it. There was also what I would call in hindsight an overestimation—the idea that Jungian psychology could cure schizophrenia. It was a time when there was a huge wave in favor of psychotherapy of the psychoses. Everybody thought that psychotherapy was the answer to psychosis. That enthusiasm has declined a bit since then, and nowadays I have a different view, but that was the initial impetus. Over the years I have seen more and more that it is not true that we can cure. I don't think we can. The rates have been one third, one third, one third: cured, improved, and unchanged. These statistics were first published in the middle of the nineteenth century, and they remain unchanged today, despite all the therapies. I heard that there are over five hundred different methods of psychotherapy. It was a bit of a crisis for me to witness the reevaluation of the role of Jungian psychology, because if it doesn't cure, what does it do? Why should we use it and run up all these expenses? Imagine what it cost to give each patient in the Clinic three hours of one-to-one psychotherapy by a Jungian specialist. That's quite an amount.

RH: So after you began the Clinic you started to get some other ideas?

TF: You interviewed John Perry. At the 1977 Jungian Congress in Rome, we decided to present our way of working at the Clinic. Then I heard that Perry intended to present a paper in which he would claim to be able to cure twenty-three out of twenty-five schizophrenic patients in three months using only psychotherapy. It was incredible, and it was clear we couldn't compete with that. So we decided to do the opposite, and my paper on the treatment of chronic psychosis was born. We formulated an alternative, which aimed not to cure but to "accompany." A certain number of chronic patients cannot be rehabilitated. If you look at our world, it is kind of crazy, and it is not for everyone. You need quite some stamina to get through life, and there are some people who can't do it, and they need a place to be. A patient remains a human being even if he is a chronic patient. If the patient has the opportunity to talk for three hours a week in a stable relationship with an intelligent partner, this will change his quality of life. It is a question of being human. And very often, of course, the impetus for both the Clinic and the patients is a religious one. Jung makes a statement in a letter dated 28 August, 1945: "I am not interested in curing neurosis. My interest is in the numinous and I have to lead my patients to an experience of the numinous. If you can have this experience you are freed from the curse of the illness."

JH: Was that your guiding principle in starting the Clinic?

TF: No, I read this passage only much later.

RH: So your whole notion of what Jungian psychology was about changed a lot from your beginnings in the Clinic.

TF: Yes, and the recognition that one cannot heal is one side of that. But the changing of my opinions was also to do with getting older. At forty you think differently about God and the beyond than at seventy. You are it bit closer to it and it gets more interesting. [Laughter.] These days, in order to get licenses and to have our therapy paid for by the health insurance companies, we have to provide statistical evidence that proves the effectiveness of Jungian methods. But in the session, Jung's concerns are very different. If the patient is cured, it's a welcome side-effect, but it is not the main objective.

RH: So the Clinic was started in about 1961.

TF: No, the Foundation was founded in 1963, and we opened the Clinic on April Fool's Day, 1964.

JH: On purpose? [Laughter.]

TF: No [laughter]...coincidence. [Laughter.]

Jung's Funeral

RH: Jung died in 1961.

TF: I remember Jung's funeral, which was a nightmare because it never ended. Everybody who spoke spoke for half an hour or so. There I had the idea that we must do something to continue. "Now we should do the Clinic!"

RH: Where did that come from? How was that connected to Jung's death?

TF: It was my own infantile, defiant reaction to want my own clinic as I already mentioned. And then there was the funeral, and I said, "Now is the moment to do it."

RH: Let's talk about Jung's funeral because you were there.

TF: I was there. It was in the church in Kusnacht, and it was packed full. One speaker spoke for almost an hour. They even had to interrupt the service for a break so that everyone could get out and have a pipe or cigarette or what have you. [Laughter.] Then we went back in again.

RH: Who was the speaker who went on for an hour?

TF: Hans Schaer.

RH: Was he a minister?

TF: He was. And for those people who had been working with Jung this was a tremendous experience, and they got carried away by their emotions. I am quite sure Schaer had prepared a manuscript for fifteen minutes, not fifty. He got carried away by his emotions and could not stop.

RH: What was it like for you to be there?

TF: Interesting! I was not deeply touched and felt no sense of personal loss. Jung was a mythical figure for me, but his death was not a personal loss. I had not lost a father or something. I needed him as a mythical figure in the sense of having a need for a huge, leading ideal.

Being a Jungian Analyst

JH: What got you to go ahead and study Jungian psychology and have it become your life work?

TF: That is a good question. It just fell into place with my own precondition for a philosophy. We all have a certain temperament and that's why we develop one philosophy or another. What Jung had to offer was very close to what I needed.

JH: Looking back do you see that your myth was to become a healer, and Jungian psychology offered you a way to funnel it?

TF: Maybe. I was always interested in religion. As a boy I was an only child, and I had an illustrated Bible I would read—especially the Old Testament because the pictures were so much more interesting. [Laughter.] I had a strong inclination towards that and to reading and being by myself. I had very strong ambitions in many directions. I was convinced that I was much better and more gifted than my peers in my classes. I had a strong drive towards power. I wanted to be somebody.

This is a myth of the Frey family, that they are better than others. And we need to prove it. [Laughter.]

JH: The notion that you were better or had to be better than others attracted you to someone who presented something that was better than what others had contributed?

TF: Yes. The notion of individuation is to be special. You have to be yourself as much as possible. That probably caught my fancy. I had always been a philosopher basically.

JH: I am getting the feeling that for you there was a value system beyond that. Your interest in religion, *et cetera*, implies…

TF: A messianic element was certainly there. I was quite convinced that I had something to offer the world, something that could improve it. And I had a very strong feeling of justice. As I was saying earlier about my daughters' involvement in the Zürich riots: I was still the offspring of a conservative Zürich bankers family, yet I was enormously proud of my daughters when they rebelled in the streets, threw stones at the police, smashed windows along Bahnhofstrasse, and showed these monied people what the values of life were. It was a very easy switch from one political view to another. It all happened within three weeks.

RH: I can identify with that. They were living your unlived life. When our kids do something like that, I can feel that same pride.

TF: Since then my relationship to much of my less immediate family has changed. I have lots of cousins around Zürich. We still see each other every year or two for a dinner, but I have lost all inner contact with them.

RH: You mean with the bankers?

TF: Yes, the Gold Coast, Zürichberg banking, Bahnhofstrasse attitude. [Laughter.] I am indebted to my daughters for how they helped me.

Working with C. A. Meier

RH: Toni, how did you actually ever hear of Jung?

TF: I lost my father in 1950. He died of a heart attack. I was then a student in the philosophy seminar at Zürich University, which consisted at that time of about twelve students and two professors. I had a colleague, Peter Walder, who was finishing his degree in psychology with a dissertation on Jung, and had lost his father on the same day that I had.

We got acquainted, and he introduced me to Jung. He became an analyst in Zürich and died about ten years ago. As we discussed Jung I began to read Jung. The first book I read was *The Psychology of Alchemy*. Then Walder started analyzing me. [Laughter.]

JH: Formally?

TF: Informally. He would invite me for tea and ask about my dreams. Then I met another guy, John Phillips, who is now an analyst in New York. He was an eternal student in Zürich and studied philosophy but could never finish. He told me that I was absolutely mad to be fiddling about with the unconscious with Peter Walder. You have to have a real analyst, and the best analyst in Zürich is C. A. Meier. I went to see C. A. Meier because I couldn't finish my dissertation. I was totally blocked. I couldn't finish my studies.

RH: That was your presenting problem to Meier?

TF: Yes.

RH: And what did Meier say to you?

TF: He never said anything. [Laughter.] He moaned and grumbled and picked the old leaves out of the plants on his desk and sometimes he cleaned his nails or had tea. He never said anything. He was an excellent analyst. I can only repeat what a colleague of mine—an old lady who is now seventy-five—said recently at a lecture she gave in California. She said she wanted to pay tribute to her analyst, C. A. Meier, for having given her such a long rope. This was one of his most impressive characteristics. He would never really tell me what to do. He was a very passive analyst, not at all prone to reacting.

RH: You know you meet people who you feel really understand Jung and maybe that depends largely on the person. For you, would you say that Meier really understood him more than others?

TF: For sure Meier was dyed in the wool. He was not just an analysand like the many others from Zürich and the rest of the world, he was Jung's Crown Prince. He was for Jung what Jung had been to Freud.

RH: Really, even more than von Franz?

TF: For Jung, Meier was his Crown Prince; and von Franz—to put it a bit sharply—was used by Jung. She had to translate his Latin and Greek quotes. She was used to large extent, and Barbara Hannah was the chauffeur. Everyone had their own function around Jung. He was great at exploiting the transference.

RH: He would do that with women.

TF: But also with men. Meier succeeded Jung at the Federal High School of Technology and had to represent him in the outside world. Meier did the traveling when Jung was old, lecturing all over the world. He wrote the textbook on Jungian psychology.

RH: The textbook?

TF: Yes, the four volumes on Jungian psychology that have only come out in English in the last ten years. These four volumes represent the fundamentals of Analytical Psychology.

RH: So would you say if you want to read the fundamentals, read these four volumes?

TF: Absolutely.

RH: As an analyst, you feel Dr. Meier was very important to you?

TF: Absolutely. He was biased in the way the Zürich school has always been biased. In his introduction to his book on the psychology of transference, Jung says that he was always glad if the transference was mild. They were not interested in transference and not at all interested in countertransference. At least they wouldn't speak about it. Perhaps they thought about it. As I told you, Meier and I fell out at the Clinic, and what went wrong, I think, was that neither of us was aware of the transference and countertransference between us. This is what I tried to show in a more general way in my article, "Oedipus in Gethsemane."

RH: You feel that is your most important writing?

TF: For me it is my swan song. I wrote that after the break with Meier, and it took me five years to get it down on paper.

JH: Was that your way of processing the break with Meier?

TF: Yes. I have always had a thing about homosexuality. As Hopcke has shown, the word homosexuality is mentioned only about fifteen times in the eighteen volumes of Jung's works—not even once per volume. And Meier was always against the homosexuals. He couldn't stand that. That's why he could not see the homosexual or homoerotic element in our relationship. We were neighbors, living two houses apart in Zürich. We were listening to the same music and had the same guests. We had everything together.

RH: Wait a minute, you were living that close together? You were neighbors?

TF: Yes.

JH: How much older was Meier?

TF: Twenty years. I went to see him just after the death of my father, which was an odd thing anyway because my father was a banker, and I was a student of philosophy, and I just felt I could not be clear about what I wanted to do. I had decided and told my father, that I would finish my studies, get my doctorate, and then I wanted to become a banker. I asked my father to be prepared to help get me introduced. That was Easter Sunday 1950, and later, after lunch, he took a nap and died. I had promised him that I would go to the bank. And with this problem I went to see Meier as my analyst, and you can imagine what happened in terms of the transference.

RH: So that is the other issue you took to him. You were blocked in your dissertation, and you had just lost your father. Do you feel Meier became like a father for you?

TF: Sure. It was the transference. We worked for half a year. I was seeing him twice a week, and one Friday he announced that he would be leaving the following Sunday for the States for six weeks. He was not interested in the transference relationship. If you are interested in transference, you don't do that to a patient—announce a six-week break the evening before. He went, and by the time he came back, I had finished my dissertation. [Laughter.]

RH: Isn't that something?

TF: You see how irrationally analysis can work. The wisdom of Meier and his clever interpretations may have been right, but it was the transference, period, that made me write my dissertation.

RH: How did the transference help you write it?

TF: I think I had found an ideal guiding figure, and I was already secretly convinced that I would be an analyst. I felt quite ashamed to own up to that and tell Meier that I wanted to become an analyst. And the unconscious helped me by sending me a dream in which I saw Jung, and he looked at me and said, "I can see that you want to become an analyst," and this dream I had to show to Meier. [Laughter.].

RH: So that was the dream that led you into your work?

TF: In the dream Jung said he could see in my face that this is what I wanted— to become an analyst. He didn't say if he thought it was right or wrong.

JH: It reflected back to you what you were feeling.

TF: Yes. And I couldn't bring it out into the world. So it came out in the form of a dream, and it was in the analytical contract that you had to tell your dreams to your analyst, so I told the dream to Meier, and he said, "Well, maybe, why not?" [Laughter.] That was his way.

JH: But you finished your studies with other programs first?

TF: Yes. I finished my Ph.D., and then I started at the Institute. I am one of these people. I would not trust a career history like mine in anybody else: being a schoolboy up to almost thirty and then becoming an analyst without having been out in the world and without having done anything. I don't think that is how it should be.

RH: So you went right from the Ph.D. to the Institute?

TF: Yes.

RH: I would think that if you were going to do that and you knew that this very important person, Carl Jung, lived right down the street, you would be rushing over to meet him or something. I would want to know him or try to work with him. None of that went on for you, right?

TF: No. But I was taken with his philosophy and the world view he had. About a year ago a supervisee asked me a question about something in analysis. After I had answered he looked at me and said, "I asked so-and-so and so-and-so, and they gave me completely different answers." And I heard myself saying, "You know those two people, they are psychologists." I asked myself, "What am I saying?", but I am quite sure that I am a philosopher. My basic impetus is philosophy and not psychology. And I am fascinated by these concepts of the archetypes and that we cannot see the world other than according to our senses and the way our brains are constructed. So we cannot possibly know the real world. That is the consequence of the archetypes, and I am intrigued by that.

RH: You were born in St. Gallen, and are now how old?

TF: Seventy.

RH: You went to boarding school?

TF: Only for a year. I was a very weak and sick child. I had polio and two severe bouts of pneumonia before the penicillin era. I almost died and could not move my left leg, so I was sent to the German boarding school in Davos, which was full of Nazis. It is funny that Adolf Guggenbühl was sent there because his family was one of the few families in Switzerland which was unconditionally anti-Nazi. His father was a publisher, and he published the first book on the concentration camps in 1935.

RH: You went to the University of Zürich for all your graduate education, including your Ph. D. You are married for forty plus years, have three daughters, three granddaughters, and a grandson.

TF: Yes. And my grandson is one of the few men in the family. He lost his father at the age of five.

RH: Were you in the first class at the Jung Institute?

TF: No, no. The Institute was founded in 1948, and I began in 1954.

RH: Who were some of your classmates that we might recognize?

TF: Adolf Guggenbühl. But he was not really at the Institute, and I don't believe he has a diploma, because he was a psychiatrist. So was Dieter Baumann who is Jung's grandson and also a psychiatrist. They were the two psychiatrists among the students. There were no medical doctors in the early days of the Institute and this caused a great deal of concern. You will find a passage in Stern's biography about how Jung scared away doctors. He treated them very badly. And the fact that the medical profession was rather anti-Jung—especially among the psychiatrists—was due largely to Jung's attitude. Also at the Institute at that time were Jim Hillman, Marvin Spiegelman, Bob Stein, Sonja Marjasch, and John Phillips. There must have been others.

RH: And yet Jung was encouraging people to become doctors?

TF: Yes he was, but when they became doctors he treated them very badly.

RH: Why did he do that?

TF: Because of the kind of person he was. During the war there were some prominent psychiatrists who took the trouble to take the train out to Kusnacht once a week for a seminar with Jung. [They couldn't drive because there was no gas.] Jung would just laugh at them and treat them in the most unbelievable way. Finally they had enough and did not come anymore. And then there was his relationship to Bleuler and all that stuff. He could have remained linked to the Burghölzli Psychiatric Hospital and linked to psychiatry in Switzerland, but he chose not to.

RH: Was he just arrogant?

TF: He had a very arrogant side. Someone would ask a question and he would say, "Of course, why do you ask such a thing!" I have a lot of sympathy for Guggenbühl's statement that we have to see Jung as a psychological genius but that his personality had a side to it that was just small, Swiss bourgeois. That is why I am against all these biographies that try to make a saint out of him. That was just not true and is strictly against his own concept of the shadow. A human being has in reality a shadow, and Jung had a big one. If you had seen his body, you would have seen that he cast a tremendous shadow.

The Shadow

JH: Did you sense that Jung was comfortable with his shadow?

TF: I think to a certain extent he certainly enjoyed it. And it was also a source of his suffering. The shadow makes you suffer.

RH: How does it make you suffer?

TF: The shadow confronts us with everything that is foreign to us, everything we don't want or that we hate. But out of the shadow also comes much that makes us and our lives valuable. Without shadows there is no creativity. We were talking earlier about Sabina Spielrein. There Jung fell into his shadow—and made one of his most important discoveries.

RH: Have you found a good way to deal with your shadow?

TF: Ah…what a question! [Much laughter.] It connects with something else—another thought that I have been having increasingly. It is not so much the analysis that you go through that is important. Of course that plays a part. But what I feel is that getting older makes a huge difference. I have always had the impression that my analytical fathers were much more shadow-integrated because they had been analyzed for longer than I had. But now I don't think so anymore. I think it is due to the fact of getting older. You can allow for much more shadow in yourself. You can allow for much less repression in yourself when the vital tension decreases. It is not so dangerous to let your shadow out. There is less energy, and therefore there is less damage. [Laughter.] You can afford to let it come out and be there, and people give you credit. Once you are an old man you can do all sorts of things.

RH: So nature takes care of things?

TF: Certainly, at least to a certain extent. But to give at least a partial answer to your question, I believe that being aware of the shadow is already part of the task. Being aware means that you must take a conscious decision about whether or not you want to act out a particular part of the shadow. You get into a conflict which you avoid by repressing. But if you manage to maintain the tension for long enough, the so-called "integration of the shadow" will take place. One can observe a similar phenomenon in mild cases of schizophrenia. I had a patient who was obsessed by the idea that he should change his job. He had already done this a few times, and it was clear that it would become more and more difficult to find employment. He would read the job ads in the newspaper, and when the nearby church clock struck five o'clock, or when a helicopter flew over the house, he would take it as a sign that he should apply for a particular job. I listened to this over several months, and one day as he was describing one such an event to me he added, "You know, I still have my spinning ideas." In time he got some distance from his paranoia. Six months later he was promoted to company director, and we stopped the treatment. I imagine that merely through my listening, he was able to free himself of his embarrassing secrets. The rest is taken care of by what Jung called "the self-healing tendency of the soul."

JH: Other people…

TF: Yes, yes…he was in treatment with a psychiatrist who told me on the phone that the man was incurable. He would not take his medication. And his delusion could not be corrected. I didn't correct the delusion. I just listened to it and let it be and then let nature take care of it.

RH: So what is the purpose of being in analysis then? Why don't you just let nature take care of everything?

TF: The analyst is like a midwife. Nature knows how to proceed in a birth. But if the woman is overcivilized and has complexes and anxieties and fears and is cramped, then things go wrong. So the midwife has to tell her to relax, breathe in the right way, and so on. Nature then takes its course.

RH: So part of the job of the analyst is to help people with nature?

TF: Yes. To allow nature to take its course. You may say it's a very optimistic idea that if you let things take their course they'll turn out all right. But the probability that a child will be born with ten fingers and not eleven is incredibly higher than the other way round. But you have to let nature take its course. Then you have ten fingers. If you fiddle around with it you may get something else.

RH: But if you let nature take its course, it does not mean that things always come out the way you wanted them?

TF: That's right. They come out not the way the ego wants, but the self. That's like in dream interpretation. If you have a dream, there's a rule of thumb: whatever happens in the dream is right in the sense of healing and individuation. Only what the ego does in the dream can be right or wrong. That's a very helpful rule of thumb.

RH: What about the person who says, "I think I will just let God take care of my life, I don't have to do anything."

TF: No, no…it's not that you don't have to do anything. You have to do quite a lot.

RH: What do you have to do?

TF: You have to follow what it—your life—wants you to do. The self doesn't do the job for you.

RH: Do you think things always come out right?

TF: No, I think they come out wrong very often. Take my example of being kicked out of the Clinic, which was absolutely traumatic.

RH: One of the worst moments of your life?

TF: One of the worst. I didn't "let it happen" at all. I fought like mad. I went right up to the Federal Court. And I lost.

RH: Fighting C. A. Meier?

TF: Yes, Meier. We last met in front of the Federal Court. Five years later I worked it through and found out that my part of it was not realizing that my time at the Clinic was up and that I should look for a successor, withdraw to the background and do something else with the rest of my life. I didn't see that at the time. So the self, in the form of Meier, took me by the neck and kicked me out.

RH: So even then, looking at it now, Meier was acting, not intentionally, on behalf of the self?

TF: Absolutely! Not intentionally but actually on behalf of the self.

RH: So your feelings about Meier now are not the same as when you were standing at the Federal Court?

TF: No. But when he was dying last November, an old friend of mine wanted to bring about a reconciliation. I asked myself very intensely whether I wanted that and I declined, saying that for me Meier had died ten years earlier. That was past, and I did not want that on a personal level. I know that he did me a personal favor by kicking me out of the Clinic, unintentionally.

RH: Why didn't you want to see him personally then?

TF: He was dead for me. It was past.

JH: Because what he had been in your life no longer existed because of everything that had gone on?

TF: To a certain extent. Taken with a grain of salt I would agree.

JH: Okay, help me understand that then.

TF: I think there is always ambivalence. But by and large I would say that this chapter was finished for me. I don't know how I will think about it in five years. Perhaps I will regret that I didn't go for the reconciliation. But at that point it made no sense to me. Don't forget that this thing has another aspect beyond the personal. The Jung Clinic was destroyed by his action. It is no longer a Jung clinic. It is now a branch of the Burghölzli Psychiatric Hospital. They are doing good psychiatry, but they are not doing psychotherapy in the Jungian sense any more. None of the members of the Board is a Jungian any more.

JH: It sounds like there were two things going on. You made reference to your personal relationship to Meier and the transference which was somehow the catalyst that brought about this split that caused the Clinic to stop. The personal relationship got mixed up and that messed up the professional one which pushed you ahead but destroyed a lot of stuff that had been important.

TF: So I must acknowledge that I am fifty percent responsible for destroying the Clinic. If I had been more aware of the background of this transference, and about my own situation both in the Clinic and in life—if I had realized that it was time to step down—then I think things would have taken another course.

RH: Perhaps you could have stepped down and appointed a successor.

TF: Yes I could have. Theoretically.

JH: You made reference to this relationship between men which I don't quite understand. One man is the mentor or father, and the other is the son, and at some point the son grows up and is challenging the father, and it falls apart...

TF: Think of the Oedipus myth. The outcome was that the son killed the father, and if you look at a book like *Power and Crowds* (by Elias Canetti), you also see that the father tries to kill the son. These chiefs and kings are afraid of their sons growing up and taking power at their expense. There is this unconscious rivalry between father and son. That's why my paper, "Oedipus and Gethsemane," is so important to me, because I think this was going on in the relationships between Breuer and Freud, Freud and Jung, Jung and Meier, and Meier and myself. God forbid that it should go further with my "sons."

JH: Are you saying that you were not aware of the competition between you and Meier?

TF: Yes, that was how it was. And it is interesting that the thing with Meier exploded with the issue of our daughter being involved in the Zürich riots.

RH: Really, it exploded between you and Meier?

TF: Yes, it was at a dinner party, and I told him that our daughter had been beaten up by a policeman, and he said that "whoever goes into danger will be hurt."

RH: He was blaming your daughter. And that is what got you going?

TF: It made the thing explode. I was furious. It was not the reaction I expected from a friend. But this is how these things go. If you miss the personal transference, if you can't see what is in the background where the shadow of this positive adoration of the analysand for the analyst is, you will run into trouble. And the extent of the resulting damage will be far-reaching. So from that little comment at the party, the shadow popped right up and took a hold of the whole relationship, and now father is going to kill son, and son is going to kill father, and you are off. My daughter had violated law and order and rebelled against the authority of the state, so her getting into trouble was her own fault. That was Meier's attitude. And I think he meant me. "You, boy, you obey. You are to obey the authority of the father."

JH: It sounds like you came out of the role when you reacted personally to your daughter, you left the value system you grew up in. You were saying, "That relationship is much more important to me than whatever system I grew up in."

TF: I think that is one aspect of the whole situation.

JH: That symbolizes your split with Meier, because he was still in the role with you, and you had gotten out of the role with your daughter.

TF: Thank you. I think you are right. And, of course, you can see an aspect of my anima in my daughter which made me break away from this imposing father figure who would not let me develop in my own way. It is the anima which meets you and challenges you and leads you into danger and crisis.

RH: I wonder also if there was a part of you that did not want Meier involved in the Clinic at all. You may have felt you needed him but…

TF: On this point you may be right.

RH: You wanted to do your own thing…

TF: But he didn't interfere very much with the clinical side. He was interested in the research. He had a sleep and dream laboratory in the Clinic on which he spent a lot of money. The Clinic had to earn this money, and the expense became increasingly an issue for me. It got addressed at a meeting of the Board. Meier had asked for a large sum of money for research, and I said that it was out of the question, that we could not afford it. But he said, "I want it." I told the Board that if they voted in favor of this payment, I would seek legal advise to dètermine whether the transaction was admissible. Meier then withdrew his demand. But then came the revenge.

RH: Your paper details how this very same dynamic went on in other relationships between men.

TF: Yes. Just after this event we had a meeting of the Swiss Society of Jungians. There for the first time the case of Sabina Spielrein was discussed. After that meeting, my wife and I went to the Swiss mountains for a hiking holiday, and on one of these hikes I started thinking about the whole thing and asked myself why things hadn't gone wrong when Jung went beyond the transference point and got involved with Spielrein and Toni Wolff, despite the fact that these women were his patients. I realized that these relationships were heterosexual and suddenly the penny dropped and I saw Breuer and Freud, Freud and Jung, and Jung and Meier. And I said, "My God! It doesn't work because that other string is homosexual." And it is much more repressed than the heterosexual. The homosexuality itself is actually the issue which has to be repressed at all costs, which is why things develop in such a destructive way.

RH: You saw this between Meier and Jung too?

TF: Absolutely.

RH: So they had a falling out?

TF: Yes. It was always concealed. I wrote about this in my paper, "Oedipus and Gethsemane." Overtly they were still together. Meier was still the Crown Prince. He was still Jung's representative in the outside world, but their personal relationship had been broken since about 1957. When Meier published his paper on projection and subject-object relation and transference, he sent the manuscript to Jung, who like a school teacher, sent it back covered in marks in red ink. Meier said, "I will not have that." Again a ridiculously small issue.

Constellation

RH: Can we talk about your notion of constellation. You say that constellation is the "becoming efficient of an archetype."

TF: The archetypes constitute the foundations of the soul. They are like sleeping dogs and occasionally one of them wakes up. Or rather, one of them becomes effective in the inner or external milieu. Another good image is a chaotic heap of iron filings on a sheet of paper. If we switch on an electromagnet under the paper, the iron filings arrange themselves according to a distinct pattern or structure. The magnetic field constellates the particles. Something switches on the current. The trigger can be the passing from childhood into adulthood at puberty. It can be the mid-life threshold; the threshold into old age or what I call "the third half" of life. It can be anything of that sort or an outside event.

During an association test, if the person being tested sits in front of the tester, he or she will get constellated. You have a tension from the expectation in the person being tested. Then the test takes its course. Then the complexes are constellated, and you can see them in the course of the experiment in the delayed reaction times. You have this in analysis too. The analyst constellates the client, which means that the analyst prompts certain aspects of the client's character to come to the fore. That is why the Jung Institute in Zürich requires part of the training to be done with a man and part to be done with a woman. Totally different things are constellated. Not only because of the gender difference but also because of the character difference. And that's the constellation. You can see this in everyday life. If you have a married couple who get along quite well and a mother-in-law joins them on holiday for eight days and stays in the same house, you will see a new constellation. [Laughter.] The word "constellation" comes from astronomy. It's the figure that the group of stars resembles. The stars don't actually create the figures, but we project the images into the sky and see things like the Big Dipper. It is not there. It is our projection. That is the constellation. And of course this conversation we are having now is characterized by the constellation between us. If I were being interviewed by someone else I would certainly come up with completely different answers. Which leads to the question, "Who am I actually?"

Dealing with the Unconscious

RH: What are your own practices of dealing with the unconscious? Do you have rituals or daily things you try to do?

TF: I don't think so. My only ritual, as far as I am aware, is to keep a written record of my dreams. When I have time and energy I keep a sort of diary where I note down things that happen. The unconscious approaches us not only through our dreams but through our daily life. Take my trouble with Meier. That came from the outside, and it was certainly constellated by the unconscious. So what happens on the outside is also meaningful and has to be taken into account. When I have some special experience in my practice or my family, I have to ask myself where it comes from. What it has to do with me? How am I responsible, not for what I do, but for what I am? How am I responsible for what happens to me?

RH: That work you do mainly by yourself? You don't talk with someone else?

TF: I sometimes talk about this with people around me—quite often with my wife and also with my daughters. Not that I give out too many details of myself. I do not think it is good to tell your dreams to everybody. But you have to work them through. Then the result can be dealt with in relationships but not the dream itself.

RH: What happens if you tell your dreams to too many people?

TF: I think you dilute the experience. Telling a lot of people gets rid of anxiety. Being unable to stand the tension of a nightmare on your own, for instance. So you tell it to somebody. Like in the Catholic Church, you go to a priest for confession, and you let off steam. That is also why I think it is not good for people to stay in analysis too long. There comes a point where you have to stand your own ground, even if it means making a blunder which could have been prevented by seeing the analyst. In the "Light and Shadow" paper, I wrote of how I was struck by the way the analysts who ran the Jung Institute in the 1950s—who were the direct disciples of Jung—would go at least once a week to Kusnacht to discuss their dreams with the old master. Jung writes about it in *The*

Relations between the Ego and the Unconscious. If you have a breakdown you can pick yourself up in the regressive restoration of the persona. And the alternative is to sit at the feet of a prophet, but this isn't a step towards individualization. If you are to individualize you have to stop sitting at the feet of the prophet. Those analysts of the fifties were still sitting at the feet of their prophet. All his life Meier wore a ring on his finger similar to one worn by Jung and smoked the same kind of pipe. He used the same kind of invoice with his patients as Jung had done. He had the same laugh as Jung had. And all of these people—Jolande Jacobi, Binswanger, Hannah, von Franz—they all went out at least once a month to talk with Jung and get their absolution.

RH: You didn't do that with Meier?

TF: No, I stopped at a certain point. After I came back to Zürich from England, I saw him once in a while for a couple of years, and then I stopped. What I can still do if I get into trouble with a client is go to a colleague and discuss the case. I am not unable to ask for help. But I think the responsibility is entirely my own. My colleague wouldn't say anything about my case anyway, he would listen and say that it was difficult, and then I would go home again and do my own thing. [Laughter.] But talking to someone triggers the constellation, and when I go home I have the answer.

Spirituality

RH: Do you consider yourself a spiritual person?

TF: I think to a certain degree I am a spiritual person. But certainly not exclusively.

RH: Would you consider your spiritual life important?

TF: Absolutely! It starts in the morning. After breakfast I sit at the piano for a whole hour. That is my hour of bliss everyday.

RH: What do you play?

TF: I play Bach, Mozart, Haydn, Chopin. I have just started with Debussy. I very often start in the morning with the preludes by Bach that I started learning when I was ten years old. Every time they seem new and fresh.

RH: You feel that is connected with your spiritual life?

TF: Absolutely. It is halfway between the spiritual and the sensual life.

RH: [Laughter.] That's interesting.

TF: Why do you find it so amusing?

RH: I think it is great.

TF: That is work. It is not pleasure. Of course it is full of pleasure. But it is mainly work that I cannot do in the evening because I am tired. Then it doesn't work.

JH: It sounds like it takes you back to yourself. And centers you before you start the day.

TF: Yes, very much.

RH: It sounds like a personal ritual.

TF: It is. And you know someone else who had the same ritual? Karl Barth. He used to play in the morning but only Mozart.

RH: Do you have a favorite piece?

TF: That changes. At the moment it is one of the posthumous preludes by Chopin which has a three-rhythm in the left hand and a four-rhythm in the right. It is hellish to play. [Laughter.]

RH: Do you read Jung much?

TF: Off and on. After I have written a paper, I read Jung and find out that he has already said the same things! [Laughter.] There are certain papers of Jung which I read every few years. The main ones are *The Psychology of the Transference* and *Answer to Job*. Another is *Psychology of Alchemy*.

RH: What do you feel Jung meant when he said that he knew God and did not need to believe in Him?

TF: I think he meant that the psyche has, by its very nature, an image of God, the self. He also described some of the influences this image may have on the individual. The self is what leads us through life, and it helps us in a very natural way. Also when we die. Jung knew that and found it superfluous to believe in something over and above that.

Death

RH: If you found yourself in heaven, and you were with Jung, would you want to talk with him, and what do you imagine you would talk about?

TF: I don't know in detail what we would discuss, but I would let him know how I feel about him.

RH: And what would you say?

TF: I would tell him I have enormous respect for his work. I am sure that his work was essential for my life and that it helped me get through life in a really meaningful way with a feeling of doing something meaningful. I needed it badly. I would tell him that his personality was not quite up to his work. But that is a human element, and I cannot blame him for it. Look at all the great men. They were all monsters.

RH: Do you think Jung would actually hear that if you said it?

TF: I think so. He would agree. Whether it's true is another question!

RH: So what do you think happens at death?

TF: I think what happens is the end of a life.

RH: So you see death as your body going into the ground, or being cremated…

TF: Yes, but my body is not me anymore. My body is me before death. But after death it is no longer me. My body will be cremated. My family will disperse the ashes somewhere around our home in the mountains.

RH: So there is no afterlife?

TF: Not for me. Not in that sense.

RH: In some other sense?

TF: Perhaps some of the pupils I have had, who now live in five continents, will practice the way I practiced. But in thirty years that will be gone too. I will live on in my grandchildren and great-grandchildren. The spirit of my grandfather is also around somewhere. One of our famous poets in Switzerland said that he had an experience when he was studying with Feuerbach, the philosopher. He said he suddenly realized that he thought death could well be the end. He wrote to a friend saying that accepting the idea that you only have one chance doesn't necessarily mean that you will become a bad person. When life's finished it is finished. No repeat performances. You can't put everything to rights after the event. You have to think about what you do before you do it.

JH: That view makes you more responsible.

TF: Yes. Lately I have had several periods of poor health. I have lost a lot of weight. My doctors were quite concerned. I felt weaker and weaker. I suddenly realized that if this was the end, it was acceptable. Life gets less and less, and then it is no longer there. It is not frightening. Dying may be frightening but not death. If you are suffering when you are dying, then death is the end of suffering.

RH: It sounds like you feel you have lived your life. Not that you want to die…

TF: No, I do not want to die. But I think I could if I had to.

RH: You don't have a lot of regrets?

TF: Oh, I do have a lot of regrets about things I wish I had done—and about a few things I wish I had not done.

JH: Are you saying that you feel that this is the given condition for all of us?

TF: I have to bear the regret and bear the guilt. And if I try to get rid of it in one way or another, I think it would be cheating.

RH: It is like the shadow of life.

TF: Exactly. But I can't say, "It was just the shadow of life and therefore I couldn't help it." I have a strong feeling that I could have done something about it on several occasions; like in the Clinic situation. If I had been more aware of my real needs and of the needs of the Clinic, things might have taken a different course. That is something I regret.

RH: Let's imagine that this interview is the last shot you would have to speak to the Jungian community in print, what would you like to say?

TF: We have talked about the function of the analyst and the notion of the analyst as midwife. Summing everything up I would say to other analysts working with the psyche, "Let it be," but not in a passive sense of just letting it go.

RH: That condenses down your life and how you have learned to deal with the psyche…just let it be.

TF: And the tension between the ego and self. The self knows where to go whereas the ego can be wrong, like in dream interpretation. What the ego does can be right or wrong, but the self is always right.

RH: Do you feel at seventy years old that your ego is better able to deal with the self.

TF: Yes, definitely. That may be an inflation on my part. I am somehow—rightly or wrongly—more at peace with myself than I was ten or twenty years ago. Again, this may well be an illusion. Who knows. [Laughter.]

RH: How would you like to be remembered in the Jungian community?

TF: I would like to be remembered as someone who eventually calmed down after he had done some valuable things such as establishing and running the Clinic and giving lectures. Someone who eventually found peace with himself and was at the same time able to share this feeling with some of his pupils so that they could take it with them.

RH: I was with you for a seminar in Zürich, and now during this interview, and I am impressed, Toni, with how open you are. You seem like a very open person.

TF: Yes, but that has to do with what I just said. I feel more at peace now and less tense.

RH: So someone twenty years ago would not have said the same thing about you?

TF: No, I was very guarded. And I had reasons to be. Because of my instinctual drives—power, sex, what have you. I would not have communicated these things with others back then. It has a lot to do with the eighties. It was very important that my daughters got into their rebellion. Their rebellion was synchronistic as it came at the right time for my own needs.

RH: Why aren't you so guarded today?

TF: I don't feel the need. I am probably very guarded, but I don't know in what ways because the resistance comes from unconscious mechanisms. [Laughter.] The unconscious is unconscious. I may well be very guarded without realizing it.

RH: You don't seem that way, and how would anyone ever really know that?

TF: Nobody would know. My wife and children would have something to say about that… They may know. Otherwise there are things we never see as we cannot exhaust the unconscious, and therefore, we cannot exhaust the shadow.

RH: So at the age of seventy do you feel that the unconscious is larger in your life or smaller than in earlier years?

TF: It is like the sea. It is immense. It has always been immense. Consciously, I am a bit less afraid of it. I have a very high respect for it and a feeling of awe. But perhaps a little less fear.

Remembering Ernst Bernhard

BIANCA GARUFI

It is difficult to speak of Ernst Bernhard, as it is always difficult to speak of a rich and complex personality and one who has had a particular importance not only in one's own life but in the lives of many others as well. Some of these, considering Bernhard a point of reference, have subsequently come together to form a group whose scope has been, and is today, the study and dissemination of the thought of C. G. Jung, of whom Bernhard was the importer into Italy, and while he lived, the promoter as well. I am referring to the Italian Association of Analytical Psychology (ATPA), founded in Rome in 1961 after twenty years of uncertainty and setbacks. From this group in 1966, another was formed, the Italian Center for Archetypal Psychology (CIPA). Together the two groups celebrated in January, 1992, their Jungian origins, with a congress in Rome at the Goethe Institute to honor the thirtieth anniversary of the School of Analytical Psychology in Italy.

Therefore to speak of Bernhard means to speak of a man who created a culture in our country, a culture of sensibility and intelligence, qualities practiced and shared by him in many ways from the beginning, that is, from when he came to Rome in 1936. It is also difficult to speak of him because it means reviving a time when the world was different from what it is now, and as a result, the ways of living and relating were also different from now, not excluding, in part, analytical relations. At the time few people were interested in Jungian thought and even fewer in

Bianca Garufi is the doyenne of Analytical Psychology in Italy. She has served on the Advisory Board of *Spring* since 1978. This article originally appeared in "Maestri Scomodi, Ernst Berhard, Buber e Jung," *Rivista di psicologia analitica nuova,* serie n. 2, 54/96, Roma, 1996.

going into analysis, in part because not many people then knew with any certainty what it meant to go into analysis. This, when you think about it, obviously had advantages and disadvantages for many reasons.

I met Bernhard in September, 1944. As I have said elsewhere,[1] the first time I visited him the war had just ended. Rome was full of military allies, and you went around on a bicycle or in a little truck. The electric lights often failed, sometimes for whole days. I remember climbing the stairs of Via Gregoriana, where Bernhard and his wife lived, in darkness, holding a candle offered to me for the occasion by the doorman.

Roberto Bazlen—better known as Bobi Bazlen, a friend of young and not-so-young intellectuals and a promoter, like few others in Italy at that time, of European culture in general and of Analytical Psychology in particular—had urged me with great insistence to meet Bernhard. Both Bobi and Bernhard had had a long experience of Freudian analysis; Bernhard in Berlin with Fenichel and Rado, and Bobi in Trieste where he had worked with Edoardo Weiss. This Freudian experience was still present in them, and especially in Bernhard, who included it in his practice, as I suppose those who worked with him at that time remember.

During my first meeting Bernhard gave me, above all, the impression of good humor and concreteness. I had come from the experience of the war and the Resistance, and during the conversation I spoke of it to him. I also told him, with fervor and the boldness of my youthful haughtiness, that I came to him to put my ideas in order; no more nor less than you go to the dentist to put your teeth in order. He received the compliment that I was paying him graciously, and to put me better at ease he told me that during the First World War in Germany, he had sympathized with the Left among the members of his regiment, and in that sense he had not changed.

He was referring, perhaps, as I realized much later, to his readings of Martin Buber and to the interests that he shared with Buber in utopian socialism.[2] Spontaneously the thought came to me that to a certain extent we could consider ourselves countrymen and inasmuch, point-blank, we could use the informal pronoun *tu* (you) with each other. Bernhard smiled indulgently and accepted. Obviously he had realized that I could not begin to work with him if it were not on an equal plane.

[1] Aldo Carotenuto, *Jung e la cultura italiana* (Roma: Astrolabio, 1977), 56, 68-69.

[2] C. Cardona, monograph of a broadcast on Ernst Bernhard, Radio Tre, 1987.

For his understanding of this and the sacrifice that without doubt it meant to him, I am today, now that I realize it, extremely grateful.

Both Bernhard and his wife, Dora, already worked with a few patients, and gradually the number increased. You went into analysis with them with the calm fervor of pioneers, even if you moved in a kind of semi-clandestineness, not only because of the cultural provincialism that still existed in Italy, a residue of the recent past, but above all because we were occupied with a psychology in many ways different from the traditional one; the one that you got only in the course of a medical degree and then only as an optional subject.

Most of us, either because we were very young or because we were uprooted from our places of origin because of the war and the postwar situation, had difficulties of every kind. Even the Bernhards found themselves pressured by the same circumstances. We helped each other more or less in turns to find work, find housing, and find food. Today no one can imagine all that, especially if you consider how the structure of the analytical setting went then. Remembering it today, notwithstanding the creative aspects already there, it was a situation altogether unrepeatable.

The Bernhards, man and wife, had come to Rome, as I already said, in 1936, both as refugees from Germany, and as a result were still isolated. He was Jewish, and his father would suffer the fate of the gas chamber, his mother a suicide out of despair. Through his own good fortune, and ours, Bernhard would have a better fate: when war broke out in Italy in 1940, he managed to avoid the worst of it inasmuch as he succeeded in being sent into confinement in Calabria, and this thanks to the intervention of Giuseppe Tucci, a member of the Italian Academy, a student of Tibetan religion, and later author of a book on the symbolism of the Mandala.

On his return to Rome and resumption of work, we patients and disciples represented for the Bernhards not only their sole contact with the world and with Italian reality, but also the best possibility of their making Jungian thought known, which they had already begun to spread with the greatest reach then possible, both scientifically and culturally.[3]

[3] In 1937, Bernhard was invited by Edoardo Weiss and by the Italian Psychoanalytical Society to give four lectures on dream from a Jungian point of view. These lectures were published for the first time in 1971 by the *Rivista di psicologia analytica* and are reprinted in "Maestri Scomodi: Ernst Bernhard, Buber, e Jung," *Rivista di psicologia analytica*, new series 2, 54/96.

The occasion for giving up the semi-clandestineness which I referred to came with the possibility of publishing some of the many important texts on depth psychology. The negotiations conducted by Bobi Bazlen between Bernhard and Meschini Ubaldini, owner of the Astrolabio publishing house, were long and laborious. Several times we feared that our hopes would be dashed. But finally the first book came out, which was Freud's *Introduction to the Study of Psychoanalysis*, as the first in the series "Psyche and Consciousness" directed specifically by Bernhard.

It was an important step also for me, since to pursue this precious series, I had to leave my job at the Einaudi publishing house. It was now 1947. Almost every book that Astrolabio sent to press in that series was a discovery for many Italian readers, often a stimulus for us and a verification of the analytical work done with Bernhard.

And here, among these memories, I should insert one which, for objective reasons, I cannot leave out. When, in 1950, it came time for me to graduate, my interest in Analytical Psychology pushed me to write a dissertation on the thought of Jung, entitled *The Psychology and Dynamic of Personality in the Works of C. G. Jung.* To discuss such a subject, you had to apply to the Faculty of Medicine, even though I was studying philosophy. My dissertation was the first in an Italian university on Jung.

My analysis with Bernhard meant a long period of minute attention to the personal unconscious. Bernhard was still relatively young, and his style of work was without doubt different from that of the last years of his life, when his mode of working, as often happens with the passing of the years and the maturing of personality, turned back greatly toward religious and philosophical interests, and then to the great problems of life and death. It was a path that made him give ever more space to consciousness and the rational, and above all to the unconscious and the irrational. It was only after returning from my long stays abroad (and already in 1965 Bernhard was no longer alive) that I could notice the process which in the meantime had changed him and his way of working. But while this transformation is not unusual in human beings and often natural, its richness often undervalued, there was also, in my opinion, another motive specifically psychological which led him in that direction—a direction which always made him prefer a psychology not exclusively based on ego, but even, if not rather, on the mystery and complexity of existence.

Only later did I guess the essence of the drive that had brought Bernhard to this deepening and this research. It happened to me in fact when I read, not for the first time but later and with greater attention, his preface to the book, *Abandonment to Divine Providence*, a book which was a spiritual guide based on the major principles of the Catholic religion, presented in the series "Psyche and Consciousness." The author, Jean Pierre de Caussade (1675-1751), was at the time the spiritual father of a convent of cloistered nuns. The publication of this book left me at the time perplexed. To see this book included among the texts dedicated to depth psychology could easily make one think, especially at first glance, that the position given to it was inappropriate. In fact I asked myself repeatedly what motive Bernhard had to include it in a series designed to forge contacts with psychoanalysts and depth psychology. It was a book different in language, level, and content from any I had read up until then, so totally different from Freud, different from Wickes' *The Psychic World of Childhood*, from Jung's *Psychology and Education*, and downright different from *The Ego and the Unconscious*, published, thanks to Cesare Pavese, in the famous anthropology series of Einaudi, and even different from *Psychology and Religion*, which appeared in a series at the publishing house of Communità (belonging to Adriano Olivetti), another supporter and benefactor of Analytical Psychology in Italy.

The content expressed in the book, *Abandonment to Divine Providence,* always seemed to me more incongruous and above all different from everything that had been discussed during my analytical sessions—two a week—*vis-à-vis* a desk between two armchairs with a book on top, which I knew to be the *I Ching*, and a box of toffies, and the round clock positioned in such a manner that I could follow the passing of time for the hour that was assigned me. I devoted only editorial attention to de Caussade's book when it came out. Much time was spent alternating between refutations and hesitations, before coming to an hypothesis which I could at least discuss with myself. All my perplexities cleared up one day while rereading with even more intense and rapt attention the penultimate page of the preface, where Bernhard had excerpted a passage from de Caussade.

In the passage in question, it seems that for this author what teaches us is only what happens to us day after day; therefore we know only what experience teaches through suffering and action. Experience is then always for de Caussade the true school, the teacher of consciousness, and everything we say to others must proceed from this fount, whose richness and light grants to us a life of making knowledge divine, a knowledge that is both natural and supernatural. The psyche, in fact, since it is a participant of these two worlds, is heard from moment to moment in such a fount and becomes a "virtuous theology" made from practice and experience. The direction of our destiny joins with our psyche in a thousand different ways in each of us; and the mode it specifically chooses is always the best for us. It is a mode therefore which reveals, with considerable evidence, the great affinity between our destiny and our psyche.

I quote now the words of Bernhard in which he comments on this thought of de Caussade:

> In *Abandonment to Divine Providence* we find, therefore, for psychology, both religious experience and a process of integration of consciousness, a rich mass of surprising parallels with the most important religious manifestations in all epochs; the religious attitude of abandonment approaches particularly that of Indian Bahkti-Yoga and Chinese Taoism[4] and includes that of modern man in the individuation process as C. G. Jung describes it. The final goal of this process—after due assimilation of the psychic contents that are removed and brought over to the responsibility of actual consciousness—is precisely in taking from that transformation of the primitive ego and ascribing it to itself. This transformation springs from the integration of consciousness through the experience lived in the psyche and in the destiny of human beings, the up until then unconscious Self, or *Selbst*, or whatever you want to call it: Divine Image, God, Christ, Divine Providence, Atman, Purusha, Tao. This transformation in *The Book of Changes* or *I Ching*, which is at the heart of Chinese wisdom, comes to be defined as follows:
>
> The benign man discovers it and calls it benign.
> The wise man discovers it and calls it wise.
> The unconscious man lives with it day by day
> and does not recognize it.[5]

As for the *I Ching* and the use—thought by many a misuse—that he made of it (Bernhard, however, consulted the *I Ching* rarely in the

[4] *Wu Wei*: the art of yielding: to say without saying, to do without doing.

[5] J. P. de Caussade, *Abbandono alla Providenza Divina* (Roma: Astrolabio, 1947), 11 ff.

classical way, and his abuse of it was rather instead in his amused but significant habit of flipping open and then closing a corner of the book after having quickly glanced at it) you could say, by way of explanation, that Bernhard's mental attitude, though solidly based on the principle of causality, would not let him disregard the principle of acausality, and this in virtue of his natural and irrepressible tendency toward the conjunction of opposites, something he also got from his readings of Jung. Here again we find the concept of abandonment to divine Providence and the relative distrust that Bernhard had—though he respected it—of the ego. In fact he limited its centrism by giving a position in the world and in the psyche to acausality and synchronicity.

As for me, what I remember of his rapid shutting of the *I Ching*, a gesture, I should say, that never bothered me for I considered it but a banal tic, I find, in this regard, the words with which Jung concludes his preface to the *I Ching* extraordinarily enlightening and liberating—a preface first done for the English edition and then translated and used in the Italian edition. He says: "Whoever is not content with the *I Ching* has no need to use it, and whoever does not understand it has presumably the best reason not to use it. It seems nevertheless that this book means something, even if it is only as a precious *document humain*."

I want to emphasize that, in my opinion, *The Abandonment to Divine Providence* was implicit, in the large and less confessional sense of the term, perhaps from the beginning, in the life and nature of Ernst Bernhard, and you have the proof of this when you read his unique book, *Mythobiography*, which seems from the first pages to be permeated with it. For Bernhard the encounter with de Caussade's book represented, in my opinion, a confirmation and contradiction of his own thought, especially in regard to his work style and to the limits he put on the ego—limits which do not lead to its deactivation but which permit a greater space and a greater freedom for the creativity of the unconscious and its images. These are in fact the inspirations, I could even say the authors, of the individuation process and the evolution of our personality.

The abandonment to Providence, which inappropriately came to be called "divine"—Providence, after all, has no need of qualifications—was considered by Bernhard the absolutely best attitude to assume in crucial situations of psychological work, and in every situation of our life, an attitude that, once acquired, will lead to a healing and decisive framework both for that particular moment and for the further conduct of existence. Suffering, the kind caused by neurosis, resides in great part in the difficulty in facing a change, in a passing phase that is necessary, even indispensable, to a point that it would be fatal to the individual to escape it. The ego, at least if it is not imaginal[6] or already a friend of the unconscious and its images, is in principle a reactionary, opposed to every change that is not imposed by itself. Through the abandonment, and therefore the relativizing of the ego—if you do not consider that a contradiction—through the legitimate support that must never be lacking or even be weakened by the ego, one can trace the path whose end, unattainable, even unfollowable, is individuation.

Mythobiography was published in 1969 by Adelphi. The book was introduced by Lanfranco Rambelli, a psychiatrist and student of Bernhard, and later a teacher in the AIPA. (Unfortunately for his many friends and dear ones, Rambelli is no longer with us.) I was still absent from Rome, so it was impossible to participate in the introduction. Some time later I had the opportunity to transcribe some of the words spoken by him on that occasion:

> Ernst Bernhard has been and is now with this *Mythobiography* an enthusiastic teacher who incited you to investigate the unknown, constellating in many of us that spirit of adventure and that profound inquiry into reality that is the prerogative of every researcher as it is of every hero of myth. The sentiments of Ernst Bernhard, which in this book blossom marvelously, are sentiments and thoughts of a great humanity and of a great affection for everyone, sentiments which, for whoever approaches them, leave one in some way touched, won over, motivated.

Mythobiography, in my memory and in the memory of anyone who has had a fruitful or corroborating encounter with the book, contains, besides the profuse religiousness evident to all, certain reflections that are notable for their psychological acumen and clinical relevance. I refer in particular to the importance given by him to the Shadow and to typology, classical concepts of Jungian thought, two subjects that are treated amply in the final section of the *Mythobiography*, whose precise title is "Psychotherapy."

---

[6] Hillman, "L'Io immaginale," *Trame Perdute* (Milano: Raffaello Cortina, 1985), 3.

The Shadow, as we know, is the side of our personality considered negative by us, everything that we believe ourselves never to be capable of, everything we believe others are capable of—disgraceful people, evil people, presumptuous people, and so on. "Me like that? Never!" Anyone who has any experience of analytical work knows well this strong denial of all our interior nastiness.

In this regard it can be interesting to consider what some of our colleagues have written concerning Freud on Shadow, on this psychic content that is so profoundly unconscious that it becomes impossible to remove and that is so exhausting to make surface and be accepted. Colleagues I have referred to—Bani Shorter, Alfred Plaut, and Andrew Samuels—note that according to Jung:

> It is to Freud that goes the credit of having called the attention of modern man to the split between the luminous aspects and the dark aspects of the human psyche. It seemed in fact to Jung that Freud, thanks to his scientific approach and immunity from any religious scope, had revealed that abyss of present darkness in human nature, which the optimism of Western Christianism and the age of science had tried to hide. Jung speaks of the method of Freud as the most profound and detailed analysis of Shadow that has ever been undertaken.[7]

As for Bernhard and his reflections on Shadow, I found his definition of Pseudo-Shadow interesting and original: it is not a real Shadow, it belongs to us only in part, and it is altogether something else from the individual, personal Shadow. The Pseudo-Shadow, then, consists in that which from darkness the individual always brings inside himself—for example, the Shadow of your cultural origins, the shadowy contents of the collective customs belonging not only to the individual but to all those that the individual, from the beginning of his existence, has had around himself. I use here the words of Bernhard: "Shadows of family, of the sphere of civilization, race,"[8] and so much else that comes from the primordial roots of humanity. They are Pseudo-Shadows, that is, not authentic Shadows, not individual, certain intrinsic inheritances of unconsciousness, of profound and distant archaicness but pregnant as well

[7] B. Shorter, A. Plaut, and A. Samuels, *Dizionario di Psicologia Analitica* (Milano: Raffaello Cortina, 1987), 105-106.

[8] *Mythobiografia*, 157.

with energetic and cultural power, that it is our job not to disdain, not to renounce but to recognize and assimilate, because they are connected with our roots. And here Bernhard adds that the Pseudo-Shadow, "the collective aspects of the Shadow, should not be repressed nor masked, but considered as collective components of our proper existence and acted on as a part with which we do not identify."[9]

Consciousness of the Pseudo-Shadow allows us, thanks to psychological work, to confront the Shadow with what does not please us about ourselves and we reject, though all of it is us, contemporaneous, actual. It imposes on us the duty to recognize this personal Shadow, to reckon with it and with our Super-Ego that sees it as odious and repellent, and instead of projecting it onto someone else, to integrate it, to make our daily life more authentic, to expand our personality, to round it off.

In regard to the Pseudo-Shadow, let us recall the essay of Bernhard on the great Mediterranean Mother, an interesting and elaborate reflection on the rapport that Italians have with this image, both from a personal point of view and from a collective and cultural point of view. "The Italian Shadow casts a cold eye on the representative of Western civilization. From its point of view, the Italian is a man who cannot be trusted, without principles, oversexed, uncontrollable, vain, vicious, sentimental."[10] It is interesting how this Shadow, or better this Pseudo-Shadow, that weighs so heavily on Italians, can find ways, even in Analytical Psychology, to be weakened enough to allow the strengths that lie in it to blossom. He discusses a problem that is alive today, stimulating for its implications—and not only psychological ones. Indeed, the sticking points of history, anthropology, and sociology that can be seen in this essay give us the possibility to better explain the behaviors and actions, both personal and collective, sometimes tragic, even bloody, that make human beings of different cultural extractions scorn, strike, and war against one another. Nonetheless I suggest to whoever today might read or reread it, that this essay, "The Mediterranean Mother," is about 1961, a time of great cultural changes which began in Berkeley in 1965 and would have, as everyone knows, their big move in Europe in 1968, a movement that has made not a few people hesitate and change their minds about things like generational authoritarianism, racism, and sexism.

[9] *Ibid.*

[10] *Ibid.*, 168 ff.

But speaking of Bernhard and bringing his image to mind, and in turn his time, it is impossible not to remember and mention the period during which I had the good fortune to work with Dora Bernhard, a woman of vast and solid culture and a specialist, in the largest sense of the term, in work on the psyche's structure. I am very grateful for the work I did with her—on the ego, the Shadow, the Persona, the Animus-Anima, the Self that this structure contained—and also for her interest in mythology, which she introduced to me, making me aware of its profound psychological significance.

But back to Ernst Bernhard and his position in the field of psychotherapy: I think one can recognize in him a particular interest and competence in work on Jungian typology and on its special functions, the therapeutic use that can be made of it, if not in fact calling clinical attention to it. In this regard, in 1976, the London based *Journal of Analytical Psychology* conducted an inquiry on the importance that is still given in Jungian analysis to typology or to work on its functions.[11] This inquiry was probably the first sign that work on the functions was becoming considered superfluous and ineffective. Perhaps it was a sign of the doubt that it was too schematic, too rational, intellectual, of little use in therapy.

We all know that the attention given by Jung to typology, to the different ways of behaving with the world that each of us uses, had its origins in the invincible diversity that, notwithstanding their mutual esteem for each other, obliged Jung and Freud in the course of time to an inevitable separation. Work on the functions constituted for Bernhard one of the cardinal points of his practice; perhaps also because it was a work that brought him into various misunderstandings with Jung, both during his analysis with him and in the period afterward. But to distinguish out of the tonality and nuances of their relationship, Bernhard brought an interesting contribution to the therapeutic use of Jungian typology; one that was perhaps not always well received by those who

[11] There were many important and exhaustive articles: W. Willeford, "The Primacy of Feeling," vol. 21, n. 2, July 1976, 115; K. Bradway and W. Detloff, "Incidents of Psychological Types Among Jungian Analysts Classified by Self and by Test," 134; K. Bradway and J. Wheelwright, "The Psychological Type of the Analyst and its Relation to Analytical Practice," vol. 23, n. 3, July, 1978; C. A. Meier and M. A. Wozny, "An Empirical Study of Jungian Typology," 226; J. Witzig, "Jung's Typology and Classification of the Psychotherapies," vol. 23, n. 4, October, 1978, 315; M. Loomis, "A New Perspective for Jung's Typology: The Singer-Loomis Inventory of Personality," vol. 27, n. 1, January, 1982, 57.

considered this typology instead, or only, as a matter of theory rather than as a clinical instrument. In fact he tried to put in relief the possibility of its advantages for analyzing, not only to integrate unconscious contents into consciousness but above all to favor the relating and developing in the patient of a greater comprehension and a more intelligent tolerance toward himself and towards the "Other." Bernhard in fact suggested working on the third function without confronting directly the final, fourth function, that which truly lies asleep in the unconscious. The attempt to hook up and draw it out can only be done indirectly through the third, or the penultimate, and working only in some auxiliary way itself, like the second function. To work directly on the fourth is improbable to give results for this function at such a point is deep, unreachable, and obscure.

I remember well, and with gratitude, this strategy that I learned from Bernhard and which I still use, because it is the best, in my opinion, for uncovering, at least in part, this function. It is a useful instrument whether for daily life and for getting in touch with that part of us that is unconscious or non-conscious, or for the inferior function, so often mixed up with Shadow, though indispensable for us and especially for the energy that is released from the unconscious and that emerges with it. In *Mythobiography* Bernhard repeats this inquiry into Shadow and the inferior function, recalling explicitly Jung's comment: "The individual Shadow, as Jung says, is tied to the inferior function. The gaining of consciousness and its integration is the final stage of the process. It only becomes possible when the Anima/Animus and the Self have been realized and differentiated, or put in harmony."[12]

On the essential confrontation with the Shadow and thus with the fourth function, I want to report here a dream of a patient with whom I worked some years ago. I well remember this dream because the patient brought it to me in writing. But before getting into the narrative of the dream and the work that it brought, I want to specify that the interpretation was focused on the fourth function only after having tried to understand the contents connected to the transference situation, and in the kind of transference that the patient had with the analyst, and thus onto me. To be moved in this direction cannot be ignored for its importance. This is by now a firm conviction because in my opinion the dream,

[12] *Mythobiography*, 158.

in the last analysis, speaks about us, only about ourselves. The images of the dream are our contents, parts of us that want to be taken into consideration, with the hope that we, in so much rationality, ego, and will, collaborate in their positive, creative intentions for our evolving process and thus for our personality. Here then is the dream:

> I found myself at a party. A lady unknown to me, dressed in black and gorgeous, came up to me and with an exaggerated outpouring took my hands and gave me the two classic kisses on the cheeks. Her cordiality had nothing authentic about it, it was only a conventional attitude dictated by the circumstances. While she continued to hold my hands with an altogether exterior impetuosity, it made the ring that I wore on the ring finger of my left hand fall to the ground, a diamond ring, a single diamond of great value. This forced me to kneel down at the feet of the lady, trying for a long time and finally succeeding in getting the jewel back.

In telling me of the dream and that unknown lady, described by the patient as pushy and affected, and who aroused in her a strong antipathy, the patient used aggressive and scornful words. It was altogether obvious that this dream awoke in her, with a decisive clarity, a real aspect of her Shadow on which she had been working for a long time; an aspect that referred to her own denial of extroversion, even of the sensation function. We agreed that that image represented in the dream these intense parts of herself, parts neglected and denied by her but which were now clamoring to be recognized and embraced.

From work previously done, we had deducted with relative certainty that the dominant function of the patient was intuition, the second, auxiliary function, was feeling, and the third was thinking. It was in fact with the thinking function in special mode (and certain readings appropriate to her case were of great help) that it was possible for her to make her denied and abhorred extroversion emerge, and to accept it within certain limits, even the existence of a function never used by her—sensation; the function that when it is the least developed in an individual hinders a good rapport with concreteness, with that which is tangible and real, and which if it is not differentiated renders us inept at using it for good common sense and having a good relationship with whatever it takes to act skillfully, to take advantage of what belongs to matter, to the body, to objects, to logic, to calculating, to socializing, to the earth.

We know that extroversion, like introversion, has importance and value for an individual's equilibrium. Thanks only to the encounter with that figure of the dream, extroverted, unknown, and entirely different from herself, thanks only to her accepting her and showing her the respect of kneeling in front of her, was she in the process of getting back her precious ring, that value which certainly belonged to her but which only in suffering the embrace of that lady, the contact of her lips, and the reaching of her hands, not to mention touching her hands and knees on the ground, was she able to find and get back, in the end making her personality more complete at the place where it mattered, on the finger that meant conjugal trust.

> The Shadow is a moral problem that puts to the test the whole personality of the Ego; no one in fact can make consciousness of Shadow without a significant application of moral resoluteness. This means recognizing as really present the dark aspects of the personality: an act that constitutes the indispensable basis of any consciousness of self, and therefore usually encounters a significant resistance. Inasmuch as consciousness of self constitutes a psychotherapeutic measure, it often requires laborious work that can go on for a long time.[13]

Let us go back for yet one more moment to Bernhard, this man who has had without doubt a decisively notable importance for many of us who are in some way his heirs, the importance that as always, in good and bad, has a parent, and in particular a symbolic one. After the death of Bernhard, some disciples posed the problem of whether now was the moment to ask about his Shadow. This problem, as far as I know, remains unsolved. Today a century separates us from his birth, and facing this still unanswered problem, an idea strikes me—an idea that he would have taken playfully and with good humor himself, as anyone once close to him would agree, even if dealing with Shadow, integrated or not, the argument remains inescapably serious. The idea refers to nothing less than God and the Devil: "As big as the Light, so big is the Shadow," where light stands for God and Shadow the Devil. This idea is rather well-known so forgive me for having repeated it.

translated from the Italian by Charles Boer

[13] C. G. Jung, "Aion: Ricerche sul simbolismo del Se," *Opere*, vol. 9, t. II (Torino: Boringhieri, 1982), 8.

The Lost Contributions of Maria Moltzer to Analytical Psychology

Two Unknown Papers

SONU SHAMDASANI

There is but one reference to Maria Moltzer in C. G. Jung's *Collected Works*. In *Psychological Types*, in the course of defining the intuitive type, Jung noted: "The credit for having discovered the existence of this type belongs to M. Moltzer."[1] Until recently little was known of the mysterious Maria Moltzer, as Richard Hull dubbed her, and still less is known of her ideas. The main reason for this is quite simple: her work appears to have remained unpublished. In *Cult Fictions*, I published a 1917 paper of hers, "The Relation Between the Club and the Zürich School," as well as establishing that she was, in all likelihood, the author of "Analytical Collectivity."[2] These papers shed crucial light on the social and intellectual world of the early circle of Analytical

[1] C. G. Jung, *Psychological Types*, *CW* 7, § 773, note 1. The editors of the English edition helpfully added "Miss" and gave a few details about her (this editorial note was not reproduced in the German edition) *CW* 7, § 773, note 1.

[2] Sonu Shamdasani, *Cult Fictions: C. G. Jung and the Founding of Analytical Psychology* (London: Routledge, 1998). For information on Moltzer, see the chapter "Sister Maria," and Magnus Ljunggren's *The Russian Mephisto: A Study of the Life of Emilii Medtner* (Stockholm: Almqvist & Wiksell International, 1994).

Sonu Shamdasani is a research fellow at the Wellcome Institute for the History of Medicine in London. His most recent book is *Cult Fictions: C. G. Jung and the Founding of Analytical Psychology* for which he received a Gradiva Award.

Psychology, and enabled the reconstruction of critical debates that are of contemporary significance. They demonstrate that far from being a monolithic entity, the "Zürich School" was characterized by difference, diversity, and division. Finally they enabled the beginnings of a reconstruction of the theoretical views of one of the most critical protagonists in the early development of Analytical Psychology.

Further light is shed on these issues by the following hitherto unpublished papers by Moltzer, "The Conception of the Libido and its Psychic Manifestations" and "On the Conception of the Unconscious." These were presented in German to the Psychological Club in 1916. Upon reading these papers it emerges that Moltzer, whilst starting principally from Jung's 1912 *Transformations and Symbols of the Libido* (*CW B*) and his 1913 "A Contribution to the Study of Psychological Types" (*CW 6*), had developed her own original concepts, an individual interpretation of Jung's concepts, and an articulate critique of prevalent practises in Analytical Psychology, such as typological reduction.

These papers are significant for understanding the genesis of some of Jung's signature concepts. This is because they can in part be seen to have arisen, or have been first articulated, in response to Moltzer's concepts. Of particular interest in this regard is the presentation of her concept of the intuitive type. If one compares Jung's concept of this type in *Psychological Types* with Moltzer's, it is apparent that their formulations, whilst overlapping, differ quite significantly. For instance, there is little place in Jung's formulations for the phylogenetic dimensions that Moltzer develops. This makes Jung's attribution to her not as straightforward as it seems at first glance. Rather, it appears that Jung developed his concept of this type through extensively reworking Moltzer's concept and recasting her trinitarian model into a quaternity.

Another aspect of the intersection between Moltzer's concepts and Jung's is the issue of the relation of the individual to collectivity and the process of individuation. These two papers of Moltzer's were delivered to the Club in the summer of 1916. The manuscripts of Jung's two critical papers on "Adaptation, Individuation, Collectivity" (*CW 18*), which he also delivered to the Club, were dated October 1916, which indicates that they were delivered after Moltzer's papers. Thus Jung's formulations in these papers can in part be read in terms of a response to or dialogue with Moltzer's positions.

While Moltzer's papers provide a crucial and hitherto missing conceptual foil for the genesis of some of Jung's signature concepts, they can also be considered in their own right. It is for this reason, together with the interest in Moltzer's ideas generated by my earlier publication, that I am first publishing them in this form, before elaborating their imbrications with Jung's concepts in more detail.

Aside from a citation of the second paper by Constance Long, in a 1917 article, "The Use of Subliminal Material," I have not come across published references to these papers.[3] However Moltzer discussed these papers with Fanny Bowditch Katz, and her notes of her sessions with Moltzer in her diary provide some further information about these papers as well as a vivid account of Moltzer's struggles. The first entry related to these papers was on Monday, June 26, 1916. Katz wrote:

> Monday, June 26: Spoke first of her paper on the Libido—of her position, her work and the resistances to her—She far harder to accept than Dr. Jung was. She rep. a far harder adaptation to life—others do not see her as she is; her human side, but see her only as a symbol—first as a *die furchtbare Mutte*r [the terrible mother] projecting all their complexes onto her, and secondly as a symbol of life—of the Christ idea. Her life, solitude, not being protected by the law, *etc.*, far harder than Dr. Jung... Her need of living too—of being a human being too. I'm beginning to see more & more how positively heroic her life is—surrounded on all sides by opposition, and standing quite alone, fighting to the death for her belief. No wonder it has nearly killed her![4]

The next relevant entries occur on Saturday, July 8, 1916. This entry gives some indication as to why she did not publish these papers. Her presentation of her concept of the intuitive type seems to have initially met with a mixed response. This entry seems to indicate a positive response:

> Her paper—third type accepted, *etc.* She very jubilant and free with me than ever before—... Spoke of experience in finding intuition—which is very important and will mean a far broader & deeper insight—she has written about it in

[3] Constance Long, "The Use of Subliminal Material in Analytical Psychology," *Collected Papers on the Psychology of Phantasy* (London: Baillière, Tindall and Cox, 1920), 82.

[4] Fanny Bowditch Katz, 1916 diary, Countway Library of Medicine, 4-5. I would like to thank the Countway Library of Medicine for permission to quote from Fanny Bowditch Katz's diaries.

> her last paper... Types the basis of the Zürich School as sexuality has been of the Vienna. She hopes the question may be kept within their little coterie until fully established—it has nearly killed her, and much harm can be done to an. by superficial workers.[5]

From internal references in Moltzer's second paper, it appears that these papers were presented on consecutive meetings of the Club. A few weeks later on Saturday, July 29, 1916, there occurs the following entry, which indicates that her concept of the third type met with some opposition:

> Spent the whole hour reading her my translation of her second paper. Spoke of the third type—of the silence following her reading of her paper—Analysis as a thing apart—and the difficulties of the analysts in accepting it because still bound up in their personal problems—this as difficult as the breaking of the transference for the patient.[6]

In a subsequent diary entry of February 12, 1917, Bowditch Katz notes that Moltzer stated that only four people had "really grasped" her paper.[7] The final entry related to these papers on February 23, 1917, gives some indication of the gulf between Moltzer's conceptions and her experience of the Psychological Club:

> ...of the Club—and of her conception of the overcoming of the *das furchtbare Kind,* [the terrible child] which differs from the *furchtbare Mutter* [the terrible mother] and the *furchtbarer Vater* [the terrible father] in being the over life, *etc.* one's experiences of the individual—all this she has experienced and known but not so the Club.[8]

The following year Moltzer resigned from the Club. However the significance of her theoretical work during this period in the genesis of Analytical Psychology between 1916 and 1918 has yet been realized.

---

[5] *Ibid.*, 10, 13, 14.

[6] *Ibid.*, 21-2. On the basis of this statement, it is likely that the translations of these papers that follow were by Bowditch Katz.

[7] Fanny Bowditch Katz, 1917 diary, Countway Library of Medicine, 4. Unfortunately, who these four individuals were—and whether she regarded Jung as one of them or not—is not recorded.

[8] *Ibid.*, 9. The ideas that Moltzer refers to here were put forward in her paper, "The Relation Between the Club and the Zürich School." See *Cult Fictions.*

The Conception of the Libido and Its Psychic Manifestations[9]

MARIA MOLTZER

It is a difficult task to explain the conception of the Libido, difficult because in itself, the Libido is not to be described and can only be understood by its manifestations. The conception of the Libido comes nearest to the conception of Energy. Whether the two conceptions quite coincide, I do not venture to judge. Unfortunately I have been unable to find the time in which to make a thorough study of the leading opinions on energy in order to see how far they coincide with the psychic manifestations. Libido can perhaps be best described by "Effect or the capacity for Effect," and that is to say, that it is capable of transformation and can change from one form into another. The metamorphosis can be a sudden one, as for instance, when one function suddenly replaces another in a moment of danger, or it can be gradual as we see it in the process of sublimation, where the libido is led over a long and difficult path, through a variety of forms into a different function.

According to my opinion, the libido cannot be said to coincide with the "*Elan vital*."[10] The *Elan vital* is rather a manifestation of the libido, an expression of the tendency towards progress or development. The libido, for instance, which expresses itself in resistances towards one's own creative power, resistances which may lead even to death, is not the expression of *Elan vital.* Neither can the libido be described by the conception of "*interet*."[11] *Interet* is a particular state of attention, therefore one more, only a manifestation of the libido.

[9] I located the German manuscript of this paper titled, "*Über den Begriff der Libido und ihre Manifestationen im Psychischen Geschehen.*" The footnotes are mine.

[10] The reference is to Henri Bergson's conception, cf. *Creative Evolution*, trans. A. Mitchell (London: Macmillan, 1954). In 1913, at the International Medical Congress in London, Jung presented a paper on "Psychoanalysis and Neurosis" in which he had identified the libido with Bergson's *élan vital. CW 4*, § 568.

[11] In his 1912 lectures at Fordham University, Jung remarked that Freud's concept of the libido "is understood in so innocuous a sense that Claparède once remarked to me that one could just as well use the word 'interest.'" *CW 4*, § 273. The first English edition of this text, published in 1913 and 1914 in *The Psychoanalytic Review*, was translated by Maria Moltzer together with David and Edith Eder.

The manifestations of the libido in human life are manifold. If we begin with the development of the child, we see that in the beginning, the libido expresses itself mainly in the function of nutrition and in the process of growth. The form of nutrition is the act of sucking. This form does not last long, and resolves itself after a comparatively short time into a new function, that of eating. With the function of eating, arises a new accomplishment—a conscious element is added to the element of nutrition, and two essential elements, that of rhythm and that of lust (which must not be understood by its sexual significance) are separated. The rhythmic element, a libido of motion, separated from the function of nutrition, now follows new channels. This libido gradually takes possession of the whole body and of the various physical sensations of the developing personality, which goes hand in hand with the spiritual and linguistic development. The sensation of desire, the second element that was bound to the first function of nutrition, also passes through this change. This desire, or lust remains an accompaniment of certain unconscious functions and pleasure, a differentiation of desire or lust, is added to consciousness. The taking possession of the various bodily functions leads gradually to the awakening of the sexual function, at which time, the pre-sexual state comes to an end and the child awakens to its personality. Here probably also the real consciousness begins.

The various functions whereby the individual can fulfill his adaptation to life are aroused, the ontogenetic development carries the collective psyche with it, with which the germs of personal thought and personal feeling are led over to collective thought and collective feeling in the consciousness. From now on, the libido manifests itself in the most far-reaching, and various ways. Just as in the first stage of childhood, the libido gradually brought the physical sensations into consciousness, through the unconscious process, the child now occupies itself consciously with itself and its physical functions as well as with its surroundings. Out of this grows gradually the separation between, or the conception of, subject and object between the introversion and the extraversion tendency, as also the individualization tendency,[12] which must be considered as differing absolutely from the above mentioned tendencies.

[12] In the German manuscript, the term Moltzer uses is *Individualisationtendenz*. This is translated as "individuation tendency" in the English translation. I have modified this throughout. It is should be noted that Moltzer may have approved the earlier translation, thus equating the terms.

The extraversion-tendency as also the introversion-tendency are mainly collective tendencies, I mean, tendencies of the libido which try to create a contact with collectivity in which they are quite different from the tendency of individualization. The individualization-tendency is that tendency which tries to create a form of its own, a form which is brought about through the combined action of a number of personal and impersonal elements. This individualization-tendency goes hand in hand with the incest barrier. The growing human being cannot find his life only in connection with collectivity; a resistance arises against being merged to the universal, a need for differentiation appears automatically and expresses itself in the incest barrier.

Collectivity is a fearful polypus—through the enlivening of the archaic functions, it reaches in thought as well as in feeling far back into the human past, encompasses the individual development united with objects and thoughts, contains all the physical sensations, and stretches its arms far out over man into the future. It is against the power of such a polypus that the individualization-tendency has to fight. No wonder that man has symbolized this tendency with the figure of the hero. The hero is a symbol of this tendency of the libido which strives to free itself from collectivity in order to create a new form out of itself, as also the personification of this tendency, and designates the man who has succeeded in overcoming these extraordinary difficulties. The tendency of individualization also contains a collective element which arises in the half conscious, half unconscious function which we call intuition. Intuition is also a collective function and has its roots in the personal and impersonal unconscious, contains elements of feelings as well as of thoughts, and tries to solve a given problem and create an adaptation in bringing together these half conscious and half unconscious elements. This adaptation coincides neither with the extraversion nor the introversion-tendency—it contains elements of both. Therefore I am inclined to accept a third type which uses mainly this intuitive function in its adaption to life. I believe this type is not as common as the other two types yet undoubtedly demands recognition.

This type of individual seems to me to appear in its perfection at times of great cultural evolution—at times when neither the mechanism of feeling nor the mechanism of thought is capable of solving the problem demanding solution. In these times of human agony, the saving work can be found through the help of intuition. In Indian mythology, this thought is expressed by the conception of the God Vishnu—one of the three principal gods of the Hindus. It is said of him that he appeared in different incarnations according to the needs of the time, as a Savior to mankind. We find the conception of the Savior also in other religions and in the legend of the Holy Grail, the redemption of the Grail is expected of the simple human being.

We too live in a time of cultural evolution—we feel humanity's distressful need and stand confronted by problems which neither the extraversion nor the introversion-tendency can solve. Why could not many people be forced by nature to live mainly by the intuitive function, whereby the adaptation would be found in the natural way?

We too are seeking a Redeemer, whom analytically, we find in the transcendental function, having its roots in the unconscious and in the conscious, that stands between thought and feeling and has grown out of intuition.

Intuition seems first to manifest itself in the age of childhood with the arising question of sexuality—the truth is sought through *einfühlung* [feeling into] and can lead over into general thinking as well as into general feeling. Through the demands of reality, education, and the school, the libido is forced into the further development of the general functions, until with the breaking through of sexuality, the individualization-tendency appears once more in the foreground. As in the earlier moments of individualizing,[13] a tearing away from collectivity is now again required, but the struggle is considerably more difficult. It is now no longer a question of the freeing of the child from the parents or its nearest environment, but of the struggle with the now aroused polypi—a struggle that in various forms has to be dealt with all through life.

The incest interdiction now appears forcibly, and with it the problem of death, which, in its psychological meaning, leads to the sacrifice. An opposing tendency of the libido, we find in the creative impulse of the individual, the shaping of the libido into an object outside the self, a tendency which will try to express itself in some form or other.

[13] The German manuscript has "*Individualisierung*," and the translation has "Individuation."

On the Conception of the Unconscious

MARIA MOLTZER

I am very grateful to Dr. Jung for opening our meeting with the very valuable presentation of the unconscious—a clue is thereby given us as to how the discussion can best be continued. On the whole I agree with what Dr. Jung has said, but would like to go more into detail on a number of points.

On the Personal Unconscious and the Consequences of its Assimilation.

There is, in reality, still another aspect of the assimilation of the unconscious—one that Dr. Jung has mentioned but has not worked out in full. I mean the recognition of the personality and of the actual demands of life. He who has been forced analytically to work the repressed personal material into consciousness, often goes through very painful experiences. To this repressed material belong namely the many omissions which, in consideration of the capability or talents of the personality, should not have taken place. The becoming-conscious of these materials has a very depressing effect and yet is unavoidable, as just through this consciousness, the individual realizes his relationship to himself and to the world—for the world can also make demands which one cannot escape unpunished.

To make this point clearer, I should like to use the following illustration: a patient of mine has for years been struggling for a scientific career and had arranged his whole life with this end in view. But besides this he had pedagogical interests which he had neglected more and more. The consequence of this attitude was that he got conflict with himself and with the world—for, losing himself in the thought of a professorship, and being able to support his family thereby, he paid no attention to the demands of the present. There was danger of his losing his position as a teacher and he was forced to accept more financial aid. This led to a moral breakdown.

This part of analysis leads to the acceptance of reality. The patient has to make clear to himself the actual conditions of life, and their acceptance forces him to find the way in which he can, in harmony with his personality, become master of the situation. His intellect had overpowered his other functions of adaptation, and the neglected portion of his personality now needs development. But the acceptance of this neglected portion means the acceptance of the Hideous Man, the symbol of the undeveloped personality—and the acceptance of the Hideous Man is a difficult problem. This announced itself by the following dream: "I am walking in a valley in Wallis. My friend (some one whose easy adaptation to life has brought him much success) and I begin to climb. I think how delightful it is to be walking in new and unfamiliar surroundings—life just now seems much more endurable. As we go on I see several people on the path: a peasant woman who asks me to take a greeting to someone up on the alp, two "cretins," a woman, and a hideous man. The woman alone takes another path and I curse her—my friend says in French that it's disgusting that she should have foisted these two dwarfs upon us; she seemed to possess a very good dress-suit case. I laugh at his saying "dwarfs," he really should have said "cretins," that would have been the right expression, but he evidently feared being understood.

This dream is extremely important. The hideous man was introduced here and manifested himself in various forms. It is also striking that this figure the still undeveloped is recognized (dwarfs, cretins).

The cretins are really dwarfs, and the archaic meaning of dwarfs is that of creatures resembling human beings, who possess wisdom, who serve man, teach the arts or guard the treasure.

This archaic meaning we find here again, for the cretins are symbolic of an undeveloped amount of libido, containing values which could be serviceable to man, but is still bound up in too small, too personal a form and is therefore particularly human. This libido can however be of service to man as it is destined to be differentiated further. The difficulty lies only in finding the proper way treat the dwarfs, in other words, in finding the attitude in which to accept them. The analysis of these two cretins was a difficult piece of work—one was a symbol of still undeveloped feeling which was lying fallow in an infantile form. The introverted attitude is always accompanied by personal feeling, but in this personal feeling lies the germ of impersonal feeling—so here also. The feeling expressed by one of the cretins showed itself in a love of excrements. In the fantasies that followed excrements were praised in all possible ways, but from the beginning it was evident that in these excrement fantasies a religious tendency lay hidden. The excrements became a symbol of God and to this God a hymn was sung. Gradually the patient saw also that this God was a terrible God, for he keeps man in solitude, in the heat of his own feelings—in the desert—and now came the realization that this was a God to be overcome, and on the whole a temporary God, for although man and beast serve him, he is also the servant of man and it is surprising that he is not seen on earth. These fantasies developed as far as the Grail conception and then stopped.

I want here to call attention to the fact that this problem brought feeling to constellation, and that the working out of feeling through the fantasies awakened a new function—that of extraversion. I say a new function, but this cannot be fully accepted, as in a rudimentary form this function had always been present. But now, becoming more fully developed, it can be of real value. The patient had come to grief with his extraversion a few years ago, and since then became more introverted. It seems to me that the pronounced types we find in analysis, expressed their former functions of adaptations regressively, and bring with them an extreme attitude which again is an expression of their neurosis.

The second cretin led to an attitude to the world expressed in infantile thought. His fantasies showed that the patient expected God to take care of him and the Lord's Prayer was to him almost an ecstatic experience. But this attitude also went to pieces, and now we are analyzing the hideous man announced by the dream. This portion of analysis will bring us to the problem of Godlikeness. I may mention here the question of infantilism. The two cretins are symbols of the infantile which first has to be accepted—but once accepted and left to its own development, unquestionably leads to the sacrifice of the early forms—so that libido, freed, can flow to new paths.

As Dr. Jung has also mentioned here the question of types, I cannot forebear to say something on this point and to consider the development of this question in retrospect. In my opinion a misuse has been made within the last years of the not yet fully developed conception of types. Oblivious of the enormous difficulties with which this question is of necessity bound up, all people were forced into one of the two categories and judged according to this very superficial diagnosis: One was extraverted and must therefore feel thus and so—another was introverted and must therefore think thus and so. This seemed to me a very rough abuse of the personality. The introvert has not only his thinking but also his feeling and must correct both if he wished to find the right attitude to life—the extravert has not only his function of feeling but also his thinking, and like the introvert must correct both. It would mean a neglect in the stage of development to treat the patient only from the point of view of type. Then must be added that a personality is not only conditioned by its type—the type indicates here that one category is to be considered. The type belongs to the collective psyche, and that which differentiates the personality from the type is just the constellation of his problems. To look only at the type means as much as obliterating the personality and identifying it entirely with its type. The solving of personal problems is difficult and there are many patients who are only too glad to find a way of escape from their tasks, and feel themselves justified in taking refuge in a new collectivity through the identification with their type. Collectivity, is, as is well known, a mother-symbol.

It has occurred to me that analysis has made a regression—a regression back to the mother, the experimental psychology out which it grew, in order to combine the real virtues of both methods. But experimental psychology was surely a terrible mother, as it failed to recognize the soul: it ruthlessly cast the soul aside and tried to force all psychic manifestations into the laws of conscious thought.

With this danger the Zürich school is threatened. Just as the Vienna school reduced practically everything to sexuality, after it discovered its value—so in the last years has the Zürich school reduced everything to types. We must guard against this danger as centralizing on two types leads to the reduction to formula of all psychic life which threatens to annihilate the new life born of the introduction of the libido-theory. Analysis based on the libido-theory which leads into the depths is perhaps in danger of making the opposite mistake, and of laying too much stress on the unconscious and the irrational—the combining of both points of view, which rightly understood, would give the proper solution.

Just as in the last years there have been only two types, so in former times there were only two kinds of human beings. The one was supposed to be so and so and called man—and the other, being so and so, was called woman. They were absolutely different and quite separated from the other, for which reason, the man must do this and the woman that. If God chose to give woman a thinking head, she was despised. Weininger was the first to declare this conception of man and woman a fiction. He put the type "man" at one end of a long chain and the type "woman" at the other; between he imagined a number of transition stages and in the middle he set the hermaphrodite, uniting the two sexes. This conception of Weininger's I should like to apply to the types.[14] Just as a type of man and a type of woman exist, so also there exist psychologically a real introvert and a real extravert; but beside these extreme types, there are also varied mixed types, with more or less developed introverted and extraverted attitudes. Here too the connecting link is supplied by the hermaphroditic symbol. The hermaphroditic problem we find in those who feel themselves the need of developing and harmoniously uniting both functions of adaptations. I have found this problem in both men and women—and in the most modern literature it is found in "The Golem."[15] I should like to call your attention to the fact that man's psychology is not quite identical with woman's—there certainly are extraverted and introverted women but their psychology is nonetheless not the same as man's.

In consideration of all these difficulties, I believe that one does the patient the most justice by analyzing him according to his problems. I mentioned at our last meeting a third type or intuitive type and called attention to the fact that with this type the function of intuition overpowered the other functions of adaptation. The conscious functions of feeling and thinking are created functions, and depend on a certain capacity of synthesis or of selection of impressions received. These functions can therefore not grasp the unusual elements produced by difficult times as the unusual quality of these times is essentially created by the predominance of foreign elements; elements which, not being accepted by consciousness, are repressed into the unconscious. Here however intuition comes to the fore, it registers the impressions received and brings the compensatory tendency over into consciousness. A beautiful example is given by Parsival, who feels within himself the suffering of Amfortas,

[14] The reference is to Otto Weininger, *Sex and Character* (London: William Heinemann, 1906).

[15] Gustav Meyrink, *The Golem*, tr. M. Mitchell (Sawtry: Dedalus, 1995).

grasps its meaning, and also its need of compensation, and wins back that which was lost—the spear.

Just as the introvert brings his function of thinking to a high development and the extravert his function of feeling, so also the intuitive type has developed his intuition. As the introverted attitude reacts with thought and the extraverted attitude with feeling, so the intuitive attitude reacts with understanding. It is with understanding that he finds his adaptation to life and asserts himself. With the intuitives, nature has made use of a former function of adaptation—intuition from which both of the other functions have been differentiated. Intuition exists, I believe, in all people, but with most it has not got beyond the biological stage which is more to be regarded as instinct. But with the intuitives, where this is the main function of adaptation, and serves to overcome the difficulties of life, it reaches a high development and acquires a universal validity.

There are also two kinds to be found in this type, those who are more inclined towards thinking and those who are more inclined towards action; and just as the one-sided development of the extraversion-tendency and of the introversion-tendency leads to a neurosis, so also does the one-sided development of intuition—as thinking and feeling are too closely connected with one another. I consider the compulsion-neurosis to be the neurosis of this type and some forms of melancholia and manic depressive insanity to be its psychosis. The artists, who are able to assimilate the unconscious and bring it to its full value, belong to a third category of this type.

The assertion that the third type does not exist is really untenable and it would not surprise me if gradually we should find this type turning up in all sorts of nooks and corners as we turn our unprejudiced attention to it. And why? Our adaptation to life is insufficient—we are searching and struggling for a new attitude, and what would be more natural than that mankind, unable to solve the difficult problems of our time, should reach back, or make a regression, to a former function of adaptation, which once furnished a new attitude to life, and out of which religion, and in the course of time, conscious thinking and conscious action developed. This regression would be made in order to find that attitude to life which would satisfy the present need.

As far as I can see intuition is the oldest human function and has grown out of instinct. I consider intuition to be the differentiation and the conscious function of instinct. Intuition stands at the threshold of consciousness and introversion of the function leads of itself to the pictures within the unconscious. I know a few intuitives who have solved the difficulties of life through their visions. To be sure, this is nothing new—the cave-dwellers have left us pictures on their walls which show us that even at that time the function of picture-making was developed, and that it was through visions that mankind was seeking its further differentiation. It is my opinion that herein lies the origin of consciously directed thought and of religion—two psychic processes which, though separated in us, are brought together in the magic arts and in occult science. In order not to digress too far from my subject, I will not say more here on this point—I wish only to call attention to the fact that it is to be assumed that the function of picture-making is found in our time.

Just as the war drives mankind into the extreme of action and of thinking, so too it must drive the real intuitives into an extreme introversion, out of which pictures will be produced, giving us an understanding of and a solution for the difficult problems of our time. This solution would be more or less universal according to the attitude and the gifts of the personality. Thus mankind will come to its transcendental function, and a new attitude gained through analysis. Through these individuals who have reached this new attitude, another type will be created, in whom, through the help of analysis, collective thinking and collective feeling as well as personal thinking and feeling are brought into harmony. In this way man finds his adaptation to himself, his soul and the world and unites the past with the present.

On Identification

I wish to mention here a special instance of identification—an identification, for example, with a well known personality. This identification shows itself most strongly when that part of the patient's own individuality, which is still undeveloped, must be accepted. This is strange and can only be explained when we remember the value of the subconscious and its influence in our conscious life. The subconscious uses this chosen personality as a symbol for a valuable function. It is as if the subconscious wanted to say: if you would accept it, your function would be as valuable to you as that which you admire in him. Its importance for the patient's own individuality lies in its symbolic value. He does not know the symbolic value of his identification, and usually thinks he must model his thoughts and actions according to the concrete personality with whom by means of his identification, he is one. The consequences of this assumption is that he fails to understand his problem and continues to project upon others, that which he ought to find in himself. Thus the most important problem escapes him.

I know of course very well that there are cases which have to follow the path of conscious identification, and who have not to accept the depth their subconsciousness, but I am not speaking of those cases, which in general, will be most common.

In order to get at the symbolic values which are unknown to the patient, one has to take up the associations attached to this personality—and out of this material, the analyst has to build up synthetically the symbolic values with the help of the patient. As these symbolic values have to be worked out consciously, which usually is a question of using already conscious material. I have called this symbolic thinking—the symbolic thinking of conscious thought, in contrast to the symbolic thinking of the unconscious, to which identification really belongs.

Some years ago, when my attention was called to this form of Godlikeness, I found no one who could accept the correctness of my assumption, but as I consider this symbolic thinking, which is one of the means of solving the transference and the "participation mystique" with the outer world, of great value, I should like to make myself clearer on this point.

A patient of mine who had given up analysis for some time, was reminded of a symptom in his hand that his unconscious demanded attention. He came to analysis and I told him it was a question of his fantasies which wanted to express themselves in drawings. Again he stayed away for some time and when he returned, he brought a dream which said that he had to accept his intellect—in his dream, his intellect was represented by a well known personality, and at once he identified the image of the new tendency which had to be accepted, with this personality itself, and wished to do what she had done to further develop her intellect. This person was, however, an introvert and he was an extravert and imitating her would be accepting collective thinking and of little use to him, for the moment. The associations showed that this personality represented the introverted personality he had still to develop within himself—if he imitated her, he had only the value of that experience, but if he understood her symbolic value, he came to his own personality. I asked him about his drawings, which supplied the further explanation of his problem which was very complicated—one difficulty was the overcoming of the terrible mother, and, as I was the symbol of problem, he wanted to free himself from me by first turning his back on me—having, of course, the most plausible reasons for so doing. The second drawing perplexed him, and the third one showed him clearly that he must overcome himself and accept his unconscious represented by myself. But it cost him much before he could bring himself to this point. When, however, he had accepted his snakes, they spoke to him and gave him the necessary insight into his situation.

Turning a Blind Eye: Misreading Jung

JAY SHERRY

These days it seems that many historians with a psychological bent are, for whatever reason, deliberately misreading Jung. The one who most annoys me at the moment is Bram Dijkstra. His 1986 *Idols of Perversity* explored male fantasies of feminine evil as expressed in the art of *fin de siecle* Europe. Its often pornographic content stimulated the pubescent imaginations of a generation of European males that included young Adolph Hitler. It was a major factor in the formation of violence-prone attitudes that culminated in the mass slaughter that began in 1914. Dijkstra's more recent *Evil Sisters* (Knopf, 1996) continues tracking incarnations of the *femme fatale* into early cinema and pulp fiction. In particular, he looks at the image of the vampire as depicted by Theda Bara in the 1915 silent film classic, *A Fool There Was*, linking it to the racialist ideology of National Socialism. Unfortunately, his far-reaching examples receive less restrained treatment than did those in the earlier book and this extends to his treatment of Jung. At first the critique is fairly reasonable, rightfully taking Jungian psychology to task for its a-historical formalism, its tendency to categorize images rather than to analyze them in relation to concrete historical situations. The best example is the work of Erich Neumann who does rate passing reference in these books. Jungians, it seems, prefer Polyhymnia, the muse of hymn and religious dance, to Clio, the muse of history.

Jay Sherry is an educator living in Brooklyn, New York. He is the author of the article, "Jung, Jews, and Hitler," which appeared in *Spring* 1986. He is currently working on a book about Jung's relation to the Swiss-German conservative tradition.

The first hint of trouble was Dijkstra's constant use of quotation marks around "archetype" and "collective unconscious," a pathetic attempt, it seemed, to establish a linguistic quarantine around words that have found widespread acceptance. Reservations turn to misreadings when in the opening pages of Chapter X we read, "After all, she [the anima] was a negative entity, Jung reminded his audience, for she represented 'the inferior Eros in man'" (394). Even a cursory reading of Jung's work makes clear that his use of the word "inferior" does not assign any inherent negativity to that psychic function. Trained in classical languages, Jung used the word in its original Latin sense of "lower," as in the name of the Roman province Germania Inferior.

Dijkstra then says, "He [Jung] helped to justify the reign of Logos over eros as the only reasonable outcome of humanity's internal battle of the sexes" (395). How do you begin to qualify this howler? With the fact that Jung dedicated most of his therapeutic praxis to a goal the opposite of what Dijkstra claims? With the fact that this approach has had a positive effect upon the lives of many ordinary and extraordinary women and men? The publication of his *Wandlungen und Symbole der Libido* (in translation as *Symbols of Transformation*) attracted widespread attention and was even reviewed by Aleister Crowley. Among those who read the book was Jack London; contrary to what Dijkstra's thesis would lead us to expect, this purveyor of Anglo-Saxon individualism was not confirmed in his prejudices by reading this book but instead was shaken out of them and spent his last years writing stories about Polynesian storytellers who relate the traditional mythology of their people. As a matter of fact, Dijkstra's slackness leads him to label things "Aryan" when "Anglo-Saxon" would have been more appropriate. This latter term had more resonance among his target population than the former.

Besides his ignorance of the basic principles of Jungian theory, he is even more likely to be ignorant of the social history of Analytical Psychology and the critical role played in it by a talented group of Anglo-American professional women. He would certainly learn something from the writings of Beatrice Hinkle, Esther Harding, and Frances Wickes to name only a few. He cannot forgive Jung any of the stereotypical elements to be found in his, or anyone's, discussion of gender or acknowledge Jung's goal of offering more, not fewer, psychological choices to modern men and women.

Where Dijkstra is taking us is down the well-trod "Jung-the-Nazi" path. Having Jung and Hitler rub shoulders in several paragraphs conjures up the subliminal image of "Carl Jung, Secret Architect of the Holocaust." In comparison, Richard Noll's thesis stands as a paragon of scholarly propriety. Well, if he was not a Nazi or an Aryan sun cultist, what was the hook upon which these projections have been hung?

Let me offer my precis. A native of Basel, Switzerland, Jung was schooled in the cultural humanism espoused by the city's most famous citizen, the art historian Jacob Burckhardt. Much of Jung's historical sensibility was derived from Burckhardt, some of it via his lifelong-long friend Albert Oeri, a grandnephew of Burckhardt's and the editor of a posthumous collection of his papers. It was a sensibility that harbored deep reservations about the hectic pace of modernization evident in everything from positivism in science to socialism in politics.

Like most young intellectuals of that time, Jung was infatuated with the philosophy of Friedrich Nietzsche. Like Burckhardt, his colleague at the University of Basel, Nietzsche decried the vulgarization of culture that he felt characterized the triumph of mass democracy; views that would be repeated by his imitators and later appropriated by the Nazis. His madness symbolized the fascination with such altered states of consciousness as hypnotic trances, dreams, and mysticism. This neo-romantic interest is evident in the works of Herman Hesse and Carl Spitteler (another Baseler whose poetry Jung used in amplifying the first part of *Psychological Types*) and was the *milieu* that shaped Jung's literary and artistic tastes as reflected in the active imaginations of his Red Book.

In the 1920s, a minor literary figure, Oscar A. H. Schmitz, became a follower of Jung's and a promoter of his work in German publications and circles, especially those attracted to Count Hermann Keyserling's School of Wisdom, Jung's most important contact there being the Sinologist Richard Wilhelm. In time Jung met Gustav Richard Heyer, a Munich doctor who would become his "crown prince." Jung entered a network that included the Indologist Jacob Hauer, who lectured on yoga to the Psychology Club in Zürich and at the 1934 Eranos Conference. This proved controversial since he had by that time become leader of the German Faith Movement, a *volkisch* religious association that sought equal status with the established Protestant and Catholic Churches. (The publication of his lecture in the proceedings of the conference resulted in one of the more notable "Freudian slips" in Jungian psychology when its title was listed as being about "Indo-Arabian" rather than "Indo-Aryan" mysticism.) Jung's 1936 article, "Wotan," focused on Hauer and demonstrates the extent to which he saw developments in Nazi Germany through Hauer's eyes. Although Jung became more critical of Germany in the late 1930s, the recent "Swiss gold" controversy highlights the compromising nature of Swiss dealings with Nazi Germany.

The deeply engraved cliche of Jung being apolitical has deterred scholars from investigating his political philosophy and affiliations. He can best seen as adhering to a nineteenth century liberalism that emphasized individual freedom and was suspicious of the excesses of state power and collectivization. His antipathy to Marxism led him to condone the Nazi invasion of the Soviet Union and become an intellectual Cold Warrior with the publication of his 1957 *Present and Future* (known in English as *The Undiscovered Self*).

What explains the fact that Dijkstra has not done his homework and is content to base his argument on a misreading of Jung? I think it can be explained by the long-standing bias academics have had against Jungian psychology. Long dismissed for its alleged obscurantism, it now seems to pose another more serious threat: increasing popularity. Examples of "creeping Jungianism" abound: the Joseph Campbell and Thomas Moore phenomena, Robert Bly and the Men's Movement, Goddess spirituality, and Jean Houston in the White House. A tone of ambivalent disdain is evident in such remarks as "...somewhere deep inside each man is a hungry hunter desperately trying to keep up with the whirlwind of women who run with the wolves" (5).

Such bias is unfortunate since Dijkstra's refusal to give Jung his due is not just dishonest but also shortsighted. He is unaware of the insights that Jung had into some of his favorite topics such as the history of early film. In his Dream Analysis Seminar (1928-30), Jung commented on such films as *The Golem* and *The Student of Prague* (an interest most likely due to the influence of Schmitz, the brother-in-law of the expressionist artist Alfred Kubin). Dijkstra acknowledges his debt to Klaus Theweleit's Male Fantasies but does not realize that one of that writer's key observations is an echo of something Jung noticed about German psychology as it was happening in the 1920's, namely the prevalence of a crude, split image of women as madonna/whore. It is one of the prime examples of Jung's talent for the kind of psychosocial insight Dijkstra thinks he is incapable of and deserves to be quoted at length.

> You know, there is a peculiar line of demarcation going right through Europe; east of the line the archetype of the *Puer Aeternas* prevails psychologically, and west of that line the psychology of the anima. One sees the characteristic difference in the literature, the novels, and *belle lettres*, also in the political aspect. For example, that whole new movement in Germany is typical of the Puer Aeternas. It is a mass movement, an intense movement, and nobody can see exactly what it means; there is a very mystical idea behind it, but it is chiefly life and movement and what it is all about, even the people themselves don't know. The psychology is also characterized by a peculiar relationship to woman. The woman is chiefly mother, virgin, or prostitute; while in the West woman does exist. If you compare German literature with French or English literature, you see the difference at once. The Puer Aeternas has all the qualities of adolescent psychology, all that hopeful one-sidedness, that hopeful attempt. They are not yet on the other side, but this movement leads very suddenly into the static world; I don't know when that will occur but it will surely come, because after the Puer Aeternas phase, the static principle always comes. We can't tell how it will develop because it will be a very great thing and it might take a long time. Now the question is of course how far the Puer Aeternas archetype reaches. We could call it the archetype of the son versus the father. The psychology of the Puer Aeternas is exclusively masculine, it is a man's world. The woman's world is nonexistent because woman as mother, as virgin, as prostitute is all seen from a man's point of view. In a woman's world there would be a woman, but in a man's world there is there is only a function, woman as function. Does that give you an idea? I cannot go into it further now.
>
> *Zarathustra Seminar*, 1107-08

Jung can be chastised for failing to realize that the static principle he was predicting in 1937 was already being put into operation by the Nazis who were constructing war memorials and death camps, the architecture of Thanatos. Touched by Wotan, Jung experienced the insight and blindness that characterize that archetype. James Kirsch said that when he told Jung in 1933 about his troubling premonitions about Hitler, Jung dismissed them saying the Nazis were a passing phenomenon.

With the success of his first book, Dijkstra decided to elaborate on his original thesis but relied on over generalizations, and in the case of Jung, serious error. Jung's life and thought deserve scrutiny, and his personal and theoretical shortcomings, criticism, but this must be based on accurate scholarship, something Dijkstra fails to demonstrate.

Erratic Visions

SONU SHAMDASANI

On reading the newly published and beautifully illustrated Bollingen Series edition of Jung's seminar, "The Interpreta tion of Visions," I was dismayed to see far more errors in the introduction and notes than in any of the previous seminars.[1] Consequently, I alerted Princeton University Press of this situation. I was asked to submit a list of "mistakes that seriously need correction." I confined myself to errors which were immediately apparent, without doing any detailed checking. Some of these may not be particularly important, and some may simply be proofing errors, but many are clearly serious and in need of correction. In any case, if something is worth noting it is surely worth noting accurately. After submitting my list, I was informed that it would be forwarded to Claire Douglas. That was the last I heard of the matter. As these points may be of interest to those who wish not to be misinformed concerning Jung, I reproduce them here, in a lightly revised form. What follows then is not intended as a review. Whilst I disagree with many interpretive points that Douglas makes in her introduction, it is surely necessary, whatever one's views, to get one's facts right.

The first points concerns confusing contradictions between Douglas' account of Jung's seminar on Kundalini Yoga and that in my

[1] *Visions: Notes of the Seminar given in 1930-4 by C. G. Jung*, ed. Claire Douglas, Bollingen Series XCIX (Princeton: Princeton UP, 1997).

Sonu Shamdasani is a research fellow at the Wellcome Institute for the History of Medicine in London. He is the editor of *The C. G. Jung Seminar Series: The Psychology of Kundalini Yoga*, published by Princeton University Press.

introduction to this seminar.[2] What is worse is that these are presented without the discrepancies noted. If Douglas considered my account wrong, it would have been preferable for this to have been pointed out. As it stands, the fact that Princeton University Press has produced two starkly discrepant accounts side by side can only create confusion for readers. The citations that follow, except where indicated, are from Claire Douglas' introduction and footnotes to *The Visions Seminars.*

> 1. "Jung finally broke with Hauer in 1937 after he learnt that Hauer had joined the Nazi party; after the war, Jung refused to resume correspondence with him (Thomas Kirsch and E. C. Whitmont, personal communications)."[3]

Jung did not break with Hauer in 1937. Hauer gave a further series of lectures at the Psychological Club in Zürich in 1938. The correspondence between them that I have read, which continues up to 1938, is cordial throughout. Further, there is absolutely no evidence to suggest that Jung broke with Hauer because he learnt that he had joined the Nazi party: there was never any doubt concerning Hauer's political affiliation. At the outset of his German Vision of God, he clearly stated that "we stand or fall with the Third Reich"[4] and I cited another statement of his to this effect.[5] In the introduction I wrote: "Their divergent views of the religio-political situation in Germany led to a break between Hauer and Jung and his circle."[6] I cited C. A. Meier's statement in a letter to me regarding the disagreement concerning Hauer's lecture on the swastika and Hauer's diary entry in Dierks' biography of him. I also drew from Meier's vivid recollections of the disagreements at the 1938 Club lectures in my interview with him. There is absolutely no evidence in the correspondence at the ETH nor in the comprehensive biography of Hauer by Dierks that they had any contact after the war nor that Jung refused to resume correspondence with him.[7] I can only presume that Douglas is

[2] *The Psychology of Kundalini Yoga: Notes of the Seminar given in 1932 by C. G. Jung,* ed. Sonu Shamdasani, Bollingen Series XCIX (Princeton: Princeton UP, 1996).

[3] Douglas, *Visions,* xviii & note 18.

[4] Wilhelm Hauer, *Deutsche Gottschau: Grundzüge eines deutschen Glaubens* (Stuttgart: 1934), 1.

[5] *Kundalini,* xli.

[6] *Ibid.,* xlii.

[7] Margarete Dierks, *Jakob Wilhelm Hauer 1881-1962:* Leben, Werk, Wirkung (Heidelberg: L. Schneider, 1896).

confusing Hauer with Gustav Heyer, with whom, incidentally, Edward Whitmont had extensive contact.

> 2. "Unsatisfied with Hauer's often protonationalistic and skewed report on Kundalini Yoga (June 24, 1931) the confusion it [Hauer's seminar] evoked in his listeners [note: See Hannah, Jung, 206] and also inspired by the analytic possibilities of his work with Miss de Witt…Jung interrupted the seminar in the fall of 1931 to delve further into the relationship of yoga to analytical psychology. He gave a commentary on this subject in four lectures on October 12, 19, and 26 and November 2, 1932."[8]
>
> "Perhaps in reaction to the lecture's [Hauer's 1931 lecture] flaws, Jung gave a different and more psychologically insightful series of four seminars on Kundalini Yoga the following autumn."[9]

I fail to see what is supposed to be "protonationalistic" in Hauer's 1931 lecture—nor do I see that there is any evidence that Jung was dissatisfied with it. At no place in the *Kundalini Seminars,* nor in the *Visions Seminars,* nor in their correspondence, does Jung refer to Hauer's interpretation of Kundalini Yoga as "protonationalistic" or "skewed." The reference to Hannah's statement is at best misplaced, as she was commenting on the supposed confusion that Hauer's 1932 lectures evoked. As to whether people found these lectures confusing, Hannah's account was strongly contested by C. A. Meier when I interviewed him. I wrote in the introduction: "Meier, who was also present, stated that while Hannah might have found Hauer's seminars confusing he found them perfectly clear, and added that there was no general confusion."[10] (The other attendee that I interviewed, Tadeus Reichstein, also gave no indication that there was any general confusion).

I find no evidence to suggest that Jung was dissatisfied with Hauer's lectures in 1931 or 1932, or that he considered Hauer's work to be skewed. If there was a general dissatisfaction with Hauer's 1931 lecture, why was he invited the following autumn to present a more extended series to the Club in 1932? And if there was general confusion then, why was he

---

[8] Douglas, *Visions*, xviii.

[9] Douglas, *Visions*, 412-3, note 1.

[10] *Kundalini*, xxxiv.

invited back in 1938? One would normally presume that this indicated that the 1931 and 1932 lectures were successful. Indeed, midway through Hauer's lectures (which ran from 3 to 8 October), Jung wrote to Jolande Jacobi that Hauer's lectures were "very interesting."[11] It is absurd to suggest that Jung's supposed dissatisfaction with Hauer's 1931 seminar was one of the instigators of Jung's 1932 seminars. Again, I cited Meier on this issue and his account accorded with my textual reconstruction of the events: "[Meier stated that] Jung's psychological commentary was from the outset part of a planned collaboration. Hauer, as the specialist, was to present a scholarly philological and historical account to provide the root support for Jung's psychological interpretation."[12]

Furthermore, what evidence is there that the Club seminars were interrupted in the fall of 1931 so that Jung could delve more deeply into the subject of Kundalini Yoga? While Jung gave one seminar on the subject on 11 October, what evidence is there that he spent the next month till the *Visions Seminars* recommenced on 11 November further researching the subject, due to his supposed dissatisfaction with Hauer's 1931 lecture and his work with Miss de Witt? (The manuscript notes of Jung on yoga that I studied were undated—as were the annotations in his books on the subject dated).

> 3. "Jung's ardent embrace of the Kundalini symbol system also reflects a secret link to Miss de Witt's analysis, which increased the Eros connection to the seminar and must have added its own singular energy to the proceedings."[13]

What evidence is there for this statement? In my introduction I wrote: "It is important to note that for those who attended Jung's seminars, they were not simply a course in hermeneutics but engendered particular experiences. Thus Reichstein recalled having dreams that depicted the movement of the Kundalini serpent during and after the seminars, and that 'at least a few' others had similar experiences."[14]

---

[11] Jung to Jolande Jacobi, 5 October 1932, ETH (original in German). I thank the *Erbengemeinschaft C. G. Jung* for permission to cite this letter.

[12] *Kundalini*, xxxiv.

[13] Douglas, *Visions*, xxi.

[14] *Kundalini*, xl.

> 4. "Jung thought Kundalini imagery was especially apt for women...because of the way it linked earth to sky and body to spirit."[15]

No source is given for this statement and I have not been able to locate it. A source would be important, as it seems discrepant with his presentation of the subject, and of spiritual traditions in general.

> 5. In the *Visions Seminars*, Jung states: "The bija-deva is an invisible, unnamed deity that has four arms—instead of four eyes; it is always inside the letter, as you remember from the Tantric Yoga Seminar."[16] [From the editor's footnote: "The bija symbolizes the mind of Buddha..." a reference to John Blofeld, *The Tantric Mysticism of Tibet*].

However, in his lectures, Hauer had stated that the term "*bija-deva*" was one that he had coined himself. He defined the *bija* as the germ of the *cakra*, and the *bija-deva* as the deity or inner working force in this.[17] As the term is Hauer's invention, and as Jung refers back to Hauer's usage, surely this would be the most apposite cross-reference—as opposed to a confusing reference to the quite distinct Buddhist Tantric tradition? (The Buddha does not feature at all in the Hindu tradition that Jung and Hauer are dealing with in this context.)

Other points:

> 1. "In 1926...Jung encouraged the greater use of active imagination."[18]

From accounts I have read, it appears that Jung and others around him were widely using active imagination in their practises during the first world war. See for instance, Tina Keller, "Beginnings of Active Imagination: Analysis with C. G. Jung and Toni Wolff."[19] Jung's 1916 paper, "The Transcendent Function" (*CW 8*) clearly describes a practice that he was already employing with patients.

---

[15] Douglas, *Visions*, xxi.

[16] *Visions*, 829.

[17] *Kundalini*, 101.

[18] Douglas, *Visions*, xi.

[19] *Spring*, 1982.

2. "Jung used the term 'dementia praecox' introduced in 1852 by B. A. Morel for any mental condition which deteriorated rapidly."[20]

Morel's term was "*démence précose.*" It was Emil Kraepelin who used the term "*dementia praecox*" in 1893. Whilst there was some descriptive overlap, Kraepelin's *dementia praecox* was a completely different disease concept. At the Burghölzli, it was Kraepelin's category that Eugen Bleuler and Jung were attempting to reformulate. Morel is not cited once by Jung.

3. "*Thus Spake Zarathustra*...Nietzsche's last book."[21]

This is not the case. *Thus Spake Zarathustra* (1885) was followed by *Beyond Good and Evil* (1886), *On the Genealogy of Morals* (1887), *The Wagner Case* (1888), *Twilight of the Idols* (1889), *Dithyrambs of Dionysus* (1892), *The Anti-Christ* (1895), *Nietzsche Contra Wagner* (1895), and *Ecce Homo* (1908).

4. "*The Upanishads* are Sanskrit commentaries on the *Vedas*..."[22]

This is also not the case. An accurate and succinct definition is given by Patrick Olivelle in his new (and excellent) translation: "*The Upanishads* came to be considered the section of the *Veda* containing salvific knowledge, whereas the other sections contained information about rites." *The Upanishads*, (London: Oxford UP, 1996), xxxiii. See also Sarvepalli Radhakrishnan and Charles Moore, *A Sourcebook in Indian Philosophy* (Princeton: Princeton UP, 1989), 37-9, for a brief account.

5. "Toni Wolff was the first president [of the Club]."[23]

Emma Jung was the first chairman. (Cf. Psychological Club, *Jahresbericht*, 1917.)

6. "Pierre Janet...a French psychiatrist and neurologist."[24]

Janet was neither a neurologist nor a psychiatrist. He first trained in philosophy and then in medicine.

[20] Douglas, 21-2, note 1.

[21] Douglas, *Visions*, 21-2, note 1.

[22] Douglas, *Visions*, 309, note 1.

[23] Douglas, *Visions*, 436, note 4.

[24] Douglas, *Visions*, 474, note 4.

> 7. "A. Samuels's introduction to *Essays on a Science of Mythology* (Princeton, 1969)."[25]

This should presumably be his introduction to Jung's *Essays on Contemporary Events.*

> 8. "Alfred Adler, Viennese psychiatrist…"[26]

Adler was a medical doctor but not a psychiatrist.

> 9. "Flournoy had studied the fantasies of Miss Frank Miller ("Some Instances of Subconscious Creative Imagination," 1906) and published a translation of them in French."[27]

Frank Miller wrote this article herself in French, and it was published in 1905 ("*CW 6*" should also read "*CW 5*").

> 10. "In the early 1920s, Jung, Eugen Bleuler, and von Schrenck-Notzing conducted a series of mediumistic experiments together, using the Austrian Rudi Schneider."[28]

While Schrenck-Notzing did many experiments on Rudi Schneider, there is no evidence that Schrenck-Notzing ever did any of them in conjunction with Jung and Bleuler. Jung did attend some mediumistic experiments with Bleuler in the 1920s, and the protocols of Schneider's seances note one held in Zürich on 21 June 1925 which Jung attended: Schrenck-Notzing was not present on that occasion.[29]

Jung's work should be edited to the highest standards of scholarship. In the latest edition of some of his seminars, this is sadly far from being the case.

---

[25] Douglas, *Visions*, 973, note 4.

[26] Douglas, *Visions*, 1319, note 8.

[27] Douglas, *Visions*, 1376-7, note 3.

[28] Douglas, *Visions*, 1377, note 4.

[29] A photo of this page is reproduced in Anita Gregory's *The Strange Case of Rudi Schneider* (Metuchen, N. J.: Scarecrow Press, 1985), 74.

Paracelsus, Goethe, Jung: Reading Jung Aesthetically

PAUL BISHOP

In July 1768, Johann Wolfgang von Goethe (1749-1832), at that time a student in Leipzig and almost nineteen years old, collapsed with a severe illness. Due to a pulmonary hemorrhage, he was forced to convalesce at his home in Frankfurt am Main for over year. During this period, Goethe was encouraged by a friend of his mother, Susanna von Klettenburg, to read various works on mysticism, alchemy, and theosophy. As a result, he immersed himself in writings on Gnosticism, Hermeticism, Kabbalah, and Neoplatonism including Georg von Welling's *Opus mago-cabbalisticum*, the *Aurea Catena Homeri*, and works by Philippus Aureolus Theophrastus Bombastus von Hohenheim (1493-1541), better known as Paracelsus. Goethe eventually set up a laboratory, and when, in March 1770, he went back to university, this time in Strasbourg, he continued his investigations into "mystical, Kabbalistic chemistry" (see *Dichtung und Wahrheit*, Part II, Book 8). On 26 August 1770, he wrote to Fäulein von Klettenberg: "Chemistry is still my secret love."[1]

It is more likely that Goethe, rather than being a practitioner of occult arts, was interested in the underlying idea of Paracelsus's

[1] See Ronald Gray, *Goethe the Alchemist* (Cambridge: Cambridge UP, 1952).

Paul Bishop teaches German at the University of Glasgow. He is the author of *The Dionysian Self: C. G. Jung's Reception of Frierich Nietzsche* and numerous other articles on Analytical Psychology.

writings.[2] In a letter to Carl Windischmann of 28 December 1812, Goethe wrote: "Throughout my works many more or less esoteric confessions crop up... The incredible discoveries of chemistry have already given powerful expression to the element of magic in nature, so that we need not be afraid to approach her in a higher sense, stimulating and encouraging a dynamic, inspired view in all men. We have no need to concern ourselves with atomistic, materialistic, mechanistic approaches, for these ways of thought will never lack for supporters and friends." To give just one example, Goethe's explanation of "The Metamorphosis of Plants" in terms of the refinement of juices is indebted to Paracelsus[3] (12, 80, 328). Indeed, the notion of "intensification" expresses the idea, recognized in alchemy, of qualitative transformation. As late as 20 July 1817 (in a letter to Georg Sartorius) and in 1819 (in *Meteore des literarischen Himmels*), Goethe quoted a favorite passage from Paracelsus. But what could it have been about Paracelsus or in his works that so fascinated Goethe? To begin to answer that question, we must first examine Goethe's conception of a key Jungian category, the Self.

Strangely enough, a precursor to the postmodern (and Jungian) concept of the Self might be sought in Goethe, who regarded the self as a multiplicity. In "The Purpose Set Forth" in *On Morphology*, Goethe wrote: "No living thing is unitary in nature; every such thing is a plurality" (12, 64). However, Goethe believed that the plural self needs to be unified, to be shaped around a central nodal point or *Mittelpunkt*. That the realization of such a central nodal point is the goal of Goethe's project becomes clearer from his review of an early psychological text, *A Psychology in Clarification of Phenomena from the Soul* (1824), by Ernst Anton Stiedenroth (1794-1858). In his review, Goethe criticized the doctrine of the rationalist philosophers Gottfried Wilhelm Leibniz (1646-1716) and Christian Wolff (1679-1707), who divided humanity into "upper" (rational, intellectual) and "lower" (sensuous, physical) functions. This division reaches

[2] As Douglas Miller has suggested, Paracelsus's philosophy "represented an attempt to come to grips with both material and non-material qualities of nature, and to find in them a reflection of human qualities; it was a kind of 'moral chemistry,' in which the chemical processes of rarefaction and purification were carefully studied in nature and related to the human spirit of life" (12 p.x).

[3] Quotations from Paracelsus are from *Selected Writings*, ed. Jolande Jacobi (London, 1951), referred to throughout as *SW*, plus a page reference.

back at least to alchemical times and the division, found in Paracelsus, between the "lower sphere" (the elemental, "animal" aspects of humanity) and the "upper sphere" (the "higher instincts," part of the "sidereal" or "astral" body). Instead, following Alexander Baumgarten (1714-1762), who founded Aesthetics as a separate discipline in Germany in 1750, Goethe argued that all of a person's faculties should be developed and integrated, organized around a unifying nodal point:

> I have often written of the dissatisfaction I felt in my younger years with the doctrine of lower and higher soul forces. In the human spirit, as in the universe, nothing is higher or lower; everything had equal rights to a common center with manifests its hidden existence precisely through this harmonic relationship between every part and itself[...] Man puts his special skills in the foreground, while seeking to reject those he lacks, banishing them from his own totality. As a correction, he needs to develop all the manifestations of human character—sensuality and reason, imagination and common sense—could be coordinated into a single totality—into a coherent whole.[4]

The image of the nodal point lies, too, at the (literal) center of his early poem, "Wanderer's Storm-Song:"

> Woe woe inner warmth
> Spirit warmth
> Center
> Glow in response to
> Phoebus Apollo
> Or cold
> His princely gaze
> Will pass over thee
> Envy-stricken
> Linger on the green of the cedar
> Which to flourish
> Awaits him not.[5]

[4] Quotations from Goethe are from the Suhrkamp edition of his *Collected Works*, referred to by volume and page number; from *Maxims and Reflections: A Selection*, ed. and trans. R. H. Stephenson (Glasgow: Scottish Papers in Germanic Studies, 1986), referred to throughout as [*MuR*] and maxim number; other references are to the *Gedenkausgabe*, refered to as [*GA*].

[5] *Goethe: Poet and Thinker*, trans. Elizabeth M. Wilkinson and L. A. Willoughby (London: Edward Arnold, 1962), 39.

In his 1797 "Self-Portrait," Goethe did not hesitate to apply this image to himself. Writing in the third person, he said: "The nodal point and the basis of his existence is a poetic formative drive, continuously and ever more deeply at work, both from within and without. Once this has been grasped, all other apparent contradictions resolve themselves."

In his review of Stiedenroth, Goethe went on to argue that four different faculties—the senses, reason, understanding, and the imagination—could be coordinated into a single totality. Because such coordination is possible, not instantaneously but over time, the totality of which Goethe speaks is a product of becoming. According to Goethe, the "basic characteristic of an individual organism" is "to divide, to unite, to merge into the universal, to abide in the particular, to transform itself[...]" (12, 303). So in *Wilhelm Meisters Lehrjahre*, the androgynous and mysterious Mignon sings: "Let me appear, until I become." And in one of his classic essays, "The Development of the Personality," Jung opened his exposition of the concept of the personality with a quotation from Goethe's *West-õstlicher Divan* (1819): "Highest happiness of earth's children / Is personality." The final words of that poem warn that "You could lose everything / If you stay as you are." Or, as in the poem "Sacred Yearning," "Die and become!"

For Goethe and, indeed, Weimar Classicism, the means by which the faculties could be coordinated was aesthetic contemplation. In the aesthetic mode, all faculties are equal, but the coordinating faculty is the imagination, referred to in the eighteenth century as *Einbildungskraft*, *Imagination*, or *Phantasie.* In a letter to the Grand Duchess Maria Paulowna (3 January 1817), Goethe offered a corrective to the comparative neglect of this faculty in Kantian philosophy:

> [In Kantian philosophy] sensuousness, understanding, and reason are cited as the main powers of our faculty of representation, but phantasy is forgotten, which means an incurable gap opens up. Phantasy is the fourth principal power of our intellectual being, it supplements sensuousness in the form of memory, it lays the perception of the external world before the understanding under the form of experience, it creates or finds forms for the ideas of reason and thereby enlivens the entire human unity, which without it would have to sink into barren inability.

In the free play of faculties that Goethe called "exact sensory imagination" (12, 46), both sense perception and mental activity play an equal, coordinated role. The realm created by the imagination—by *Einbildungskraft*, by imagination, by phantasy—is, of course, the aesthetic.

There are numerous correspondences between Jung and Goethe on the doctrine of the Self. In "The Relations between the Ego and the Unconscious," Jung sets out what he means by this concept:

> It may not be immediately apparent what is meant by a "mid-point of the personality." I will therefore try to outline this problem in a few words. If we picture the conscious mind, with the ego as its centre, as being opposed to the unconscious, and if we now add to our mental picture the process of assimilating the unconscious, we can think of this assimilation as a kind of approximation of conscious and unconscious, where the centre of the total personality no longer coincides with the ego, but with a point midway between the conscious and the unconscious. This would be the point of a new equilibrium, a new centering of the total personality, a virtual centre which, on account of its focal position between conscious and unconscious, ensures for the personality a new and more solid foundation (*CW* 7, § 365).

In Jungian psychology, the equivalent to the four faculties are called psychic "functions," described as thinking, feeling, sensation, and intuition. Although Jung's psychological functions do not map onto the faculties as classically understood, his distinction between "rational" and "irrational" functions corresponds to the distinction between "upper" and "lower" faculties. Like Goethe, Jung is insistent upon the need to coordinate all such drives, faculties, or functions. And, like Goethe, Jung found an image of this combination of the upper ("noble") and lower ("ignoble") faculties in alchemy, whose secret he described as "the transformation of personality through the blending and fusion of the noble with base components, of the differentiated with the inferior functions, of the conscious with the unconscious" (*CW* 7, § 360).

The Goethean emphasis on becoming through appearing is central to Jung's notion of the "individuation process," which Jung described as "coming to selfhood," "self-realization," "the process by which a person becomes a psychological 'individual,' that is, a separate, indivisible unity or 'whole'" (*CW 7*, § 266; *CW 9/i*, § 490). Ultimately, Jung argued, the unification of opposites could only be brought about through the creation of symbols. He defined the symbol as "an expression for something unknown or not yet knowable" (*CW 11*, § 713). Of such symbols, Jung believed, those representing the Self are the most important, especially the symbol of the divine child: "The Self is the *teleois anthropos*, the whole man, whose symbols are the divine child and its synonyms," such as Tammuz, Adonis, Balder (*CW 11*, § 755). Like Goethe (and Schiller), Jung emphasized the suprarational quality of the symbol, claiming that both the creation and the apprehension of the symbol demands "a certain amount of intuition" (*CW 6*, § 171). What Jung calls here intuition might well be understood as an aesthetic faculty and, as if to hint at this, Jung speaks of "the enchanting spring-like beauty of this divine youth" (*CW 11*, § 715). One of his therapeutic techniques, "active imagination," involves such aesthetic activities as the creation of mandalas, for "the mandala is the center. It is the exponent of all paths. It is the path to the center, to individuation"[6] (*MDR*, 222).

The following themes emerge from Paracelsus's work as important for Goethe and, in turn, Jung. To begin with, his approach is underpinned by the notion of macrocosm and microcosm, a common belief in medieval and post-classical thinking. On this account, Man is a "small world," a miniature of the larger universe created by God. Concomitantly, correspondences are held to exist between, on the one hand, the realm of Man and, on the other, the cosmos:

> The whole world surround Man as a circle surrounds one point. From this it follows that all things are related to this one point, no differently from an apple seed which is surrounded and preserved by the fruit, and which draws its sustenance from it[...] Similarly, Man is a seed and the world is his apple; and just as the seed fares in the apple, so does man fare in the world, which surrounds him[...] Each thing has its own origin; partly in the eternal, and partly in the temporal. And wisdom, whether it be heavenly or earthly, can be achieved only through the attractive force of the center

[6] Quotations from Jung's *Memories, Dreams, Reflections* (London: Routledge & Kegan Paul, 1963), are referred to throughout as *MDR*, plus a page reference.

and the circle. (*SW*, 1112)

Implicit in this view is the idea that self-knowledge is also knowledge of world: "Everything that is within can be known by what is without[...] Everything external in naturc points to something internal; for nature is both inside man and outside man" (*SW*, 194, 165). As Goethe wrote in his review of a book by Johann Heinroth: "The human being knows himself only insofar as he knows the world; he perceives the world only in himself, and himself only in the world" (12, 39). Goethe gives to the notion of a reciprocal relationship between the Self and the world a characteristic twist, emphasizing not just the inner search but the connection back to the external world, too: "My whole inner activity proved to be a living heutistic that, acknowledging an unknown, intuited rule, sought to find it in, and introduce it into, the external world" (*MuR*, 328).

Correspondingly, in his definition of the individuation process (*Individuationsprozeß*), Jung wrote: "Individuation does not shut one out from the world, but gathers the world to oneself" (*CW 8*, § 432). In *Memories, Dreams, Reflections*, Jung embraces the doctrine of microcosm-macrocosm: "Our psyche is set up in accord with the structure of the universe" (368). In the same chapter, Jung professed that he sought to examine the profound relationship between intrapsychic experiences and the external world: "I try to see the line which leads through my life into the world, and out of the world again" (352). Here, a complex chiasmic parallelism expresses, both rhetorically and conceptually, a Goethean sentiment in a Goethean manner.

In *Das Buch Paragranum* (written 1530, published 1565), Paracelsus set forth his method of analogy, which sought to provide a link between explanations on a physical and ethical principles. For Paracelsus cosmology turns out to provide a basis for ethics, for if "the center of all things is man, he is the middle point between heaven and earth" (*SW*, 112), then "everything that man accomplishes or does, that he teaches or wants to learn, must have its right proportion; it must follow its own line and remain within its circle, to the end that a balance be preserved, that there be no crooked thing, that nothing exceed the circle" (*SW*, 116).

The underlying idea in Paracelsus's position is thus correspondence or analogy. In his aphorisms on natural science, Goethe wrote: "There is nothing to criticize about thinking in analogies" (*GA* 17, 732). For Goethe,

the principle that "everything that exists is an analogy for all that exists" (*GA* 17, 706, 733) leads on to the claim that "a human being, in full sensuous awareness, is the greatest and most precise physical apparatus there can be." (*MuR*, 706).[7] Equally, Jung's approach proceeds along lines close to the principles of morphological idealism, and the insights that provide the basis for successful therapy receive thereby their ethical justification. Furthermore, the principles of alchemy provided the basis for the empirical science of chemistry. For Paracelsus, alchemy and chemistry involved the dual procedure of dissolution (or analysis) and coagulation (or synthesis). The principles of analysis and synthesis of elements became central to chemistry as a "hard" science. In "Analysis and Synthesis," Goethe highlighted the reciprocal relationship between these principles: "An important point is apparently overlooked when analysis is used alone: every analysis presupposes a synthesis" (12, 49). And, in the eighteenth century, Goethe's was by no means the only attempt to reconcile analytic and synthetic faculties.[8] Furthermore, Goethe argued that both principles were predicated on the notion of totality, asking: "What higher synthesis is there than a living organism? Why would we submit ourselves to the torments of anatomy, physiology, and psychology if not to reach some concept of the whole, a concept which can always restore itself to wholeness no matter how it is torn to pieces?" (12, 49). Although Jung based his distinction on Kant's distinction between analytic and synthetic judgements in the *First Critique*, Goethe's questions may well have been behind Jung's own rhetorical interrogative in his letter to Freud of 2-12 April 1909, he wrote: "If there is a 'psych[o]analysis' there must also be a 'psychosynthesis' which creates future events according to the same laws."

At the root of Paracelsus's approach to medicine lay his conception of the universe as cosmic organism (the basis of panpsychism). In his *Maxims and Reflections*, Goethe wrote: "The rational world is to be considered as a great immortal individual, that incessantly brings about the necessary and thereby masters even chance" (*MuR*, 444). Similarly, Jung

[7] "[A]ll knowledge, and all science, has value only to the degree that it enhances, sooner or later, the intrinsic (that is, aesthetic) value of human life." R. H. Stephenson, *Goethe's Conception of Knowledge and Science* (Edinburgh: Edinburgh UP, 1995), 8.

[8] H. B. Nisbet, *Goethe and the Scientific Tradition* (London: Institute of Germanic Studies, 1972), 12; and compare with R. H. Stephenson, 3-5.

not only regarded the psyche as being subject to precisely the same regulatory and compensatory mechanisms as physical organism, but had recourse to the notion of the world soul (*anima mundi*) (8, 931). In his *Opus paramirum* (written 1531, published 1562), Paracelsus went further, explaining not only that the world consisted of three primal substances (sulphur, mercury or quicksilver, and salt, representing the principles of combustibility, fluidity, and consistency) but that, as an organism, the cosmos consisted of concentration (microcosm) and expansion (macrocosm). This dynamic model is consistent with those of Goethe and Jung. In his writings on natural science (such as *On Morphology* and *Theory of Colour*), Goethe uses the principles of *systole* and *diastole* to refer to expansion and contraction in both physical and psychological contexts. Correspondingly, in *Psychological Types* (1921) Jung proposed the psychological mechanisms of introversion and extraversion (*CW 6*, § 6, § 428).

Finally the outcast, eccentric, and quite possibly fraudulent doctor of medicine provided a prototype or precursor of the great symbolic figure of the late sixteenth century, Faust. As a child, Goethe saw a puppet-play version of the story of the erring academic and read of one of the Faust chapbooks. Just as there is a continuity between the historical figures of Faust and Paracelsus, there was, according to Jung, a continuity between Goethe's early interest in alchemy and his vast, two-part verse tragedy, which became the "main business" of his life: "It is no secret that Goethe, as is evident from the second part of *Faust*, still felt the impact of the powerful spirit of Paracelsus" (*CW 13*, § 145). Beneath "the strange arcane terminology of philosophical alchemy" (*CW 13*, § 157), as Jung put it, there lay an intellectual core that Goethe absorbed: "The subject is abstruse and wrapped in obscurity, but it constitutes an essential part of the Paracelsan spirit and exerted a profound influence on Goethe, so much so that they formed the matrix for *Faust*" (*CW 13*, § 159).

Even on a textual level, Jung detected echoes of alchemical ideas. For example, in the line spoken by Thales "An old coin must/ Gain extra value from its rust," he saw a reference to the notion in *Das Buch Paragranum* of the "the leprosy of copper." Goethe's dramatic version of the story of Faust became a significant work for Jung who as a child was urged by his mother to read it. Significantly, one of Jung's longest discussions of

Faust is appended to a collection of his writings on alchemy (*CW 12*, § 558-563).

Jung believed he had uncovered a hitherto ignored tradition in German literature and thought. In fact he himself formed part of it: "Not for nothing was Paracelsus the prototype of Faust, whom Jacob Burckhardt once called 'a great primordial image' in the soul of every German. From Faust the line leads directly to Nietzsche, who was a Faustian man if ever there was one" (*CW 13*, § 154). Jung explained, albeit with dark reference to the political events and technological developments of the 40s, how he saw the link with Nietzsche:

> Alchemy was the dawn of the scientific age, when the daemon of the scientific spirit compelled the forces of nature to serve Man to an extent that had never been known before. It was from the spirit of alchemy that Goethe wrought the figure of the "superman" Faust, and this superman led Nietzsche's Zarathustra to declare that God was dead and to proclaim the will to give birth to the superman, to "create a god for yourself out of your seven devils." (*CW 13*, § 163)

Zarathustra's injunction, in a text replete with alchemical imagery, is to embark upon a process of self-transformation.[9] In "Of the Three Transformations," the spirit becomes a camel, then a lion, then a child. Zarathustra explains: "The child is innocence and forgetfulness, a new beginning, a game, a self-propelling wheel, a first motion, a sacred Yes-saying[…] A child is concealed in the true man: it wants to play." ("Of the Three Transformations," "Of Old and Young Women"). Jung, too, recognized in the child a symbol of the potential for totality: "The 'child' is all that is abandoned and exposed and at the same time divinely powerful; the insignificant, dubious beginning, and the triumphal end. The 'eternal child' in Man is an indescribable experience, an incongruity, a handicap, and a divine prerogative" (*CW 9/i*, § 300).

In his third, and longest discussion of Paracelsus, Jung offers a reading, characteristically full of interruption and digression, of the treatise *De vita longa* (1562). Indeed, one might even apply to Jung's commentary the same description that he gave of Paracelsus's writings:

[9] See Graham Parkes, *Composing the Soul: Reaches of Nietzsche's Psychology* (Chicago: The University of Chicago Press, 1994).

"Long dreary stretches of utter nonsense alternate with oases of inspired insight" (*CW 15*, § 18). Like much of Paracelsus's writing, *De vita longa* dealt with alchemical themes. However, according to Jung, the alchemical adept was engaged upon a psychological enterprise. For Jung, the goal of that enterprise was totality:

> The alchemical operation consisted essentially in separating the prima materia, the so-called chaos, into the active principle, the soul, and the passive principle, the body, which were then reunited in personified form in the *coniunctio* or "chymical marriage." In other words, the *coniunctio* was allegorized as the hierosgamos, the ritual cohabitation of Sol [sun = gold] and Luna [moon = silver]. From this union sprang the *filius sapientiae* [son of wisdom] or *filius philosophorum* [philosophers' son], the transformed Mercurius, who was thought of as hermaphroditic in token of his rounded perfection. (*CW 13*, § 157)

Jung argues in the *De longa vita* that the *prima materia* is identifiable with a principle called the "Yliaster" (= *hyle* [matter] and *astrum* [stars]). On Jung's reading, the symbolic names of the *prima materia*—as a center, a sphere, the tree of paradise with many flowers—"paint a picture of the Self, the indescribable totality of Man" (*CW 13*, § 173). The transformation of the Yliaster lies at the heart of the Paracelsan process of *retorta distillatio* (distillation): "The purpose of distillation in alchemy was to extract the volatile substance, or spirit, from the impure body. This process was a psychic as well as a physical experience" (*CW 13*, § 185).

According to Jung, "the accentuation of the center is again a fundamental idea in alchemy" (*CW 13*, § 186). He points to Paracelsus, who remarks that the distillation must start *ex medio centri* ("from the midst of the center"), and two of his alchemical contemporaries, Michael Maier and Gerard Dorn. In *De circulo physico quadrato*, Maier writes that center contains "the 'indivisible point,' which is simple, indestructible, and eternal," and in "Physica Trithemii," Dorn writes of "the culmination of all knowledge and of the mystic art, and the infallible midpoint of the center (*infallibile medii centrum*)" (*CW 13*, § 185, § 186, § 188). For Paracelsus the heart, "the sun in the microcosm" (*De pestilate*), is the seat of the imagination (*CW 13*, § 201). From these and many other examples, Jung concludes: "The *retorta distillatio ex medio centri* results in the activation and development of a psychic center, a concept that coincides psychologically with that of the self" (*CW 13*, § 189).

Whereas the alchemists required a physical laboratory to perform their experiments, their tools included "spiritual" or psychological techniques. In *De vita longa*, the Yliaster is purified through *imaginatio* (Book IV, Chapter 6; quoted 13 172). Through this process, "a 'new form is impressed' on the impure body" (*CW 13*, § 172). Although Jung translates *imaginatio* by "meditation," his gloss of this procedure shows that the faculty that performs the task of *imaginatio* is the imagination: "Here we encounter the psychic factor in alchemy: the artifex accompanies his chemical work with a simultaneous mental operation which is performed by means of the imagination" (*CW 13*, § 173). Similarly, "active imagination," developed in the course of clinical experience, consists of "intense concentration on the background of consciousness, that is perfected only after long practice" (*CW 7*, § 366). In *De occulta philosophia*, Paracelsus spoke of the foundation-stone of Christianity as resting on prayer, faith, and the imagination. Further on, Jung refers to Martin Ruland, a pupil of Paracelsus, who interprets what Paracelsus called "the four Scaiolae" as "spiritual powers of the mind" [*spirituales mentis vires*] (*Lexicon alchemae sive Dictionarium alchemisticum*, 1612). For Jung, these four aspects—*phantasia*, *imaginatio*, *speculatio*, and *agnata fides* [inborn faith]—correspond in his own psychological typology to the four psychic functions (*CW 13*, § 207). In *Vom Ursprung und Herkommen der Franzosen* (1529) (a treatise on syphilis!), Paracelsus wrote that "four things play a part in conception and birth: body, imagination, form, and influence." Within this scheme, the child "receives its reason" from "the 'imagination' and its objects" (*SW*, 105). Apart, of course, from the quadripartite division, it is hard to see any direct correspondence between Paracelsus's four forces, Ruland's fourfold faculties of the mind, Goethe's four human faculties, and Jung's psychological functions. But what they do have in common is notion that these forces, however they are described, must be combined and thereby transformed into a totality.

Jung compared the goal of Paracelsan alchemy—"higher self-development," or the production of the *homo maior*—to what he termed "individuation" (*CW 13*, § 220). And he emphasized the role of the imagination in the work of the lonely alchemist: "This rigorous solitude, together with his preoccupation with the endless obscurities of the work, was sufficient to activate the unconscious, in other words, as Dorn says, to set the *imaginatio* into operation and through its power of images make things appear that apparently were not previously present" (*CW 13*, § 220). Moreover, for Jung, what is most significant about the archetype is its effect upon the imagination: "Every archetype is psychologically a *fascinosum*, i.e. it exerts an influence that excites and grips the imagination" (*CW 13*, § 207).[10]

The role of the imagination in alchemy throws a different light on its claim to be a secret "art." One alchemical motto ran: *quod natura relinquit imperfectum, ars perfecit* [what nature left imperfect, the art perfects] (*CW 13*, § 195). Instead of an occult science, alchemy begins to look instead like an aesthetic enterprise. There is a hint of this view in Paracelsus's rhetorical question: "The lover goes a long way to meet a beautiful woman; how much farther should one go to discover a beautiful art?" (*SW*, 234). The alchemical contrast between Nature and Art quoted above implies, at the same time, their mutual interdependence, and from here there is just one step to the position embraced by Goethe: "Nature, it seems, must always clash with Art,/ And yet, before we know it, both are one" (1, 165). And in one of his aphorisms, Goethe wrote of *Kunst* ("art[ifice]") as "a second nature, also mysterious, but more intelligible; for it arises from the understanding" (MuR, 1105).[11]

In terms of analytical psychology then, the alchemical transformation represents the "individuation process." Part of that transformation requires the intervention of Melusina, beautiful water-nymph of French legend (whose story Goethe retold in modified form in "The New Melusine," part of *Wilhelm Meister's Journeyman Years*). Jung assimilates the figure of Melusina to that of the anima, and describes it as being at once "a psychic vision" and yet "a distinct objective entity" that demonstrates "the psyche's capacity for imaginative realization" (called "Ares" by Paracelsus) (*CW 13*, § 216). In his commentary (1583) on *De vita longa*,

[10] In 1929, Jung claimed that, for Paracelsus, "nature swarmed with witches, incubi, succubi, devils, sylphs, undines, etc." (*CW 15*, § 12), but in his second 1941 lecture he explained that "it is clear from numerous passages in his writings that [Paracelsus] was aware that homunculi and such-like beings were creatures of the imagination [*éImaginationé*]. His more primitive cast of mind [*éAnschauungé*] attributed a reality to these projections" (*CW 13*, § 195).

[11] Here, Goethe expresses an idea that goes back to Aristotle. The "perennial aesthetic" stretches back further than there is room here to explore.

Dorn speaks of Melusina as *apparentem in mente visionem* ["the vision appearing in the mind"] (*CW 13*, § 180, 214). According to Jung, the alchemical figure of Melusina appears in Goethe's *Faust* in many guises: "Faust's hopelessness leads him straight into the arms of Gretchen, in which Melusina would doubtless remain were it not for the catastrophe which drives Faust still deeper into magic: Melusina changes into Helen." Yet, in Goethe's play, the most important transformation is that of Faust himself: "Faust has to change himself at death into a boy, the *puer aeternus* [eternal youth], to whom the true world will be shown only after all desirousness has fallen away from him" (*CW 13*, § 220).

In the language of alchemy, the outcome of the *coniunctio* is described as the "Aniadus" (or "Aniadum"), the "exaltation of both worlds," the "true May" or the "exaltation in May;" or in the words of Dorn, the *rerum efficacia* [efficacity of all things] (*CW 13*, § 190). Ruland defined "Aniada" as promoting longevity "through influence, imagination, appraising judgement [*aestimatio*] and phantasy" (*CW 13*, § 193,) In his commentary, Dorn speaks of the "imitation of Aniadus" as occurring *per influentiam imaginationis, aestimationis vel phantasiae*. Jung interprets this process as "active imagination," comparing it with the *consideratio*, *contemplatio*, *ponderatio*, and *imaginatio per sensus* of which Ignatius of Loyola speaks. Dorn also speaks of "Adech" (another term for "Aniadus") as the imaginary inner man (*CW 13*, § 201, n.11). Another alchemical term, the "Aquaster," is described by Paracelsus as a "mental [or 'intellectual'] vision" which is born "supernaturally: from the Aniadic mother, with the aid of Adech and through the power of the imagination, comes the great vision, which impregnates the supernatural matrix so that it gives birth to the invisible foetus of longevity, that is created or begotten by the invisible or extrinsic Yliaster" (*CW 13*, § 204). For Jung, the springtime condition of alchemy meant "a 'scientific' union of the natural with

[12] A difference between Paracelsus and Goethe is their attitude towards the body. As Jung points out, "Paracelsus has nothing good to say about the body" (*CW 13*, § 190). It is Paracelsus' Christian view of the body which makes it un-Goethean: "Man should not turn to the carnal part of his body; for all this is animal. He should concern himself only with that part of the body which is invisible and intangible—the light of nature" (*SW*, 236). However, Jung said "the supreme Paracelsan principle is thoroughly materialistic." This does not mean that Paracelsus thought "mechanistically, in terms of inert, chemical matter," but "in a primitive, animistic way" (*CW 15*, § 12). The Paracelsan principle that the body corresponds to Nature at large implies that the cure of physical ailments requires a holistic approach, including the body.

the spiritual man with the aid of arcane techniques of a medical nature" (*CW 13*, § 194).[12] In other words, the physical and intellectual aspects of humanity were brought together. According to Jung, just such a union was the goal of alchemy:

> Paracelsus, like all the philosophical alchemists, was seeking for something that would give him a hold on the dark, body-bound nature of Man, on the soul which [is] intangibly interwoven with the world and with matter[...] Not separation of the natures but union of the natures was the goal of alchemy[...] Nature not only contains a process of transformation—it is itself transformation. It strives not for isolation but for union, for the wedding feast followed by death and rebirth. (*CW 13*, § 198)

As Jung emphasizes, for the alchemists the outcome of this transformation can only find expression in symbolic form. According to Jung, the *hierosgamos* of light and darkness in the form of Sol and Luna, the union of the opposites, can only be approached through the symbol: "What takes place between light and darkness, what unites the opposites, has a share in both sides and can be judged just as well from the left and from the right, without our becoming any wiser: indeed, we can only open up the opposition again. Here only the symbol helps, for, in accordance with its paradoxical nature, it represents the 'tertium' that in logic does not exist, but which in reality is the living truth" (*CW 13*, § 199). Such a unification in the "higher sense," Goethe wrote, can take place "whereby the separated parts are first developed and heightened, so that the combination of the two developed sides produces a third being, something higher, new, and unexpected" (*GA* 17, 708).

[13] "We should not begrudge Paracelsus and the alchemists their secret language: deeper insight into the problems of psychic development soon teaches us how much better it is to reserve judgment instead of prematurely announcing to all and sundry what's what. Of course we all have an understandable desire for crystal clarity, but we are apt to forget that in psychic matters we are dealing with processes of experience, that is, with transformations which should never be given hard and fast names if their living movement is not to petrify into something static." (*CW 13*, § 199). See Goethe's *Farbenlehre*: "We are insufficiently aware that a language is, in fact, merely symbolic, merely figurative, never a direct expression of the objective world, but only a reflection of it. [...] How difficult it is, though, to refrain from replacing the thing with its sign, to keep the object alive before us instead of killing it with the word" (*Collected Works 12*, 227).

Jung's reflections on the esoteric language of alchemy resemble Goethe's awareness of the problems of language.[13] Hence for Jung, the need for myth and for the symbol:

> The protean mythologem and the shimmering symbol express the processes of the psyche far more trenchantly and, in the end, far more clearly than the clearest concept; for the symbol not only conveys a visualization of the process but—and this is perhaps just as important—it also beings a reexperiencing of it, of that twilight which we can learn to understand only through inoffensive empathy, but which too much clarity dispels" (*CW 13*, § 199).

Yet in his encomium of the symbol, Jung hints at but does not state what lends it its power: its aesthetic qualities:

> Thus the symbolic hints of marriage and exaltation in the "true May," when the heavenly flowers bloom and the secret of the inner man is made manifest, by the very choice and sound of the words convey a vision and experience of a climax whose significance could be amplified only by the finest flights of the poets (*CW 13*, § 199).

Every rule of beauty is at the same time a discovery in psychology.
Moses Mendelssohn

According to *Dichtung und Wahrheit*, it was Goethe's encounter with Herder in Autumn 1770 that brought to a conclusion his preoccupation with alchemy and started him upon his self-conscious realization of his destiny as a poet (Part II, Book 10). Yet in Herder's works we find a striking continuity of alchemical themes—for example the quest for wholeness. To begin with, numerous remarks in Herder's writings mediated basic concepts that Goethe, in turn, made his own. For example, the concepts of attraction and repulsion—"in the universe everything is attraction and repulsion"—could be found in Herder, not to mention his former teacher, Kant.[14] And in *Vom Erkennen und Empfinden der*

[14] See Herder, *On the Sense of Feeling*. In *Vom Erkennen und Empfinden der menschlichen Seele*, Herder discussed "the great phenomenon of effect and rest, contraction and expansion" at greater length, whilst in "Love and the Sense of Self" (1781), Herder noted the pre-Socratic origins of "attraction and repulsion" in Empedocles, and described them as the "pulse of the soul."

menschlichen Seele (written 1774), Herder claimed: "The most healthy individuals throughout time excluded nothing: in them, cognition and feeling flowed together to give rise to human life, to deeds, to blissful happiness."

However above all, what Herder taught Goethe was the definition of the aesthetic as a coordination of "upper" and "lower" drives, of the intellect (or *Gefühl* as "inner sense") and the body (*Gefühl* as physical sensation, as touch), of the head and the heart, of the eye (the supreme organ in neo-Platonism) and the hand (symbolic of tactile and sensuous activity). Centuries earlier, Paracelsus had declared that "from his own head a man cannot learn the theory of medicine, but only from that which his eyes see and his fingers touch" (*SW*, 124). Himself drawing on Diderot, Herder taught that "*Be-griff*" (the concept, something "grasped") and "*Ge-fühl*" ("feelings," inner sensations) were of equal value. In *Plastik* (written 1768-1770), Herder wrote that "the eye is only the guide, only the reason of the hand; the hand alone provides forms, concepts of what they mean, what inheres in them." To make his point, Herder pointed to the fundamental role of actual experience in the education of a decidedly unalchemical child:

> Enter the playroom of a child, and see how the little man, learning from experience, clasps, grasps, takes, weighs, touches, measures with hands and feet, in order to secure for himself the difficult, first and necessary, concepts of bodiness, forms, size, space, distance, and the like. Words and precepts cannot give them to him; only experience, experiment, trial and error can do that[...] Here, by unceasingly combining sight and touch [Gefühl], checking one against the other, extending, raising and strengthening each by means of the other, he forms his first judgement. (*Plastik*, section I, 2)

This union of "upper" and "lower" functions, of mind and body, of eye

[15] "What Herder made available to Goethe during that crucial winter of 1770-71 was, on the one hand, empirical evidence for a doctrine of the psyche which assumed the closest possible independence between sense-perception and the mental activities of knowing, feeling, and willing. On the other, the possibility of deriving from that same empirical evidence an all-embracing aesthetic." E. M. Wilkinson and L. A. Willoughby, "The Blind Man and the Poet," *German Studies Presented to W. H. Bruford* (London: G. G. Harrap, 1962), 36.

and hand, Herder argued, could be found alone in and through art in general, and in particular, the aesthetic use of language.[15] The poet Herder wrote, "should express feelings," but he must do so artistically ("artificially"): "You must present, in an artificial way, the natural expression of feeling." In the poetic (aesthetic) use of language, "how everything cleaves to the expression here: not in individual words, but in every part, in their development, and in the whole." (*Fragmente über die neuere Deutsche Literatur* [1767]).[16] Later Goethe's closest contemporary, spoke of "aesthetic discourse," where both the logico-conceptual and the rhetorico-aesthetic aspects of language exist at the same time in a relation of reciprocal subordination.[17] In his major work of 1795, the *Aesthetic Letters*, Schiller argued that it is only the aesthetic mode of perception that makes a person a whole (Letter 27, § 10).

Herder's view had an immediate impact on Goethe's development as a poet.[18] His views are reflected in his letter to Herder of July 1772; then, after the visit to Rome, in erotic form, in his fifth Roman Elegy—

> Also, am I not learning when at the shape of her bosom,
> Graceful lines, I can glance, guide a light hand down her hips?
> Only thus I appreciate marble; reflecting, comparing,
> See with an eye that can feel, feel with a hand that can see. (1, 107)

—and finally, in esoteric form, in the "Mothers Scene" of *Faust II* which, replete with alchemical imagery, as Jung was only too aware, offers an allegory of aesthetic creativity. So when Jung writes that "the second part of Goethe's *Faust* presents only incidentally and in doubtful degree an aesthetic problem, but primarily and in far greater degree a human one" (*CW 13*, § 210), his antithesis is a false one.

Yet there are indications that reading Jung aesthetically not only helps

---

[16] The poet must "think of language as a 'body'—not just a collection of referential signs, but a medium whose every aspect can be made a vehicle of meaning. His thought must be made to 'cleave to language' [*am Ausdrucke kleben*] through art and artifice, and must inhere in every formal relation, not just in the relations between the meaning of the words" ("The Blind Man and the Poet," 47).

[17] See Wilkinson and Willoughby's introduction to Schiller's *On the Aesthetic Education of Man*, (Oxford: Clarendon Press, 1982).

[18] See E. M. Wilkinson and L. A. Willoughby, "Goethe to Herder, July 1772: Some Problems of Pedagogic Presentation," *German Life & Letters*, 15 (1961), 110-122.

us understand him but also places him in the tradition that reaches back to Goethe, and quite possibly, to Paracelsus. Take another look at his description of the symbol of the "true May" quoted above: in the German edition of Jung's works, a quotation from Goethe's poem "*Selige Sehnsucht*" is appended to this passage in a footnote and closer examination of the original also shows that Jung is talking about the "vision" or *Anschauung* by which "the secret of the inner man is made manifest" (*CW 13*, § 199). In Goethe's writings the expression *Anschauung* had important connotations. It needs to be set aside from, on the one hand, *schwärmen* (an excess of abstraction, spiritualization, intuition) and *sehen* (mere passive physical apprehension). By contrast, the term *schauen*, although derived from German mysticism, can perhaps best be translated as "aesthetic intuition."[19] According to Goethe, this kind of *schauen* is achieved by a coordination of the faculties of perception, reason, and imagination.

In one of his maxims, Goethe wrote: "Thinking is more interesting than knowing. But not more than *Anschauen*." (*MuR*, 1150; cf. *MuR*, 744, 1147). And when the musician Johann Christian Lobe met Goethe in Jena in 1820, he was told: "There is nothing unimportant in the world. It all depends on how you look at it [*Es gibt nichts Unbedeutendes in der Welt. Es kommt nur auf die Anschauungsweise an*]."[20] Centuries earlier Paracelsus had written: "He who knows nothing loves nothing. He who can do nothing understands nothing. He who understands nothing is worthless. But he who understands also loves, notices, sees..." (SW, 237). Likewise, for his part, Jung claimed that psychology was concerned with the act of seeing: "*Die Psychologie befaßt sich mit dem Akt des Sehens*" (*CW 12*, § 15).

From the essay entitled, "Judgement though Intuitive Perception," it is clear that Goethe regarded such *anschauen* not only as consonant with

[19] E. M. Wilkinson translates *Anschauung* as "intuitive explanation," but she explains it as "a combination of mediate knowledge éabouté with the immediacy of knowledge *of*, a fusion of conceptual reason with thought which is visual and tactual" (*Goethe: Poet and Thinker*, 177).

[20] As R. H. Stephenson has written, "*Anschauen*, freshly equipped with the latest innovations of theoretical reason, is always at the cutting edge, seeing ever deeper into the unfathomable mystery of things. In other words, what Western thought has always privileged—the Faustian masculine mastery of Nature—needs always to be supplemented and offset, in an unending reciprocal interchange, by the aesthetic, feminine, 'eavesdropping' on Nature than *Anschauen* enacts" (89).

[21] See Kant, *Critique of Judgement*, 77.

Kantian philosophy but as precisely that regulative faculty that Kant had called *intellectus archetypus* (12, 31).[21] Such perception, Goethe argued, enables humanity to "participate intellectually" in the eternal creativeness of Nature [*durch das Anschauen einer immer schaffenden Natur zur geistigen Teilnahme an ihren Produktionen*] and to strive to represent what he called "primal image and prototype." Elsewhere Goethe ascribed four qualities—"ideal, real, symbolic, identical"—to the "archetypal phenomenon:" "ideal, as the ultimate we can know; real, as what we know; symbolic, because it includes all instances; identical, with all instances" (12, 303).

Therefore it is by no means insignificant that there are several similarities between Goethe's conception of the *Urpflanze* (primordial plant) and the origins of Jung's archetypal theory. In one of Jung's earliest works, his doctoral dissertation, *On the Psychology and Pathology of So-Called Occult Phenomena* (1902), he explained the formation of visions in somnambulistic states as "independent transmutations of simple stimuli." Jung went on to point out that there were analogies to such experiences in conscious, waking states as well, describing these stimuli in Goethean terms as "the primary phenomenon [*Urphänomen*] in the formation of somnambulistic dream pictures." He cited Goethe's conjuration of the image of a flower as an example: "Goethe, for instance, says that when he sat down, lowered his head, and vividly conjured up the image of a flower, he saw it undergoing changes of its own accord, as if entering into new combinations of form" (*CW 1*, § 28). In a footnote Jung quoted the following passage from Goethe's review of *Das Sehen in subjektiver Hinsicht* (1819) by Johannes Purkinje, a famous anatomist and physiologist:

> I had the gift, when I closed my eyes and bent my head, of being able to conjure up in my mind's eye the imaginary picture of a flower. This flower did not retain its first shape for a single instant, but unfolded out of itself new flowers with colored petals and green leaves. They were not natural flowers, but fantastic ones, and were as regular in shape as a sculptor's rosettes. It was impossible to fix the creative images that sprang up, yet they lasted as long as I desired them to last... (*CW 1*, § 28, n.1)

What Goethe intuits here—intellectually but also sensually and hence aesthetically—is the *Urphänomen*, or in Jungian terms, the archetype of the flower. In the case of both the Goethean *Urphänomen* and the Jungian archetype, they only reveal themselves to the appropriate form of *Anschauung*. Jung rarely admits the importance of the aesthetic in such explicit terms, but in one of his early papers, he does.

In "The Transcendent Function" (written 1916), Jung warns of the dangers of the "merely aesthetic" (*CW 8*, § 176) but goes on to write that "attention to form" and "attention to [logical] meaning" exist in a reciprocal relationship: "One tendency seems to be the regulating principle of the other; both are bound together in a compensatory relationship… So far as it is possible at this stage to draw more general conclusions, we could say that aesthetic formulation needs understanding of the meaning, and understanding needs aesthetic formulation. The two supplement each other to form the transcendent function" (*CW 8*, § 177). This reciprocal subordination of logical and aesthetic modes is precisely the mode of discourse borrowed from Schiller and employed by Goethe called "aesthetic discourse."

According to Walter Pater, "producers of great literature do not live in isolation but catch light and heat from each other's thought." Goethe called this associative process filiation, telling Eckermann on 1 January 1827: "A filiation runs through all art. If you see a great master, you will always find that he used what was good in his predecessors, and precisely this makes him great. Men like Raphael do not just spring up from nowhere." Nor did Jung just spring up from nowhere. For what is true of art is equally true of intellectual ideas, and this article has tried to suggest the "filiation" between Paracelsus, Goethe, and Jung. Yet it is wise not to ignore the different historical contexts in which each lived and wrote. Each had a keen awareness of his own historical position, and Jung enjoyed the advantage of an historical perspective on his two predecessors and regarded himself as occupying an equally significant if not unique position in intellectual history.

Paracelsus (who was the first person to deliver lectures in German instead of Latin at Basel and who soon left the University to take up an itinerant life), occupies a position midway between the Middle Ages and the Renaissance age of the "New Humanism." According to Jung,

"Paracelsus had a mind typical of a crucial time of transition" (*CW 15*, § 15). At such times Jung wrote, "when a particular view of the world is collapsing, sweeping away all the formulas that purported to offer final answers to the great psychological problems of life," then the archetypes make themselves felt (*CW 15*, § 11). In Paracelsus Jung saw a remarkable symbolic figure:

> The secular conflict that broke out at the turn of the sixteenth century, and whose living image stands before our eyes in the figure of Paracelsus, is a prerequisite for higher consciousness; for analysis is always followed by synthesis, and what was divided on a lower level will reappear, united, on a higher one (*CW 13*, § 238).

Goethe's life spanned the period of the Enlightenment, from the collapse of the Holy Roman Empire, the French Revolution, the American War of Independence, to the invention of photography and steam locomotives. In his scientific writings Goethe was critical of the times in which he lived: "The present age has a bad habit of being abstruse in the sciences. We remove ourselves from common sense without opening up a higher one; we become transcendent, fantastic, fearful of intuitive perception in the real world, and when we wish to enter the practical realm, or need to, we suddenly turn atomistic and mechanical." (12, 309). Goethe's numerous interventions in the scientific discussions of his day—with Newton, about the nature of light; or the debate between Cuvier and Geoffrey de Saint-Hilaire—and his own theories, especially the *Farbenlehre*, were designed as a corrective to these imbalances. More generally Goethe saw for the nineteenth century a project that, while reliant on the advances of the eighteenth century, was distinct from it: "One sings the praises of the eighteenth century for concerning itself chiefly with analysis; the task now remains for the nineteenth to uncover the erroneous prevailing syntheses and analyze their content afresh" (*MuR*, 666, my translation). In his autobiography Goethe called his age "the epoch of challenge" (4, 481), noting more specifically that "the conflict between knowledge and faith was not yet the order of the day" (4, 451).

However that conflict was high on the agenda of the age of Jung when the transition to modernity in almost every sphere of life was nearly complete. In his relationship with his father and in his own spiritual struggles, Jung experienced "that conflict between knowledge and faith which poisoned the spiritual atmosphere of the nineteenth century" (*CW 13*, § 149) that Paracelsus and Goethe did not. Of Paracelsus Jung wrote: "As a medieval Christian, he still lived in a unitary world and did not feel the two sources of knowledge, the divine and the natural, as the conflict it later turned out to be" (*CW 13*, § 149). And unlike his contemporary Agrippa von Nettesheim (who declared himself in *De incertitudine et vanitate scientiarum* (1527) to be "philosopher, demon, hero, God, and all things"), Paracelsus did not, Jung said, rise "to such unfortunate heights of modernity." The nineteenth century's equivalent to Agrippa's boast was the ambition, expressed by Marx and Engels in *The German Ideology* (1845/46), that a person could be a hunter in the morning, a fisherman in the afternoon, a shepherd in the evening, and a critic after dinner. Yet it is to precisely such a totality that Jungian psychology, following Paracelsus and Goethe, not to mention Herder and Nietzsche, aspires—a totality which, according to Jung's autobiography, found mythological expression in his experience of becoming the lion-faced god, the Leontocephalus, and yet which might without recourse to mysticism also be achieved, if we are to believe Goethe and the Weimar Classicists, through the aesthetic.

Paracelsus, Goethe, and Jung are three links—not so much in the Golden (or Homeric) Chain that begins with Hermes Trismegistos—but rather in the continuous and ever more consciously elaborated chain of reflection on the role of the aesthetic. In 1530 Paracelsus wrote: "Give heed to your inner garden[...] and also to yourself that you may learn that which no one can teach you, and which will amaze everyone" (*SW*, 177). Although that, like other alchemical precepts, sounds mystical, it becomes less so when compared with Goethe's claim, made in his last letter (written to Wilhelm von Humboldt on 17 March 1832), that humanity's faculties could, through their proper use, be forged into a totality: "The organs of Man, by means of practice, theory, reflection, success, failure, support and resistance and, time and time again, reflection, link unconsciously, freely and actively what has been acquired with what is innate, producing a unity that astonishes the world."

"There is," Jung says, "no linear evolution; there is only a circumambulation of the self" (*MDR*, 222). For all three thinkers the totality of the self finds expression in the symbol of the circle, “a small spark of the eternal invisible fire” (Paracelsus), whose motion, “the rotation of the monad around itself, which knows neither rest nor peace” (Goethe, *MuR,* 391), represents the mysterious power of life.

Against the Times:
Henry Corbin and the Other History of Being

TOM CHEETHAM

If there was a single first step on the road to the cosmos which Henry Corbin invited us to enter, it was the simple, passionate refusal to accept the understanding of ourselves and the world which dominates modern consciousness. The foundations for this were historical and materialist throughout. All of our means of understanding converge upon a single, unified vision of reality.

History, sociology, psychology, biology, physics, and engineering—all of the "human" and all the "natural" sciences—are versions of the same reductive program. All are based on laws of historical causality in a world composed of matter in space. In a world so conceived, nothing could be more real than anything else. In a world so conceived, consciousness was reducible to and explicable in terms of physical, biological, social, and historical forces.[1] Such a world was radically incompatible with the existence of persons.

As long as we feel alienated and exiled in such a world, there is hope. But the very real danger, as he saw it, is that we will abandon ourselves to this world in our hopelessness, abandon ourselves to those impersonal

[1] Corbin says, tongue-in-cheek, that chromosomes are a fascist invention. "De la Theologie Apophatique comme Antidote du Nihilism," *Le Paradox du Monotheisme* (Paris: Editions de l'Herne, 1981), 258, n. 32.

Tom Cheetham is an adjuct professor at The College of the Atlantic in Bar Harbor, Maine and is working on a book about Henry Corbin.

forces which drive us blindly to our ends, and in doing so, disappear. There would no longer be persons.[2]

All of this Corbin refused in its entirety. His claim was that in order to understand how it came about, and in order to escape from it, we must understand it as a spiritual, philosophical, and metaphysical problem. This does not mean that it is an abstract and merely philosophical undertaking; the only "philosophy" that interested Corbin was one which was effective. In fact, that we conceive of metaphysics and philosophy as "merely intellectual" is symptomatic of our problem. An understanding of ourselves and our situation which is true—and therefore effective—requires metaphysical comprehension at the personal level.

An existential focus on the immediacy of the human person in reaction to the scientific rationalism of the Enlightenment, the abstraction of Hegelian Idealism and Marxist ideology, took many different forms in the European thought of the late nineteenth and early twentieth century. But of immediate importance for understanding Corbin's writings is the phenomenological philosophy of Husserl, especially in the form given it by Martin Heidegger.

The significance of Heidegger's *Being & Time* for Corbin was not so much that it caused a revolution in his outlook, but rather that it provided a crystallization of themes and issues which were gathering in his thinking. He was studying Islamic thought, particularly the writings of Suhrawardi, in which he had become immersed well before reading Heidegger. Like Corbin, Heidegger had been deeply engaged in the study of medieval philosophy and theology and wrote his first academic treatise on Duns Scotus. This provided a significant link between Heidegger's intellectual background and his own.[3]

Heidegger's life work involved a fundamental critique of Western thought and of the course of Western history. That this rather sweeping plan was intended from the start is evident even at the beginning of *Being & Time*: Section six is somewhat immodestly titled, "On the Task of Destroying the History of Ontology." He hoped to provide the most

[2] Corbin, *op. cit.*, 240.

[3] See "De Heidegger a Sohravardi, entretiens avec Phillipe Nemo," Henry Corbin, *Cahier de l'Herne*, n. 39. Consacré a Henry Corbin, Paris, 1981, 28ff. Corbin discussed in detail the influence of Heidegger's early work, and I rely on that here. Robert Avens has examined Heidegger's relation to Corbin and Hillman. See Avens, *The New Gnosis* (Dallas: Spring Publications, 1984).

radical kind of critique possible by getting at the roots of what it means for us to "be" at all. *Being & Time* is ostensibly about "the question of the meaning of 'being.'" Of the utmost importance is Heidegger's choice of standpoint for his task:

> Looking at something, understanding and conceiving it, choosing access to it—all of these ways of behaving are constitutive for our inquiry, and therefore are modes of Being for those particular entities which we, the inquirers, are ourselves. Thus to work out the question of Being adequately, we must make an entity—the enquirer—transparent in his own Being. The very asking of this question is an entity's mode of Being; and as such gets its essential character from what is inquired about—namely, Being. This entity which each of us is himself and which includes inquiring as one of the possibilities of its Being, we shall denote by the term "Dasein."[4]

"*Dasein*" is Heidegger's way of naming that about us which has "ontological priority over every other entity,"[5] that about us which allows anything to appear at all. This *Dasein* that we are has a complex structure which has not been noticed explicitly before, and which Heidegger intends to uncover. In order to begin the revelation of these structures of being, he distinguishes those aspects which pertain to the fundamental structure of *Dasein* from those which are characteristic only of our everyday existence in the world. The former, deeper level, he calls "ontological" and "existential," the latter more superficial level he calls "ontic" and "existentiell." This distinction is basic. It is on the more obscure level that the ontological priority of *Dasein* resides.

Dasein is, literally translated, "being there." It provides the condition for the possibility of anything being present at all. This is the crucial intuition which made Heidegger's work so important for Corbin. He stresses that the "*da*" of *Dasein* is the "act of Presence."[6] The analysis

[4] Martin Heidegger, *Being & Time*, trans. J. Macquarrie and E. Robinson (San Francisco: Harper San Francisco, 1962 [1929]), 26-27.

[5] *Ibid.*, 62.

[6] Corbin, *op. cit.* 32. We might ponder here a comparison between Heidegger's attempt to provide a transhuman centrality to something like "consciousness" and Jung's "African revelation" on the Athi plains in November, 1925. *Being & Time* bears a dedication to Edmund Husserl, dated April 8, 1926.

thus begins with Presence as the fundamental given—not with a knowing subject, or with matter, and not with any kind of "thing." This presence is ontologically prior to the appearance of a subject or of consciousness. Thus Heidegger attempts to stand outside the metaphysical dualisms phenomena/noumena, subject/object, idealist/materialist. He wanted to provide a way of understanding ourselves and the world which was at once rigorously philosophical and metaphysical but not in any way abstract. On the contrary, this "analytic of *Dasein*" was to be rooted in the multitude of ways in which we are and situated "outside" of any of the traditional categories of physical thought.[7] Heidegger takes as fundamental a close analysis of the ways in which we are in the world.

The analysis of *Dasein* is phenomenological—that is, it begins with how phenomena appear. It is not an attempt to reduce or explain one thing or appearance by another. The aim is the disclosure, the uncovering, of that which shows itself in the appearances. Corbin's understanding of the methods and goals of phenomenology was influenced by his understanding of Heidegger, but at the same time, he found resonances in this method with aspects of Islamic thought which allowed him to go beyond Heidegger's analysis.

Everyone who reads Heidegger seriously is confronted with the task of making sense of his numerous neologisms. The text is subtle and complex. But the notoriously tortuous writing is not difficult because it is abstract. It is difficult because he is attempting to create a vocabulary which can break through the traditional categories of Western thought into a concrete language which could reveal what is hidden from our everyday consciousness. Corbin's response to the challenge was revealing: his copy of *Being & Time* was marked by glosses in Arabic.[8]

[7] Heidegger's writing style is difficult because he is attempting to break through common categories into a language which is concrete. Whether he succeeds in accomplishing this has been the subject of academic writings since 1927. Avens cites Hans Jonas, an expert in both historical Gnosticism and a former student of Heidegger's. Heidegger objects to calling man a "rational animal" since it places humans too low. Jonas says, "in reality, the lowering to Heidegger consists in placing man in any scale, that is, in a context of nature as such." Cited in Robert Avens, "Things and Angels: Death and Immortality in Heidegger and in Islamic Gnosis," *Hamdard Islamicus VII*(2) Summer, 1984, 17. For Corbin and his mystical sources, there is no autonomous "natural order" except the one we deceive ourselves into positing when we immobilize Nature by means of unconscious Idolatry, or what Hillman calls "literalism."

[8] Corbin, *op. cit.*, 24.

Corbin's genius was in part as a "comparative phenomenologist," and his work was to make real, to "valorize," as he liked to say, the worlds of other times and other cultures. He moved in worlds where the basic conditions of experience were radically different from those of the modern West. It was partly through Heidegger's understanding of the primordial priority of *Dasein* that he found the philosophical justification for doing so. As a powerful philosopher placed between two cultures, Corbin was in a position to stand on the boundaries of worlds and feel the full force of the encounter. He needed to orient himself, to find the center he was seeking, and that need helped him towards it.

A phenomenology of primordial presence goes to the root of our experience of space and time and of the very "stuff" of the world. If space and time are founded upon something deeper, on a mode of presence which in some way determines their characteristics and which is not separable from how they "appear," then it is to that mode of presence that we must go if we are to understand ourselves and the world. Here is the place to focus if we wish to free ourselves from it. It is upon the "mode of being" of this *Dasein*, this presence, that all else depends.

However, we, as *Dasein*, are not in space the way in which we have come to believe we are. It is truer to say that we "spatialize" a world.

> Orientation is a primary phenomenon of our presence in the world. A human presence has the property of spatializing a world around it, and this phenomenon implies a certain relationship of man and the world, *his* world, this relationship being determined by the very mode of his presence in the world. The four cardinal points, east and west, north and south, are not *things* encountered by this presence, but the directions which express its sense, man's acclimatization to the world, his familiarity with it. To have this sense is to orient oneself in the world.[9]

This is difficult enough for a modern consciousness to accept, but with Corbin's "Heideggerian" analysis of time, an even more radical break with the rationalist tradition occurred. As "presence" provides the possibility of orientation in "space," so there is a primordial structure which provides the possibility of the "time" of history. For Heidegger,

---

[9] Henry Corbin, *The Man of Night in Iranian Sufism*, trans. N. Pearson (New Lebanon, New York: Omega Publications, 1994 [Fr. 1971]), 2.

one of the fundamental characteristics of *Dasein* is "historicality."[10] Historicality is a characteristic of *Dasein*, and it is this that provides the possibility for the occurrence of anything like "history." That is, in terms which Corbin came to use, the manifest history of human events is only possible because there is a deeper, hidden structure within the Presence of *Dasein* which holds the characteristics of "time" in a more fundamental sense. Again, the deep structure is covered over by the everyday, the commonplace. Heidegger's treatment of time was pivotal for Corbin:

> I must say that the course of my work had its origin in the incomparable analysis that we owe to Heidegger, showing the ontological roots of historical science, and giving evidence that there is a historicity more original, more primordial that which we call Universal History, the History of external events, the Weltgeschichte, History in the ordinary sense of the term... There is the same relationship between historicality and historicity as between the existential and the existentiell. This was a decisive moment.[11]

Because the history of "external events" is somehow subordinate to and takes place within this more basic structure of Presence, we are not entirely at its mercy. The phenomenology of Presence means that we do not confront a world of

> ...things that are separate from the soul in the manner of objects...that form "currents" in the manner of a river... [F]or then the dilemma can arise: either to throw oneself into the current or to struggle against it.[12]

Corbin wanted neither to be submerged in the current of the time of material things nor to fight it. Neither option sufficed, because each way is at the mercy of independent objects in quantitative space.[13] We must realize that it is not "things" or "history" which have us, which give us

[10] *Being & Time*, 41.

[11] *Ibid.*, 28. The German "*geschichtlich*" is often rendered "historicality" in English. Corbin translates it into French as "*historialite*."

[12] Henry Corbin, *Avicenna and the Visionary Recital*, trans. Willard Trask (Princeton: Princeton UP, 1960, [Fr. 1954]), 10.

[13] In a study of the relationship between Jungian psychology and philosophical phenomenology, Roger Brooke comments that "what analytical psychology calls images, phenomenology, following Heidegger, calls things." Roger Brooke, *Jung and Phenomenology* (London: Routlege, 1991), 149. He also relates archetypes to the notion of Presence. This is very much in the spirit of Corbin.

life or death, it is we who have them. The phenomenology of Presence thus understood provides the grounding for Corbin's greatest refusal:

> This historicality appears in effect as motivating and legitimating the refusal to let ourselves be inserted into the historicity of History, into the web of historical causality, and which we are calling an uprooting[14] of the historicity of History. For is there is a "meaning of History" it is not at all in the historicity of historical events; it is in this historicality, in the secret, esoteric, existential roots of history and the historical.[15]

Corbin did not claim that to step out of history or out of the "Faustian space" of modern science was easy or simple. Quite the contrary. It required "spiritual combat" of the highest order, but the intimation that it could be done at all was the necessary and crucial realization in our materialist world. To realize we are not irremediably bound by the deepest, most far-reaching presuppositions of "our time," an aptitude for "the secret, esoteric, existential roots of History" was required. The image of the current of history has profound resonances for Corbin.

The way out was through gnosis. More than once Corbin quoted the sixth Imam of the Shi'ites: "We, the Imams, we are the Sages who instruct; our Shi'ites are those initiated by us; as for the rest, they are as the foam rolled along by the torrent."[16] Throughout the entire range of Corbin's work, the emphasis was upon the hidden realities of soul. It was here that one had to turn to escape the secular, the superficial, the material, the public, the merely literal. Corbin saw in Heidegger's program an intent comparable in part to that of the Shi'ite gnostics whose struggle is to protect and guard the realities of the hidden Divine Trust, which is the true reality of Creation. The spiritual combat of Shi'ism is against all the literalizing, secularizing tendencies of any age. While Heidegger's strategy includes breaking away from any theology, it is clearly directed against narrow materialism or any "commonplace," everyday interpretation of the world and human life.

We require far more than an abstract intellectual recognition of the possibility to "tear ourselves away" from historical time. For Corbin,

---

[14] The French "*arracher*," is translated "to tear out, tear away, pull out, uproot."

[15] "De Heidegger a Sohravardi," 28.

[16] *En Islam Iranienne: Aspects Spirituels et Philosophiques, Le Shi'isme duodecemain,* Vol. I (Paris: Gallimard, 1971), 117.

phenomenology implied a movement of the whole being, since the phenomena in question include all the emotions and sympathies of the human person. We require a movement of soul, a desire, a resolve, and the "courage of love."[17] This is a far cry from Husserl's original, rather passionless, intellectual conception of phenomenology. There is no coolly observant "transcendental ego" for Corbin. Heidegger, too, took phenomenology more to heart than his teacher, Husserl, ever did. His emphasis on Resolve is notorious and rather somber. Corbin's use of the notion was most un-Heideggerian. For Heidegger, we must be Resolute in our Being-towards-Death, since our being-towards our authentic future and our essential mortality is constitutive of our deepest reality. But Corbin said there was no necessity whatever to remain Present in Heidegger's *Weltanschauung*. What to Heidegger seemed our rock-bottom mode of being, that is, "Being-towards-Death," is really not ontologically foundational, but rather part of Heidegger's historically conditioned *Gestalt*, which we need not adopt. Corbin used the key Heidegger gave us to free himself from his world as well.

For Corbin, the modern world had fallen prey to a deadly agnosticism which could only end in nihilism and had nearly lost the capacity for those modes of being which are oriented towards the eternal, towards that which is "on the other side of death."[18] There are modes of Presence and the World they entail, the World they make possible, which have become lost to modern historical consciousness, and that World has become for us a "lost continent" because the modes of Presence it requires are oriented towards the Eternal. This is the World which Corbin wanted to make accessible once more, and he found it in the Islamic world and in pre-Islamic Iran.

The move to Islam was a move out of linear, historical time. Nwyia says: "Schooled in the Qur'an, Muslim consciousness is spontaneously anhistorical, that it to say mythic…the historical event evaporates and all that is left is a vague memory submerged in a story which has become mythic."[19] Norman O. Brown comments further on this idea:

[17] *En Islam Iranienne*, v. 1, 38.

[18] "De Heidegger a Sohravardi," 32-33.

[19] Cited in Norman O. Brown, "The Apocalypse of Islam," *Facing Apocalypse* (Dallas: Spring Publications, 1987), 156. I use the term mythic here to refer to those modes of consciousness which are not rationalist, materialist, and historicist, and which pertain to the archaic consciousness of traditional cultures.

> The Qur'an backs off from that linear organization of time, revelation, and history which became the backbone of orthodox Christianity, and remains the backbone of Western culture after the death of God... Islam is committed by the Qur'an to project a meta-historical plane on which the eternal being of historical events is disclosed... History *sub specie aeternitatis*.[20]

Thus there was more at stake here than the claim that we could step out of the current of history of material causality. What we were stepping into was mythic time, mythic space, a mythic reality, where the historicist priority of time over space is reversed. This step out of secular, linear temporality required a relation to Eternity. Corbin was engaged in reawakening our "archaic" potential for archetypal, transhistorical experience, and his royal road lay through soul. It led into the transhistorical consciousness of mystical Islam.[21]

Corbin was concerned throughout his work to counter the forces of nihilistic materialism which he saw destroying the fabric of the "traditional cultures" of Islam. But his efforts apply to all such cultures threatened by the spread of modern consciousness and its social and economic results. In a world which is rapidly losing biodiversity and cultural diversity, Corbin's work can be seen as an attempt to safeguard human spiritual diversity against the ravages of narrow-minded idolatries, whether spiritual or scientific. Within Islam, that most monotheistic of all the Abrahamic religions, Corbin, student of the Islamicist Louis Massignon, revealed a primordial relation to the world and to divinity. Norman O. Brown writes:

> The Islamic imagination, Massignon has written, should be seen as the product of a desperate regression, back to the primitive, the eternal pagan substrate of all religion... Islam stays with the dream life of the masses...discarded by the Enlightenment as superstition...[22]

---

[20] *Ibid.*, 154-157.

[21] This kind of analysis of mythic versus historical time is central to the work of Corbin's friend and colleague at the Eranos Conferences, Mircea Eliade. See for example Eliade's *The Myth of the Eternal Return, or Cosmos and History* (Princeton: Princeton UP, 1954). Especially pertinent is the last chapter which expresses many of the same feelings about the dilemma of modern humanity which drove Corbin's research.

[22] *Ibid.*, 160.

In his late work, Heidegger's analysis of Presence and its relation to time can be seen as a move towards mythic, and perhaps mystic, consciousness. He begins to develop his early intuition and describe both the past and the future as somehow contained within an expanded sense of Presence. In his late work, "past and future are...articulated as hidden powers that approach us, offering and opening the present while nevertheless remaining withdrawn, concealed from the very present that they make possible...[H]e writes of the past and the future as absences that by their very absence concern us and so make themselves felt within the present."[23] Yet even in his early work which so deeply impressed Corbin, the "horizons" of time are contained in the act of Presence. The "primordial" phenomenon of the future is that it "comes toward us."[24] The past and the future are both somehow contained "in" the "present."

The implications of Heidegger's analysis are made explicit by Abram when he says that the primordial experience of the future can be found in the Present as "beyond-the-horizon" and that of the past in the "under-the-ground."[25] A similar experience of the world underlies Corbin's comment about Islamic thought:

> Forms are thought of as in being in space rather that in time. Our thinkers perceive the world not as "evolving" in a horizontal and rectilinear direction, but as ascending: the past is not behind us but "beneath our feet."[26]

This emphasis on space rather than time and on the eternal significance of the present moment runs throughout Islamic consciousness. The space of a mosque "is as if reabsorbed into the ubiquity of the present moment; it does not beckon the eye in a specific direction; it suggests no tension or antimony between the here below and the beyond, or between earth and heaven; it possesses all its fullness in every place."[27]

---

[23] David Abram, *The Spell of the Sensuous: Perception and Language in a More-Than-Human World* (New York: Pantheon, 1996), 211-212.

[24] Heidegger, *op. cit.*, 372.

[25] Abram, *op. cit.*, 212-213.

[26] Henry Corbin, *A History of Islamic Philosophy*, trans. P. Sherrard (London: Kegan Paul, 1993[Fr. 1964]), 5. This attitude towards time and change underlying Islamic thought explains the vehemence of the attack on "evolutionism" in such a sophisticated thinker as Seyyed Hossein Nasr. See Nasr, *Knowledge and the Sacred* (Albany: State University of New York Press, 1989). From the view of modern science, his critique is absurd.

[27] Titus Burckhardt, from *Art of Islam: Language and Meaning*, cited in Brown *op. cit.*

So Corbin's "uprooting" of soul from the current of historical causality was a freeing from its entrapment in a secular world in which it is swept along to an inevitable demise. It was a freeing to a world of archetype and myth. It is therefore in a double sense that Corbin said we are freed to "give a future to the past"—the past as the merely no-longer-present of other cultures, other histories, and the Past as the Eternally Present. The past and the future

> are not attributes of exterior things; they are attributes of the soul itself. It is we who are living or dead, and who are responsible for the life and death of these things.[28]
>
> Life and death are attributes of the soul, not of present or past things...The decision of the future falls to the soul, depends upon how the soul understands itself, upon its refusal or acceptance of a new birth.[29]

What gives a future to the past, to a "history of being" other than that of the modern West, is soul opening that possibility. For Corbin, it was up to us whether we succeed or fail in making a future for the past. But this does not mean that we can necessarily take some past "system" and adopt it from the outside as our own. For instance, Corbin says of Avicenna,

> It may prove that the letter of his cosmological system is closed to the immediate consciousness of our time. But...[his] personal experience...reveals a situation with which our perhaps has something in common. In this case his whole system becomes the "cipher" of such a situation. To "decipher" it is not to accumulate a vain erudition of things, but to open our own possibilities to ourselves.[30]

So a "history of philosophy" or a comparative study of philosophical or religious "systems" was for Corbin always based upon a phenomenological method which assumed the potential effectiveness of the system under scrutiny for soul in the present. Any other kind of history was vain erudition. Corbin's philological, historical, and comparative research is the work of a man devoted to *philosophia*, a

---

[28] *En Islam Iranienne*, v. 1, 37.

[29] *Avicenna and the Visionary Recital*, 10.

[30] *Loc. cit.*

seeker. He himself emphasized the unity of his quest:

> What I searched for in Heidegger, what I understood thanks to Heidegger, is the same thing that I searched for and found in Irano-Islamic metaphysics... But with this last, everything was situated from then on at a different level.[31]

Heidegger's search for an alternative to modern materialistic nihilism remained within the Western philosophical tradition. His attempt to escape the "Cartesian" world led him in the end to the origins of Western thought in the pre-Socratics, searching their texts for the roots of a failed metaphysics. He wanted to uncover the "history of Being" and "destroy the history of ontology," and so recover the phenomena of a lost world. Corbin's path led east to Iran, "a world where the "History of being" was something entirely other than that imposed by the transition for Greek to Latin.[32] It led to an alternate history, but one having roots in both the primordial monotheism of Abraham and in the philosophy of ancient Greece.

[31] "De Heidegger a Sohravardi," 24.

[32] Henry Corbin, "Prophetic Philosophy and the Metaphysics of Being," *The Voyage and the Messenger: Iran and Philosophy*, trans. Joseph Rowe (Berkeley: North Atlantic Books, 1998, [Fr. 1990]), 215. For Corbin and Heidegger, because our language, our thought, our mode of being, and our mode of presence, are inextricably interwoven, the history of language is crucial for understanding who we are and how we have come to "be" the way we are. In this passage from Greek to Latin and beyond the linguistic distinctions between the essence and the existence of a thing are correlated with "a fundamental dissociation between thought and being." This dissociation is not accepted, for instance, by Mulla Sadra. Corbin says, "The words which serve in Arabic to designate the act of being...could not semantically have the same vicissitudes of vocabulary." Iranian theosophers, thinking in Persian and writing in Arabic, did not fall prey to the same ontological mistakes as did the philosophers of the West.

Broken Promises

GINETTE PARIS

This is our eighth Convivium and the questions is: "Has psychotherapy reached the 'End of the Road?'" A chilling title—at least for those of us who identify with the profession of psychotherapist. Knowing Noel and Eva,[1] the founders and organizers of our Convivium, I know that the choice of such a title is not meant as an attack. It is, rather, a defense—a reaction to the inflammatory book title, *We've Had a Hundred Years of Psychotherapy and the World is Getting Worse* [James Hillman and Michael Ventura, 1992].

It is getting worse? Is it our fault? Will therapists be able to earn their living? Are we obsolete?

Although Hillman made it clear that he believed psychological help is still possible, and although readers should, by now, be accustomed to his martial style, many psychotherapists felt uneasy with the title, if not with the content, of the book. Of all the books written by the same author, this one is certainly not the highest on my list. Nevertheless, I thought the title was splendid—an expression of pure Hillmanian

[1] *Editors' Note*: Noel Cobb and Eva Loewe were for many years the editors of *Sphinx: A Journal of Archetypal Psychology and the Arts*, which was and is printed in London. Since Eva Loewe's recent and untimely death, Noel Cobb has continued editing *Sphinx* and organizing the London Convivium Conferences.

Ginette Paris is the Research Coordinator for Mythological Studies at Pacifica Graduate Institute in Santa Barbara, California. She is the author of numerous books and novels including *Pagan Meditations* published by Spring. This lecture was first presented at the Eighth Annual International Conference of the London Convivium for Archetypal Studies, May 27-29, 1994.

fierceness, a punch. I felt relief: someone from inside the trade was exposing the root of our doubts. These doubts were there all along in most of us, but only now are we allowing ourselves to discuss the issue. Clients and society are forcing it on us by asking, "Is therapy worth our money? Our time?"

This past winter I taught a course called "Jungian-based Psychotherapy" at the Pacifica Institute for Depth Psychology, [now Pacifica Graduate Institute] in Santa Barbara, California. All the students there are adults, training to become therapists. One morning, Charles Asher, the Dean, with whom I was teaching the course, wrote a question on the blackboard: "What are the people who pay you paying for?" Here are some of the students' answers:

—Presence.
—To be listened to. To tell their story. To be heard, seen, witnessed, mirrored, appreciated, differentiated.
—To build their confidence, to correct their self-image.
—To carry the pain, to heal, to gain some distance.
—To change, to have emotions, to connect, to communicate, to open and heal the imaginal.
—To find soul, authenticity, peace, wisdom, empathy, safety.
—To learn serenity, centredness, engagement, risk, descent, ascent.
—To prepare for death, for birth of a new self, for a transition.
—To accept a loss, a rejection, to get through a tragedy.

The point of the exercise was to show how each answer leads to a correspondent lack in the culture. For example, the need for "presence" is an indication that our culture breeds isolation and alienation; the need "to be listened to" reveals we do not listen to each other, so busy are we with television, shopping, and running against the clock; the need "to tell their story" reveals there are not many places, except maybe at an AA meeting, were can I tell my story, and so on, for each answer.

It is easy to conclude that culture needs therapy. But one can draw another conclusion: the profession of psychotherapist may well be one of those accidents in history, a profession that appears out of the blue because there is a lack in the culture and dies when the need is fulfilled some other way. If instead of the question, "What are clients paying for," one would ask, "What is the function of a god or goddess," the same answers would do. The function of a divinity (and of a therapist) seems to be similar: to give a feeling of presence in the Universe, to make us feel that we are being listened to, to tell our stories, to be heard, seen, witnessed, mirrored, appreciated, differentiated, *et cetera*.

Or if you dislike the reference to "divinity," and prefer the Jungian terminology, one may ask, "What is the function of an archetype?" Again the same answers will fit the new question: an archetype will carry the pain, heal, give us distance, make us change, have emotions, connect, communicate, open and heal the imaginal, prepare us for death, for the birth of a new self, for a transition, help us accept a loss, a rejection, get through a tragedy.

We should not forget that psychotherapy's prosperity coincided with the decline of religion, that psychotherapists are needed when gods and goddesses are silent, when collective myths cannot hold our individual stories, when archetypes are turning into crushing stereotypes. Freud's father was a rabbi, Jung's father was a pastor, and the culture was offering to the sons ways to update their father's businesses. The best way to go, then, was to become a medical doctor. Science was highly valued, its myth alive and strong, and an alliance with medicine provided Freud and Jung with an alternative to the moral discourse of traditional religions. Freud and Jung stepped into psychology not so much as sons of religious fathers, but as doctors. I believe it is because of medical science's status in the culture that the doubts about the effectiveness of psychotherapy were so long to surface.

If one looks carefully at the disillusionment suffered in the last century by philosophers, historians, sociologists, and anthropologists, it is astonishing to see how protected and privileged psychotherapy has been. It took more time, more attacks from the outside, as well as more criticism from the inside, for psychotherapy to reach the same point of self-doubt as other social scientists and humanists. I remember when my colleagues in sociology suffered their disillusionment more than twenty years ago. The implicit promise had been that sociology could help predict, control, and prevent destructive social behaviors. Graduates in sociology entered *en masse* into government positions where the promises of their discipline were put to the test and failed—sociology could not cure social diseases, and at best, it could only sometimes help predict them. Faculties of sociology, in order to survive, had to do what faculties of philosophy had done many decades earlier—lower their expectations and admit students with less discrimination. Anthropologists also failed to keep their profession's promise and had to admit that, no, they were not very helpful in bringing peace between nations and tribes. Although criminologists were supposed to help lower the crime rate and political scientists give us better politicians, none of these promises were kept. Student populations dropped and professors were displaced like refugees from troubled countries. But there were no such problems for psychology departments. They were reaping considerable rewards for longer than any of the other social sciences, thanks to the belief in psychotherapy's capacity to cure life's injustices, failures, and pain.

Only today has psychotherapy reached the top of its credit limit. In most health insurance plans, many forms of therapy will no longer be reimbursed and a whole slew of new, psychoactive drugs are considered to be more effective and less costly than some therapies. Even at health-food stores products are sold which are supposed to influence moods. These quick-fixes are tempting and pervasive. Even I, a teacher of Jungian theory according to which the *anima* is responsible for our moods, found myself buying a little bottle of amino acid whose label declared it a "mood enhancer." I have met young cyberpunks for whom identity is something that a drug can re-design for you without the need for self work. Ecstasy can be purchased both over the counter and in the illegal drug market, and depression is understood by many as a chemical imbalance in the brain.

Given the new trends, what will remain of our clientele a few years from now? Nothing, if we let the failure of psychology as a science destroy the credibility of psychotherapy. Already in the academic world, the kinds of research on psychotherapy which still receive government subsidies are those with a theoretical background in cognitive, behavioral, or experimental psychology. Depth psychology is more than ever accused of not being scientific enough.

The disdain of depth psychology by universities is highly evident in the North American academic tradition which is more positivist and pragmatic in its definition of science. To be scientific one has to use the experimental, hypothetico-deductive method. Period. In Europe where psychology has been traditionally connected to philosophy, the definition of science has retained some of its original meaning: science is almost any form of disciplined knowledge. But the damage does not stop at the doors of the academy. While scientists are rejecting depth psychology because it failed to prove itself as scientific, the New Age spiritualists are rejecting depth psychology because of our attempts to de-literalize their angels. If one is "into" channeling, one needs a literal angel not a metaphorical one. For channelers and others that carry certain spiritualist traditions, angels are not imagined, they are to be believed in. Why should these New Agers study imaginal theories when faith will do the job?

The confusion around the word therapy is getting thicker by the day. Tarot reading is therapy, astrology is therapy, rituals are therapy, pastoral counseling is therapy, story telling is therapy, art is therapy, music is therapy, dancing is therapy, smelling aroma is therapy, psychodrama is therapy, writing in a personal diary is therapy. I have a friend who has a special talent: when I feel down and depressed, she makes jokes, she makes fun of me. Her method works. Her jokes make me see how absurd it is to make myself miserable by this or that. I gain some distance. I found a name for her ability: ridiculo-therapy (therapy by mockery.)

Does the preponderance of "therapies" for sale mean that anything with the word soul or therapy in it call be sold as psychotherapy? "Where does psychology belong?" James Hillman asked almost thirty years ago in *Re-Visioning Psychology*. He argued then that the study of soul had a way of its own, that it was closer to a humanism than to a medical specialty. But instead of a humanistic psychology, Hillman called the study of the soul a *humanitas,* like that of the Renaissance—a concern, an interest, a passion for the contents of the imagination. His conclusion was that we need to explore and yet do more than explore: we need to reinvent a psychology inspired, but not copied, from the Renaissance. In order to accept the twist Hillman was then giving to psychology, the culture as a whole may have needed to be faced with the actual failure of psychology's medical model. In other words, we may only now be ready for a redefinition of psychotherapy.

If psychotherapy is to become a Renaissance psychology and survive its crisis of transformation, we will need not only all our imaginal power but every bit and parcel of our Western heritage. Some remarkable gifts given to us by the Renaissance have been neglected, and it is now time to unpack them. I will call the first one the gift of historical consciousness.

Historical Consciousness

To profit from this gift one does not require to regress to either the Renaissance or antiquity. We do not need to become born-again pagans to become archetypalists. Many historians dislike the term "Renaissance" because it implies the rebirth of Greek and Roman antiquity. But the antiquity the Renaissance was returning to was not historical, it was imaginal. In fact, although Renaissance scholars and philosophers admired Greek and Roman culture, they showed a surprising lack of respect for the relics of the past. Archeologists today still cringe at the thought of sixteenth century artists who, when the Etruscan sculpture of the she-wolf was found on the Capitole, simply added in Romulus and Remus, the twin babies that were missing. The genius of the Renaissance was not in reviving antiquity but in using antiquity as an inspiration to create something new and original. If it was necessary to steal, distort, and appropriate the materials and ideas they were rediscovering, leaders of the Renaissance did so with no second thoughts.

If the Renaissance was not a rebirth of antiquity, where is the value in Greek revival either then or today? I believe it is in the value of historical consciousness. We may resist the idea that history could inspire psychotherapy. Historians, like sociologists, criminologists, and so many others, fell into the trap of making promises that they could not keep. Maybe some of you remember how the study of history was believed to be a panacea: it was supposed to prevent the repetition of the same old mistakes. But because of their broken promises, historians were under attack: hundreds of brilliant analyses on the fall of the Roman Empire could never prevent the fall of another empire, be it French, British, or Russian. Historians could have published a book called, "We've Had Hundreds of Years of History and the World Still Doesn't Learn from It." History's language became more modest, and the lesson in humility has done historians some good; they have been allowed to return to their true passion. The passion of a historian is not predicting, nor is it preventing or curing today's ills by understanding the past. A historian's vocation is not a call to action. The true historian wants to understand humanity and to tell its story, to compare stories, to keep stories, to tell them anew in every generation. Historical facts do not change any more than the facts of our biographies do, and yet the historians can exhaust neither the desire to understand anew nor the desire to weave that understanding into a story.

Where do we come from? Who are we? In those seemingly simple questions lies the work of the historian, and it could be ours too if we were ready to be modest. If we were ready, the relationship with the personal past would no longer be explored with the goal of preventing neurosis or restoring mental health. It would instead be offered as an avenue to deepen the knowledge of who I am and where I come from. When a client asked, "What am I getting for my money?", we could answer, "A gift of personal (historical) consciousness." No need for false promises. We could tell them beforehand that a person unaware of his past is not necessarily less happy, nor is he more neurotic or less functional. We could say that person is simply less rich, like a city without museums, a nation without historians, without writers, and without artists. In a psychology which is seeking knowledge of the soul, there would be no point in asking a question like, "Am I cured?" The question would instead be, "Did I learn something?" I see this as a way of returning psychology to its original function—learning about the soul.

I am not denying that the current forms of psychotherapy can have a healing effect. Clinical benefits are evident. But I think we need to strategically retreat from the clinical front. It would be to our advantage to consider the clinical benefits of therapy to be secondary benefits; something insurance cannot force us to guarantee, not because they are unimportant, but because the therapist has no power over these issues. In order to do that we may find it useful to de-emphasize the image of the therapist as doctor, pastor, or healer in favor of imagining the therapist as teacher whose task is then to help the client learn something. What the client does with his newly found historical consciousness is no more our business than it is the business of professors to choose a profession for our students. And God knows that what students end up doing with their lives is, most of the time, immensely different from what we thought we were preparing them for.

The theory that places soul-making in a different category from mental health has been written. Hillman did a good job at it. One has only to go read the books. But once the old notions are gone, one needs a multitude of new ways to express the new consciousness. One goal of a therapy oriented toward historical consciousness would be to allow one to say, "I am my past," like history allows us to say, "I am Greco-Roman," "I am Jewish," and "I am Christian." Now, let's look into a second gift from the Renaissance: *humanitas*, the Greek notion of humanism.

Greek Humanism

The kind of humanism that I see as our gift from the Renaissance can be summarized in one idea: a human being cannot exist without a culture. That kind of humanism is in opposition to the Christian world view where man is supposed to stand alone in his conscience and be seen and judged only by the eye of God. It may seem paradoxical that the Renaissance insisted that we are cultural beings while at the same time it de-emphasized the notion of individuality. But the paradox dissolves with the assertion that humans are free—individuality becomes individuation.

The insight that a human being cannot exist without a culture came with another that said all the elements of a culture work as a whole. Art, science, religion, philosophy, history, psychology—one may need to separate them in different fields for practical reasons, but we must never forget that they work only as a whole, all mysteriously connected, as in the person of Leonardo Da Vinci, the Renaissance personified. Following that insight, I think psychotherapy should try to reconnect with parts of our culture that we used to be closer to. The old forgotten allies I am thinking of are literature and philosophy.

Literature

When writing this paper I remembered how often reading a novel or viewing a film raised my consciousness. Some novels and movies were for me truly initiatory. Even the choice to study psychology came after reading Marcel Proust—one of the intellectual heroes of my youth and a genius at seeing through souls. Almost as a nostalgia for these years where I was a devoted "Proustophile," I once took a sabbatical leave to try my hand at being a novelist. Nothing in my life was as therapeutic as writing fiction. Although it was incredible therapy, writing a novel was costly: as a novelist one has to be prepared to live a monastic life, earn little if any money, and lose friends and career opportunities because one's mind is possessed by the story and its characters. I had to put a stop to being a full-time novelist because I was not ready to accept the risks involved. (One benefit, though, is that I almost look forward to old age and retirement, when I can go back to writing fiction.)

Returning to my life as therapist and professor, I could not forget the therapeutic power of fiction writing. As a result I ended up stealing and adapting insights and ideas learned from practical books about writing fiction (like John Gardner's *Art of Fiction*) for use in psychotherapy. For example, one mistake all amateur novelists will do is to tell the story as if things were happening to the protagonist. It does not work. One cannot write a novel in the victim's mode. The novelist's task is to show what the protagonist does with what was done to him or her. A story may start with abuse and victimization. Okay, and then what? Where do you go from there? A novel cannot be written from the point of view of victim because a victim does not make things happen: a victim is harmed by what happened, and the story stops there. To have a story, the protagonist has to transform fate into destiny; very much what Sartre was trying to do with his notion of radical freedom. To become active in one's destiny happens to be the goal of therapy. Therapy starts with a patient who feels he or she does not make things happen: a victim is harmed by what happened. A victim does not write the script of his or her life: the script feels imposed. Therapy, defined by a novelist, is a process by which a victim is transformed into a hero, and a hero is defined as a character who departs from expected ways, learns, has will, takes control, and expresses freedom.

Life lived in the victim's style is as boring and meaningless as a bad novel. As therapists we assist our patients while they rewrite, edit, enhance, speed up the action, and delete and add to the fiction by which they live. Some other basic rules for the development of a narrative inspired me as a therapist. Here are some more of these practical rules and their applications to therapy.

> a) In order to have dramatic tension, the protagonist has to want some thing strongly. In therapy, that means one has to help the patient identify what he wants strongly.
>
> b) There has to be a force (another character or a situation) that opposes the protagonist's will. In therapy, identify

that opposition.

c) Every hero needs a villain. Who are the villains in your client's life?

d) A villain does not need to be bad. Does the client understand that?

e) Show, do not tell. Beyond the telling, what is the client really trying to show? One client says, "My father was a hostile personality" and by that he wants to show how the father did not talk much at the dinner table. Another says, "My father was a hostile personality" and by that he wants to show that his father viciously beat him for years and finally killed his mother. The therapist and the patient have to see through the telling.

f) Surprise creates suspense. A surprising painful emotion sometimes has a specific value.

g) The most interesting traits of a character can be complex, viewed as favorable by some, and unfavorable by others. Therapy is not about goodness, but complexity.

Enough for literature. I would now like to talk about another neglected friend and ally of psychotherapy: philosophy.

Philosophy

It may take a little more imagination to renew therapy's old alliance with philosophy, or maybe I have a personal problem there. I come from a family where many of the men were teachers, translators, or writers of philosophy. My older brother is a publisher of philosophy textbooks. When I was an adolescent, I loved to talk philosophy with my brother, but I hated it when he pushed me into a philosophical corner. It seemed at the time that the point of philosophy was precisely that: to silence the opponent with a thorough argument that would leave me with an open mouth and an empty mind. He would count the points: I would usually quit arguing between zero and ten. I played this game not because I was a masochist, but because I loved the books my brother gave me to read in order to be able to beat me with his superior mind. Despite his tortuous games as a young man, I now love the wise and sensitive man my brother has become. Likewise, I wish psychology would now give philosophy another chance.

The poverty of today's philosophical culture is appalling. I read the other day that the average American, when asked, "How did the Universe begin?", cannot give more substantial of an answer than, "It started with the Big Bang." That is it, a two word cosmogony. Sadly, the average student of psychology does not fair much better because of a lack of philosophy. From Socrates to Montaigne, the philosopher's task has been to address basic questions: what is beauty, truth, good, and evil. This kind of philosophy we all need. Even as children we yearn for a good philosophical talk once in a while. Philosophy is something the soul needs from childhood until the moment of death. A psychotherapist is not there to give his clients lectures on truth, beauty, the nature of good and evil, nor is his function to define morality.

The Greeks complained about the younger generation being morally lax, and then the Romans complained about the same thing, and then the Christians, and now we do. This complaint shows us is that morality changes or that there is more than one standard to judge a situation. As polytheists, we should well be aware that Hermes' morality is not that of Zeus' and that a behavior that is good in one context may be totally wrong in another. It is not our business as psychotherapists to decide what the reigning archetype should be. But it is our business to identify it and to make clear by which standards the patient is judging a situation.

This kind of work one could call philosophical. Some patients who ask for our help are not conscious of the morality by which they live, so of course they have trouble deciding what for them is good from what for them is evil. They hate their impulsive behavior and contradictory emotions. If we treat their moral confusion only as an emotional problem, then we risk ignoring their philosophical needs. Again, I am certainly not suggesting that we start lecturing our patients. All I am suggesting is that our image of ourselves as therapists could benefit from the example of Socrates who said that being human means having a philosophy about life. What is that philosophy? Some of us need help to discover it. There is as much a need to be aware of our philosophical assumptions as there is a need to be aware of our emotions. Socrates' method was to assist when the mind was giving birth to a coherent system of values to live by.

A therapy open to the influence of philosophy would help the individual place his disordered values into a coherent system. A coherent philosophical system, even if homemade and imperfect, is more comfortable than confusion. Now, let's look at a third gift from the Renaissance: a model for the integration of religion and psychotherapy.

Religion and Psychotherapy

The Greeks did not have what we call a psychology because it was included in their religion. In fact they did not have a word for religion: it was all couched in their stories and images about gods and goddesses. With the exception of Ficino, not much attention was given by the Renaissance to the psychology inherent in Greco-Roman mythology. The fact that it was pagan was a big enough obstacle. It was much less risky to insist on the greatness of the Greeks in mathematics, science, architecture, art, and medicine and to leave the pagan mythology alone. One consequence is that the value of this incredible archetypal system has only begun to be explored.

Here I must confess that while I have the unsettling feeling that archetypal psychology has just started to draw inspiration from pagan mythology, already there is a danger that gods and goddesses will be literalized, as are the angels in channeling. I fear they will be turned into relics, petrified into dogma, turned into boring clichés, or converted into esoteric jargon. I am sometimes afraid that my beloved pagan gods and goddesses will die of overexposure in "pop psychology." I fear academic *rigor mortis* stemming from well-intentioned mythologists who are horrified that archetypalists like us should want to renew and push the stories forward. These mythologists sincerely believe these stories have no meaning for us today, that they had meaning only then and there for the Greeks and Romans. They express the same emotions as those archeologists who were horrified to discover that the Renaissance not only adapted and borrowed, but transformed, distorted, and stole from antiquity. I can understand the desire to preserve the objects from the past by sealing them in plastic bags and cataloging them into a huge data base. But I would rather keep them alive.

Some mythologists put us in the ranks of archeologist Sir Arthur Evans who committed the unthinkable. In 1900 Evans bought the land that contained the ruins of the Palace of Cnossos and began his excavations. In his desire to restore the basic structures and the proportions of Minos' palace, he raised walls and columns and redrew half erased drawings with what he thought were the original pigments. His intention was similar to ours: to give a new life to ancient images. But we are fortunate because we do not deal with stones and buildings but with words. Adding to a myth need not be like adding a new coat of paint that destroys the original painting. But nevertheless, the scorn coming from some parts of the academic community is equally dangerous, and if we are not careful, it may dry the well of inspiration.

Conclusion

Understanding our roots and being able to tell our story, feeling and seeing through the culture we live in, communicating with the right words, finding the rituals for transitional moments, brings in itself an incredible satisfaction. It is not problem-solving, and it is not the treatment of suffering either. But it is specifically human, and that should be validation enough. It is no longer necessary to make promises we cannot keep—promises insurance policies are no longer willing to cover; promises that are responsible for the absurd legalism that is starting to corrupt the foundations of the relationship between analyst and analysand, a mistake much worse then that of Evans. Insofar as we imagine ourselves to be educators, historians, or Socratic midwifes of the content of the conscience, our work, like that of all educators, is a cultural operation. This change in our imagination would not be a radical turning point, simply a return to origins.

Historically, those interested in psyche have linked their understanding of it to an understanding of the culture. One cannot read Freud, Jung, or Hillman without noticing how psyche cannot be separated from culture. They constantly refer to history, mythology, literature, art, and alchemy. At the same time, they are careful not to equate psychology with any of these. A tarot, an astrological, or an *I Ching* reading can all be soulful activities, but opposed to psychology they are a-historic, out of this time and space. They are non-rational tools. This is where psychology differs: our job should be to take care of psyche in the cultural, historical context that we live in. Psychotherapy should try not to copy the a-historical, non-rational, anti-intellectual trend—not because these approaches are inferior—but because memory and rationality, like our propensity to think philosophically, to imagine artistically, to understand historically, are part of who we are. Anything that is part of our culture is part of our psyche and so should be part of our *psyche-logos*.

Once we stop making promises that we cannot keep, we will discover that we have more than enough material to work with. One of the inscriptions on the pediment of Apollo's temple at Delphi, "Know Your Self," is an extraordinary agenda, one that could keep us busy for a long time to come.

Wolfgang's World

SHEILA GRIMALDI-CRAIG

Wolfgang Giegerich. *The Soul's Logical Life*. Frankfurt-am-Main: Peter Lang, 1998. 282 Pp. Paper. $42.95.

In 1975 James Hillman took Jungian psychology out of Protestant Switzerland on a voyage to Catholic Italy, where he introduced it to the suave mood-swings of Marsilio Ficino, a chronic melancholiac who nonetheless inspired the Renaissance to its highest highs. A side trip to Henry Corbin's mystical Islam grounded the strategy in an image-oriented elegance from a culture long lost to the West (and little consulted even today by archetypal psychologists after Hillman).

Around the same time, Rafael Lopez-Pedraza took Jungian psychology on a voyage of his own, not to Renaissance Italy but to baroque Spain and Latin-America, where he refracted its classical imagery through the broken lenses of Don Quixote and Pablo Picasso, widening the soul's range to a dimension that included even more of the twentieth century's wayward, perverse psyche. These two voyagers (and their merry crews) created what is now called archetypal psychology, a reading of Jung based more on adjectival projections than substantivized universals, more on imaginal tendencies than literal problems, more on fragmented pieces than individuated wholes, more on floundering souls and less on fulfilled Selves.

Now another great Jungian voyage is under way, not as geographically far from Protestant Zürich as these other two but in some ways

Sheila Grimaldi-Craig taught for many years in the Connecticut public schools. She is a regular book reviewer for this journal.

much further, almost like "Wayne's World" in its inside-out (or insight-out) approach. Wolfgang Giegerich, an Jungian psychologist in Stuttgart, Germany, has taken Jungian psychology (and its archetypal stepchild too) back to school for a course in the rigorous dialectical thought of his fellow Stuttgartian, Georg Wilhelm Friedrich Hegel (1770-1831).

The result is the most thorough-going, engaging, and original criticism of both Jungian and archetypal psychology that I have ever read. I think it is the most important single book in this field since Hillman's *Re-Visioning Psychology* first sent things plunging a quarter century ago. However unlike its predecessors it is not, nor is it intended to be, a congenial read. The pupils, both old Mr. Classical Jungianism and young Ms. Archetypal Psychology, get whacked so hard and so often by Herr Professor Hegel's ruler as the course proceeds that it is not clear whether either of them makes it home or can ever sit up straight in a chair again. This book will at times infuriate you as well as astonish you with its brilliance and dagger-thrusts of insights. ("In a psychology that really means what it says," the author writes, "the form of speaking and writing would have to be such that its statements would in themselves be the cutting edge of a sword...") But Giegerich is so scornful of what he sees as archetypal psychology's mental laziness, its drift into media success, and its abandonment of "truth" for the sake of "playing with images" that he takes no prisoners.

> The time for indulging in myths and images of the Gods, the Self, the daimon, etc. is past. We no longer live in a psychological age where the image as a content of consciousness would and could have any truth for us.

He finds these "images" as worn out and pointless as "the images we watch on TV," which he claims we all place a little border or fence around to protect ourselves from taking them seriously (or as "truth").

Archetypal psychology is now and always has been, he says, simply ego-consciousness playing at a subtle game of not being ego-consciousness, of pretending, of polite fictions.

> To the degree that consciousness focuses on archetypal contents, consciousness itself becomes ego-consciousness. Today's psychological problem can no longer be dealt with on the level of contents (images, symbols, rituals, nymphs,

> Gods, doctrines). Our problem is, has long been, the problem of the logical form of consciousness.

To break through to that level of consciousness—to *The Soul's Logical Life*—we have to give up pretending that ancient poets and medieval alchemists, Renaissance philosophers and modern painters, the founding geniuses of Jungian and archetypal psychology, are the last word in thought.

> Can we really imagine that psychology could get away with employing basically the same naïve logical form of thinking with which the people of antiquity and the Middle Ages responded to their problems, and with descriptions and theory that can be and are presented in such easily accessible, everyday form, that any newspaper reader could also understand them effortlessly at first sight?

Giegerich abominates the media today—especially television—but also computers and cyberspace, technology, and capitalist finance, advertising and "the black tide of mud" that he calls the information society, all because they hold us and we hold them at a carefully bounded, fenced distance from "truth."

> But this age does not want truth. Apart from quick profit, it wants an avalanche of: information, images, stimulation, feelings, happenings, and of course automated processes. Our age enjoys systematically "deconstructing" our entire metaphysical ("logocentric") tradition and our cultural heritage as it happily moves into "virtual reality" which is a reality that is absolutely fenced in, because it is absolutely truth-free.

I have to admit I do love most of the above, both my TV and computer, my stereo and the movies, I like shopping, and I certainly would not turn down a quick profit if somebody would please show me how the heck to make one. But frankly I have never considered that "logical truth" had much to do with it, with what I buy or eat, what I watch or listen to or read, other than is the price right and does it taste good, is the program interesting or the music pleasant or the book enjoyable? Even books like this one, I review for you, dear reader, because I think you might find them stimulating, not because I wish to put you on the track of truth in life. I am even one of those who thought Clinton was right to lie under oath about "sex with that woman." (I swear only on the "Homeric Hymn to Hermes" in such matters.)

Giegerich would hate me: I am what he means by "the little house in the suburbs mentality," what he detests in Jungians who "are more and more placing themselves on the wrong side of the gulf, fraternizing with the common sense mentality prevailing in society." My book reviews, I'm sure, must be part of what he denounces as "psychological kitsch," and I know I'm deep in the "petty-bourgeois character of present psychology," to judge by the kind of letters I get from some of you readers. While my husband, Douglas, thinks I'm a dreamer, I have to admit I've never been one to "dream the [Christian] myth onwards," as Giegerich, quoting the master, insists Jung's true followers are supposed to do. But since he also says that the time for "dreaming" it onwards is now past, it would appear that I, and you, are being given a second chance, heralded by this book. ("Since the myth that needs to be dreamed onwards is the particular Christian myth, to 'dream' it onwards can only mean to sublate the mythic mode and the mode of 'dreaming' the myth altogether.") Ready for Wolfgang's World?

Alas, dreaming it would have been so much easier than the "relentless," "rigorous," even "brutal" logic of what he now insists we must do, to subject psychology to the movement of Hegelian "thought."

> Its movement has to be that of absolute negative *Er-innerung* (Hegel), absolute negative "recollection," reflection, interiorization of itself into itself. This is not for the purpose of autistic or narcissistic introspection, but for the purpose of approaching the phenomena of the world, seeing them and it only as reflected in the mirror of the negativity of its Notion of soul, much like Perseus could afford to see Medusa only via his mirror.

All I know about Perseus is that he used that mirror to kill the Medusa, who he was told had turned a lot of heroes like himself into stone. That mirror was itself maybe the all-time ultimate defense mechanism, or border, or "fence," to avoid the big bad monster. But it is now Giegerich's most valued weapon as before him it was Hegel's. ("Without this mirror, the positivity of the facts turns the viewer into stone, i.e., into a scientist [just as conversely the vision of the scientist inevitably turns reality into positive, stone-like facts]), and psychology has become impossible.") That is a large claim to be making, given the fact that we all need a few hard facts to live by, what science calls "observables" or windows on reality. But Giegerich is, like all good dream-the-dream onward Jungians, or now think-the-thought onward Hegelians, trying to preserve a psychology that is not "scientific" psychology.

> Psychology happens when there is a mind that while looking into the (inner or outer) world is able to stay within itself (within the mind and its Notion, not within the private subjectivity of the person's fantasies or feelings). It must be able to relentlessly hold its place in the bottomlessness and infinity of the black hole that its constitutive internal identity (the soul of psychology = the Notion of soul) is, and to see whatever there is to be seen (external facts as well as facts known through introspection) exclusively within the confines of this mirror. Psychology is the discipline of interiority.

To see things only in the inside-out mirror that Hegel invented as the truth test of realness (*Wirklichkeit*, as opposed to the *Realität* or "reality" where I do most of my shopping) is, to put it mildly, a demanding challenge for those of us who find it hard enough just keeping the roof over our little house in the psychological suburbs. Do we really need Hegel's all-encompassing mirror to honor the psyche, or is it only in concrete-laden Stuttgart that people think the Medusa is still turning everything into stone?

Legend has it that Hegel himself once said, "One man has understood me, and even he has not." So don't quote me on any of this, but here is what I think Hegel was doing. His basic struggle, as he saw it, was with a world firmly set on relying on the evidence of the senses to determine reality. In *The Phenomenology of Spirit*, his most important book, he looks at the six ascending attitudes of consciousness toward reality (ordinary consciousness, self-consciousness, reason, spirit, religion, and absolute knowledge). Intellectual conceptions intervene, he says, when we think we can just rely on our senses, and these conceptions are elusive. So consciousness and the real world remain at odds. But by going, carefully and logically, to higher levels of consciousness, we come to religion, which is the nearest step we can get to absolute knowledge, and, when properly understood, represents the fullest comprehension of all the other forms of consciousness, what he calls "the actuality, truth and certainty of its throne." Neither "idealistic" nor "realistic," then, Hegelianism is a philosophy where idealisms and realisms themselves have to be faced—"negated" from their positivity—"sublated"—before you can get to the ultimate idealism, which is the ultimate realism too, the absolute, unyielding, crowning truth of existence. In the view of Hegel's contemporaries, religion's highest form, the nearest step anyone had ever taken to the absolute, was the personal Christ of Evangelical fundamentalists, a figure that Hegel, by contrast, sublated to the universal, the ideal, the spiritual, the "logical" Christ.

As for the lowly natural world, located in some small and detestable part of which is my little house in the suburbs, it proceeds only from "the idea," while the spiritual world (Mind) proceeds from the idea and nature. So the natural world can't explain the mind, but it is necessary for starters. Reality, however, is forever independent of my individual consciousness. The basis of both Mind and Nature must be thought. But this thought is not based on the kind of consciousness that makes distinctions of ego and non-ego. There is a primary thought, a logic in other words, that was there before creation created a natural world, and before thought started growing there. It is this primary thought, what Hegel calls simply "the idea," which appears in consciousness as "the crowning development of the mind." And you can only get there—and only if you are fiercely resistant to the positivities (the stone-hard facts) that will distract and waylay you from truth—by use of the most rigorous logic conceivable.

Hegel thought Kant's categories, those *a priori* principles behind everything (including Jung's archetypes), were petty distinctions of a mind that simply couldn't see how things were "really" related. Instead of categorically dividing things into their opposites in order to distinguish them, giving them a separate and phony reality, Hegel insisted that abstract ideas, when you really "abstract" them, are interchangeable with their opposites, so that extremes meet, opposites coincide, and we would all be better off looking at things in their unity.

That's what Hegel was doing. By applying Hegel's truth system to Jung, that is, by locating all the positivities that have crept into a subject that never should have had any, Giegerich demands a sublation of psychology as it now stands.

> We have to realize that the term "unconscious" has long become a positive term, the negation it expresses being totally overheard. This ultimately positive and personalistic use of the term—despite Jung's vehement disclaimers—is one of the severest shortcomings of Jung's psychology... He lacked the logical means, and he willfully refused to see it as a logical problem...He stubbornly wanted to do his work by means of observation ("empiricism") and intuition alone. He rejected rigorous thought in psychological matters as a kind of "metaphysical speculation" that he felt was prohibited to him as a Kantian.

Archetypal psychology early on saw the limitation of Jung's use of the term "unconscious," saw how it was becoming a stone-hard fact instead of remaining an alchemical idea ("the stone that is not stone," as the alchemists put it), and opted for the term "imaginal" to replace it. And Giegerich approves. ("Archetypal psychology was sensitive to the fundamental shortcoming of the conventional use of 'the unconscious' and, following Henry [*sic*] Corbin, more or less replaced the term 'unconscious' with the term 'the imaginal.'") But Giegerich claims that term, too, has become calcified, no longer negative, and its once subtle use now vulgarized by the lot of us who go about playing archetypal psychology games: "my" Hercules complex, my Poseidon personality, my anima problem. We have got to stop this anti-alchemical slippage back into such positivities, he says, but the way out is not the same as the way in.

Giegerich is really calling for a post-alchemical soul, because we are wasting our time and our soul life, he says, by not using our brains.

> Today, 180 years or so after Hegel, it is possible to know and say more clearly what the reality we mean is, without succumbing to a positivistic or personalistic reduction that so easily goes along with the idea of the "unconscious."

Talk about a *via negativa*! Giegerich makes up for those lost one hundred and eighty years of thought by shooting down, sublating, negativizing, and killing almost every hardened tenet of the Jungian/archetypalist schools of psychology. It goes without saying that he so utterly disdains the literalisms of all the other schools—Freudians, behaviorists, clinicians, academics, *et al.*—that he saves almost all his arrows for his friends. He claims, at any rate, to be only trying to help.

> When I say that the imaginal approach of psychology does not go far enough, this expresses exactly the spirit of my criticism of archetypal psychology. I am not trying to retract its convictions and fall back behind them. I want to push archetypal psychology with its imaginal approach forward beyond the half-way mark at which it stopped.

Fundamentally he repudiates "the unshaken position of the ego" in archetypal psychology which continues to prevent the psyche from being a person-free proposition. The psyche can never be itself, can never represent its "truth," if it is always imagined as something filtered through people, whether imaginal people or otherwise. Giegerich writes:

> Even though the imagination admittedly does not theoretically and implicitly posit its contents as actually existing and does not claim to express philosophical truths, but rather appears as narrative, fantasy, fictions, metaphor, play, humor, etc. —nevertheless, by its very form, it does primarily posit beings, persons, animals and so on as positively existing. It thus constantly reaffirms the 'natural' ontological prejudice, supports our habitual sense of positivity, perpetuates the ordinary, perceptual and sensual, form of experiencing the world as the eye and, may I be forgiven this pun, the I (ego-personality) would perceive things; and then, secondarily, it retracts this positing again.

All those "as-if" propositions that Hillman made in *Re-visioning Psychology* Giegerich characterizes as only "a half-way movement out of the ego's city into the world of soul—and only a half-hearted surrender to the (logical) demands the notion of soul would make on a psychology." As long as you posit imaginal characters—inevitably with egos of their own—you are resisting the logical thought of the soul for the ego game of soul fictions, soul theatre, soul play. Hillman had imagined a one-way movement into soul by way of a "bridge" between the ego and the unconscious, a dream bridge. But Giegerich says the problem with archetypal psychology is that you get to keep running back and forth to the other side of the bridge, depending on whether you want to fend off the charge of "nothing but" fantasy (the soul side) or the charge of literalism (the ego side). Giegerich wants that bridge "burned" behind you—because you must enter the soul's logical life and be done with such positivities of the imaginal style once and for all. ("The imaginal style with its 'as-if' indeed provides an alibi or a secret refuge for the ego's (openly scorned) positivity (the literal, the ontological) by avowing that imaginal psychology is not concerned with truth or Being...") In Wolfgang's World the bridge is to be burned before you even cross it!

> The real crossing over would presuppose the burning of the bridge. Or better: the burning of the bridge would itself be the beginning of a real crossing over, and the only way of crossing over! You can only get across by burning what was supposed to serve as your bridge. The very act of burning is the movement across it, because it is the movement away from the stationary image of a bridge to thought as movement. This is how contradictory, how "crazy" the way of the soul is.

Maybe. But that fire is going to burn more than the bridge: in that same conflagration of positivities will go the Gods as well (what he calls "the psychological obsolescence of God and Gods"), and myths ("what goes under the name of myths does not refer to real myths and real Gods") and poetry ("even poetry, which was the only refuge for a kind of mythological logic from the end of the pagan world through the Age of Romanticism, cannot bring sky and Zeus together in a credible way anymore"), and, even as we gasp, the imagination itself.

> Every concrete reality is the unity of itself and the whole logic of being-in-the-world in the given cultural situation they belong to. The imagination cannot comprehend this, because it does not want to comprehend to begin with. It only wants to envision...If it were not blind to the logic of the soul, it would not be 'imagination.' It would be sublated imagination—thought.

So, as we stand around this immense bonfire of the positivities, will not someone ask why we are doing this? As someone afraid of bonfires ever since I was a child, someone still taken in by what Giegerich abhors as "the innocence of the anima-only soul," I volunteer. Where are we going here? Won't the soul's logical life be the deadest place ever, the ashes of a sublated universe, about as exciting as everything was before the Creator, out of cosmic boredom, surely, decided to start the ball rolling and made the word, as the *Bible* says, "flesh?"

No, says Giegerich. "It means nothing less than to trespass into infinity, into the sphere of the absolute." In that "wilderness," as he calls it, of (negative) truth, we will really "live dangerously," but not as Nietzsche proposed when he advised people to live that way. Nietzsche, according to Giegerich, was "one of the greatest destroyers of the notion of truth," for in proclaiming that "God is dead" he was proclaiming the death of the Absolute. The twentieth century followed Nietzsche into the dangers of a world where the Absolute was dead. So now the danger, the real wilderness, can only be back on the other side.

Giegerich comes to this idea of the new "wilderness" by way of a brilliant—if outrageous—analysis of the Actaeon myth. Actaeon, as the poet Ovid tells us, was a youth who went one day deep into the wilderness while hunting, where he stumbled upon the naked Goddess Artemis as she was bathing with her nymphs. Embarrassed, she threw water on him, turning him into a stag. His own dogs then tore him apart. Giegerich first presents an analysis of Thomas Moore's discussion of the Actaeon myth (in Hillman's *Puer Papers*), which he criticizes for its typical, archetypal psychology approach.

> Actaeon is almost talked about as if he were a patient in the consulting room, an analysand with such and such character traits, with a certain consciousness, preferences and attitudes, with his kind of behavior (e.g., his hunting passion), his kind of sexuality (his voyeurism), his particular pathological features (his innocent puer masculinity, his excessive spirituality, his sense of impotence) and thus also with a fate particular to him (his being 'hounded' by his own dogs).

The problem with Moore's approach, as the reader can by now guess, is that he is inevitably treating Actaeon "as some kind of existent being" and as an "ego-personality." We are imagining Actaeon instead of thinking him. Only if we insist on an allegorical reading, a "thinking" reading of myth—where we presume from the start that the myth means something other than what it says—can we avoid the trap. (The trap is imagining Actaeon as a real person even though we've been hoodwinked into proclaiming ourselves deliteralizers and good Hillmaniac "seers-through.")

"Imaginal psychology has to eat its own medicine," Giegerich declares and stop prescribing deliteralized figures which it never-the-less proceeds to take literally. "But if it did this," he adds, "it would, of course, sublate itself and cease being imaginal psychology. It would realize that the actual nature of the soul's life is 'other than imaginal.'"

Giegerich's own reading of the Actaeon myth—fully sublated—comes at the end of the book. Logical thought, as we have by then learned, takes us to a unity of opposites. Instead of Actaeon the stag-hunter-male-patient-in-the-waiting-room versus Artemis-the-virgin-goddess of wilderness, the two are united.

> How else could you behold Artemis, the huntress, but through the killing of the hunted stag? Just stumbling through the forest as some dude without being a hunter and without as such being akin to Her, being Her counterpart or complement, you could never behold the naked Goddess. Like is exclusively seen by like... Artemis is not a positivity, not an empirical-factual reality. Without an Actaeon, there is no Artemis, no bathing Goddess, no naked truth...both are the two sides of one and the same archetypal reality.

It is a fascinating line of thinking through this myth, a kind of structuralism into a psychological syzygy, if you will, but not exactly the kind first offered by the French anthropologist, Claude Levi-Strauss, when, in his massive, computer-based analysis of the diachronic/synchronic layout of Bororo mythology, he found a dialectical unity: it wasn't about birds or flying monkeys or the sky, it was code for "up," over and over again in many different "up" images, or "down" in many different "down" images. And when the code of all these is spelled out by the computer, we are able to read the "logic" or "structure" of "primitive" society's myths—almost all of which (in *The Raw and the Cooked* and the three other books of his grand opus) deal with table manners, a first attempt at civilization. (When Levi-Strauss applied the same structuralist approach to Greek myths, he boiled them all down to a single sentence dealing with incest taboos.)

Giegerich is not quite reading the Actaeon myth through structuralism's framework—where "the medium is the message," a dominant slogan of the 1960s' assault on Absolute Truth. He insists in fact that the medium is not the message if the message is going to be truth, for the medium (myth) is only a way of getting there (and not a very good way). The medium will not be the message if you read myth thinkingly, dialectically, until you see the unity of the idea as an allegorical thought. Structuralism is also a method of contrast, a way of showing the underlying logic of myths, but it all but ignores their explicit statements as nothing but *bricolage*, the stuff at hand that an amateur builder might use to prop up his hut. Giegerich's allegorical structure stays with the explicit tale, because for him myth is articulating (if in a *passe* way) the soul's logical structure. In one of the most amazing pages in the book, he presents a list of myths, from Actaeon and Artemis to Bluebeard and his wife, and including Hades, Pan, Odysseus, Hercules, Orpheus, and the rest, all of which he says show how "the soul has many other moments from within which the whole truth about its nature can be portrayed."

The list seems so summary, so abrupt, so complete in its way that you want to cry, "Stop!" For Aphrodite and Ares, for example, that wonderful story, the "unity" or "whole truth" of the soul is simply that it "delights in its own nature (beauty and war)." The single-unity idea reduces them, stripping them of their passion, their appeal, their very emotion. Is it just my "innocent anima-only soul" that feels something is wrong here and wants to hurry back to the other side of the bridge? But we have burned the bridge that is archetypal psychology, the bridge that let our egos hold our hand as we stalked across, step by scary step. The bridge is gone. The myths are gone. The Gods are gone. The soul's logical life is being laid out before us, and chilly as it is, if we turn back we will be accused of not wanting the truth, only warmth.

> Dodging the question of truth can be seen as a defense, as an attempt to remain at a distance to the soul, to stay out of it as ruthless wilderness, and instead to restrict oneself to a mere imagining things and envisioning the whole range of the polytheistic pandemonium of images.

"More light, more light," Goethe is supposed to have said just before dying. "More warmth, more warmth," Miguel de Unamuno said, under the same circumstances. What a difference a culture makes. But the only warmth you're going to find on this bridge is from the fire consuming it.

I feel a little like Dorothy here, in *The Wizard of Oz*. I'm scared, but I do want to see the Emerald City. I do, I do, I do. And yet, I don't think Giegerich is even promising that it will be emerald, if he can be said to be promising anything to such kitsch-clutchers like me. Wolfgang's World, the house of Hegel, is in black and white, not color. He leaves me at the end of this powerful book still in my imaginal mode, but now I am imagining that I am in Hegel's house. ("Not in a million years," I can hear the reply, "you're still dreaming in your petty-bourgeois little house in the suburbs.") Yet, as the poet T. S. Eliot wrote, "Oh, do not ask 'What is it?' / Let us go and make our visit." The house is hard to find, hidden behind a huge hedge that is so overgrown it is hard to see what's behind it. A smiling young man named Charles Darwin, who is collecting rocks and plants from a nearby quarry, assures us that this is the place. It is unbelievably dusty inside, after 180 years of neglect. The musty smell that permeates everything offends my American housewife sense of things, but when I send my husband to open a window—you didn't think I'd cross the bridge of the soul to Hegel's house without Douglas, did you?— he opens one in the front of the house. It looks out onto the vast, relativistic, existential abyss of the twentieth century, onto Nietzsche's world, and Sartre's, onto Walmart's and Woody Allen's.

"Shut that window," I tell him, "And open one in the back." Let's see what the house of Absolute Truth looks back on. If opening windows makes for "new observables," as the scientists say, let's let some air into this place from Hegel's back window, not his front. But Douglas, who's a lifelong epicurean, God bless him, has already started down the stairs to the basement.

"I'm going down to the wine cellar, dear," he calls up to me. "Imagine the cognacs that must be down there, the Margauxs, the ancient grappas that have been waiting for us all this time we were drinking nothing but diet cokes."

But what is that sound? I go to open the back window and I am amazed at what I see. Every inch of Hegel's backyard is filled with this gigantic mechanical clock, a mass of cogs and wheels and bells and whistles, and they are all still turning, still grinding away loudly with a precision of movement. It is the kind of clock you can still see in some town squares in Europe. There are two giant carved figures, one on each side of the clock, and each one takes his turn monotonously winding the gearbox as the wheels turn round. Oh, I recognize them now—the one on the left is the French philosopher Rene Descartes and the one on the right is Sir Isaac Newton. Neither seems to be showing any emotion, not even satisfaction that their efforts to keep the mechanical clock perpetually turning have been successful. It's a fine clock, I'll say that for it, even though as I check the time on my Swatch I see that the clock behind Hegel's house is a little off. But, then, as Einstein once said, all time is relative, depending on the position you're standing on when you measure it.

Oh, oh—someone's coming. I'm going to have to stop this fantasy right now. It might be Hegel's insane sister, Christiane, who once went to the post office and tried to mail herself as a package to someone, perhaps only now being returned to sender. She, too, once lived here, a constant reminder of the madness of the soul for her brother and his "all-encompassing, self-defending systematic philosophy as a typical product of paranoid thought" (James Hillman, *Re-Visioning Psychology*, 240).

Book Reviews

Ann Bedford Ulanov. *The Female Ancestors of Christ.* Einsiedeln: Daimon Verlag, 1998. Pp. 131. Paper, $15.95.

Starting with the genealogy of Christ found in the book of *Matthew*, Ann Bedford Ulanov analyzes the traditions of the four known ancestresses of Christ. In a thoughtful and insightful work, she calls attention to their previously overlooked contributions to our understanding of the role of the feminine in the divine. In the lives of Tamar, Rahab, Ruth, and Bathsheba, we find woman revealed as subject as well as object; as bold trickster as well as compassionate mediator of transformation.

> In all of these women, we find the closest association of sexuality and spirituality, something often de-emphasized if not actually attacked in the teachings of our tradition. These women reconnect us with the instinctual basis of our faith, revealing it as a central resource, not something to be cast aside and triumphed over. They bequeath to Jesus, and through him to us, the seeds of woman as person and as believer… Jesus redeems woman from being seen only in terms of men's images of her. She is fully herself, to be judged, forgiven, blessed; to be used in parables to represent God's actions and to reveal God's truths; to be a loving follower, a beloved friend, a lover.

¤ ¤ ¤

Emma Jung and Marie-Louise von Franz. *The Grail Legend.* Trans. Andrea Dykes. Princeton: Princeton UP, 1998. Pp. 452. Paper, $15.95.

In a mature and thoroughly considered survey of the Matter of Britain and works such as Wolfram's *Parzival* in relation to alchemy and depth psychology, the authors have provided a valuable extension to the works of C. G. Jung, who demurred to his wife on this topic so central to his deepest concerns. After Emma's death in 1955, her work was taken to completion (and reworked) by M.-L. von Franz. In covering a wide range of literary and alchemical sources, the authors bring the broadest possible range of scholarship and analytical insight to bear in this landmark work.

> It is as if a further enrichment of the symbol of the Self...were taking place in the Grail story, by which the continued tearing asunder by the opposites might be ended and their reconciliation striven for. For this task the individual human being serves as a vessel, for only when the opposites are reconciled in the single individual can they be united. The individual therefore becomes a receptacle for the transformation of the problem of the opposites in the image of God.

¤ ¤ ¤

Michael Allen Williams. *Rethinking Gnosticism: An Argument for Dismantling a Dubious Category*. Princeton: Princeton UP, 1999. Pp. 335. Cloth, $19.95.

Jungians have long been interested in "gnosticism." *In Psychology and Alchemy* (1944), Jung wrote, "I hope the reader will not be offended if my exposition sounds like a Gnostic myth. We are moving in those psychological regions where, as a matter of fact, Gnosis is rooted. The message of the Christian symbol is Gnosis, and the compensation effected by the unconscious is Gnosis in even higher degree." But what is Gnosis in any degree? What did this term refer to historically? In *Rethinking Gnosticism*, Michael Allen Williams, Professor of Comparative Religion at the University of Washington, argues that the term is really a modern construction and has no ancient self-definition, that many of the religious features people usually associate with it (for example, that it was a rebellious protest against mainstream Christianism) are questionable, and that the term is now more of an impediment to understanding than a help. In one fascinating chapter after another, Williams shows that some Gnostics were "Anticosmic World-rejectors" (one Gnostic myth claimed that the real Creator God was a dark demiurge and the world was, as result, an evil place), and other Gnostics were simply people who favored "socio-cultural accommodation," some hated the body while others looked to perfect it, some were ascetics while others were libertines. He is particularly lucid in his analysis of the Nag Hammadi collection of books, a 4th century library that was discovered in 1945 in a rural area of Egypt. These books form the largest single collection of surviving books from the "Gnostics." Williams, at this point, is so put off by the term that he will only refer to it indirectly, as in "the thinkers and movements that have been the subject of this book." He ends this extremely enlightening study with a comment from Morton Smith (who wrote a hilarious movie review of Martin Scorceses's film, *The Last Temptation of Christ*, for *Spring 49* [1989]):

> The late Professor Morton Smith of Columbia University gave a paper in 1978 at a major conference on the topic of "gnosticism" in which he laid out an argument against the appropriateness of this category. At the end of his paper, he nevertheless remarked with mock resignation and lovable sarcasm that 'gnosticism' has become in effect a brand name with a secure market.' But I wonder. I wonder if the market is not in fact softer than it once was. And in any case, I wonder if the record of product performance does not indicate that it is time for scholars as responsible modern 'producers of knowledge' to issue a massive recall, and to focus collective attention on developing not merely a repackaging program but a new model altogether.

John Weir Perry

1914-1998

Albert S. Cook

1926-1998

Joseph B. Wheelwright

1906-1999

Ariadne's Clue
a guide to the symbols of humankind
ANTHONY STEVENS

C. G. Jung
The Psychology of
Kundalini Yoga
Edited by Sonu Shamdasani
BOLLINGEN XCIX

ANALYTICAL PSYCHOLOGY SOCIETY
OF WESTERN NEW YORK

Program Announcement: Fall 1999

The listing below gives selected titles and presenters. Time, place, and costs are included in the complete program, which is printed three times a year.

MAPS OF THE SOUL: SOME QUESTIONS ABOUT FAIRY TALES
A Presentation by Joan Goldberg, Storyteller

EROTIC SHADINGS: LOVE'S SWEET AND BITTER TRACES
A Lecture and Workshop by David L. Miller, Ph.D.

INTRODUCTION TO JUNGIAN PSYCHOLOGY
Classes with John R. Segmen, Ph.D.

THE FORCE OF CHARACTER: AND THE LASTING LIFE
A Reading from his new book by James Hillman

THE LEGACY OF THE DEAD: GENEALOGY OF A JUNGIAN METAPHOR
A Lecture by Paul Kugler, Ph.D.

THE LABYRINTH: THE NEVER ENDING STORY
A Lecture and Workshop with Sylvia Senensky, M.Ed.

ERANOS & ARCHETYPAL PSYCHOLOGY: A HISTORY IN IMAGES
A Slide Presentation By Paul Kugler, Ph.D.

The Analytical Psychology Society of Western New York, founded in 1976 as a non-profit membership-supported organization, focuses on studies and concerns in analytical and archetypal psychology. Membership is open to the public; dues are tax-deductible. Benefits include reduced prices for books, workshops, classes, and lecture series.

For further information or to receive a program, write to: Analytical Psychology Society of Western New York, 100 Coniston Road, Buffalo NY 14226-4660 or call (716) 854-7457